Communication and Channel Systems in Tourism Marketing

Communication and Channel Systems in Tourism Marketing has also been published as *Journal of Travel & Tourism Marketing,* Volume 2, Numbers 2/3 1993.

The development, preparation, and publication of this work has been undertaken with great care. However, the publisher, employees, editors, and agents of The Haworth Press and all imprints of The Haworth Press, Inc., including The Haworth Medical Press and Pharmaceutical Products Press, are not responsible for any errors contained herein or for consequences that may ensue from use of materials or information contained in this work. Opinions expressed by the authors(s) are not necessarily those of The Haworth Press, Inc.

The Haworth Press, Inc., 10 Alice Street, Binghamton, NY 13904-1580 USA

Library of Congress Cataloging-in-Publication Data

Communication and channel systems in tourism marketing / Muzaffer Uysal, Daniel R. Fesenmaier, editors.

     p. cm.

"Has also been published as Journal of travel & tourism marketing, volume 2, numbers 2/3 1993"–T.p. verso.

     Includes bibliographical references and index.

     ISBN 1-56024-580-8 (alk. paper).–ISBN 1-56024-581-6 (alk. paper)

     1. Tourist trade–Marketing. I. Uysal, Muzaffer. II. Fesenmaier, Daniel R.

G155.A1C534 1993

338.4'791–dc20

                                        93-30947

                                           CIP

INDEXING & ABSTRACTING

Contributions to this publication are selectively indexed or abstracted in print, electronic, online, or CD-ROM version(s) of the reference tools and information services listed below. This list is current as of the copyright date of this publication. See the end of this section for additional notes.

- *ABSCAN Inc.*, P. O. Box 2384, Monroe, LA 71207-2384
- *Centre des Hautes Etudes Touristiques (CHET)*, Fondation Vasarely, 1, avenue Marcel Pagnol, 13090 Aix-en-Provence, France
- *GEO Abstracts (GEO Abstracts/GEOBASE)*, Elsevier/GEO Abstracts, Regency House, 34 Duke Street, Norwich NR3 3AP, England
- *Journal of Health Care Marketing (abstracts section)*, Georgia Tech-School of Management, Ivan Allen College-225 North Avenue NW, Atlanta, GA 30332
- *Leisure, Recreation & Tourism Abstracts (LRTA/CAB ABSTRACTS)*, Cab International, Wallingford, Oxon OX10 8DE, England
- *Lodging & Restaurant Index*, Purdue University, Stone Hall Room 220, West Lafayette, IN 47907-1002
- *Management & Marketing Abstracts*, Pira International, Randalls Road, Leatherhead, Surrey KT22 7RU, England
- *Sage Urban Studies Abstracts*, Sage Publications, Inc., 2455 Teller Road, Newbury Park, CA 91320
- *Social Planning/Policy & Development Abstracts (SOPODA)*, Sociological Abstracts, Inc., P. O. Box 22206, San Diego, CA 92192-0206
- *Sociological Abstracts (SA)*, Sociological Abstracts, Inc., P. O. Box 22206, San Diego, CA 92192-0206
- *Urban Affairs Abstracts*, National League of Cities, 1301 Pennsylvania Avenue NW, Washington, DC 20004

(continued)

SPECIAL BIBLIOGRAPHIC NOTES

related to special journal issues (separates)
and indexing/abstracting

☐ indexing/abstracting services in this list will also cover material in the "separate" that is co-published simultaneously with Haworth's special thematic journal issue or DocuSerial. Indexing/abstracting usually covers material at the article/chapter level.

☐ monographic co-editions are intended for either non-subscribers or libraries which intend to purchase a second copy for their circulating collections.

☐ monographic co-editions are reported to all jobbers/wholesalers/approval plans. The source journal is listed as the "series" to assist the prevention of duplicate purchasing in the same manner utilized for books-in-series.

☐ to facilitate user/access services all indexing/abstracting services are encouraged to utilize the co-indexing entry note indicated at the bottom of the first page of each article/chapter/contribution.

☐ this is intended to assist a library user of any reference tool (whether print, electronic, online, or CD-ROM) to locate the monographic version if the library has purchased this version but not a subscription to the source journal.

☐ individual articles/chapters in any Haworth publication are also available through the Haworth Document Delivery Services (HDDS).

Communication and Channel Systems in Tourism Marketing

CONTENTS

Introduction   1
       Muzaffer Uysal
       Daniel R. Fesenmaier

Communicating Tourism Supplier Services: Building
   Repeat Visitor Relationships   3
       Laurel J. Reid
       Stanley D. Reid

Market Structure Analysis of Media Selection Practices
   by Travel Services   21
       David Snepenger
       Mary Snepenger

Effects of Distribution Channel Level on Tour Purchasing
   Attributes and Information Sources   37
       Charles R. Duke
       Margaret A. Persia

Communication Channels to Segment Pleasure Travelers   57
       Sheauhsing Hsieh
       Joseph T. O'Leary

Using Travel Brochures to Target Frequent Travellers
   and "Big-Spenders"   77
       Bruce E. Wicks
       Michael A. Schuett

State Slogans: The Case of the Missing USP   91
       John Richardson
       Judy Cohen

Design of Destination and Attraction-Specific Brochures   111
    Donald Getz
    Lisa Sailor

Functional and Aesthetic Information Needs Underlying
    the Pleasure Travel Experience   133
    Christine A. Vogt
    Daniel R. Fesenmaier
    Kelly MacKay

Effects of User and Trip Characteristics on Responses
    to Communication Messages   147
    Francis P. Noe
    Muzaffer Uysal
    Claudia Jurowski

The Influence of Tourists' Characteristics on Ratings
    of Information Sources for an Attraction   171
    Kathleen L. Andereck
    Linda L. Caldwell

Image Formation Process   191
    William C. Gartner

Collaborative Alliances: New Interorganizational Forms
    in Tourism   217
    Steven Selin

Competing and Cooperating in the Changing Tourism
    Channel System   229
    Frank M. Go
    A. Paul Williams

Index   249

ABOUT THE EDITORS

Muzaffer Uysal, PhD, is Associate Professor of Tourism in the Department of Hotel, Restaurant, and Institutional Management at Virginia Polytechnic Institute and State University, Blacksburg. He has extensive experience in the travel and tourism field and has authored or co-authored more than eighty articles and several book chapters related to different aspects of tourism marketing, demand/supply interaction, and international tourism. Dr. Uysal is Associate Editor of *Leisure Sciences* for tourism related areas and methods and serves on the editorial boards of three additional international journals. He is a member of the Travel and Tourism Research Association, the National Recreation and Park Association, and the International Association of Scientific Experts in Tourism. Recently, he was invited to serve on the Education Advisory Council of the National Tour Foundation.

Daniel R. Fesenmaier, PhD, is Associate Professor at the University of Illinois and Tourism Specialist with the Illinois Cooperative Extension Service. He holds positions as Adjunct Associate Professor in the Department of Geography at the University of Illinois and Southern Illinois University-Carbondale. Dr. Fesenmaier currently serves as a consultant to a number of tourism development programs, including the strategic planning committee for the Illinois Bureau of Tourism and a USAID tourism development project in Ghana. He has conducted over 100 tourism marketing and development studies for a number of federal, state, and local tourism agencies. Associate Editor for the *Journal of Travel & Tourism Marketing* and *Leisure Sciences*, he is co-author of two books and author of over seventy-five articles dealing with the economics and marketing of tourism.

Introduction

Muzaffer Uysal
Daniel R. Fesenmaier

The nature and content of tourism marketing research have grown dramatically in recent years and this research is evolving into an accepted field of scholarly endeavor. One of the key strategic components of travel and tourism marketing is the area of communication and channel systems.

This is a special volume on *Communication and Channel Systems in Tourism Marketing*. The purpose of this work is to present tourism marketing research that incorporates communication and channel systems of marketing as an integral component.

First, we wish to acknowledge the *Journal of Travel & Tourism Marketing* Editor, Dr. K. S. (Kaye) Chon for his support in developing this book. We owe a great debt to all the referees and authors for their help and comments. We also sincerely thank the authors for submitting their papers. Lastly, this volume would not have been possible without the help and assistance of the people listed below who gave both time and effort to act as referees. Their contribution is greatly acknowledged.

Kathleen Andereck, University of North Carolina at Greensboro
Kenneth F. Backman, Clemson University
Sheila J. Backman, Clemson University
Michael A. Blazey, California State University-Long Beach
Mark A. Bonn, Florida State University
Linda Caldwell, University of North Carolina at Greensboro
William C. Gartner, University of Wisconsin-Stout
Richard Gitelson, The Pennsylvania State University
Jonathan N. Goodrich, Florida International University

[Haworth co-indexing entry note]: "Introduction." Uysal, Muzaffer, and Daniel R. Fesenmaier. Co-published simultaneously in *Journal of Travel & Tourism Marketing* (The Haworth Press, Inc.) Vol. 2, No. 2/3, 1993, pp. 1-2; and: *Communication and Channel Systems in Tourism Marketing* (ed: Muzaffer Uysal, and Daniel R. Fesenmaier) The Haworth Press, Inc., 1993, pp. 1-2. Multiple copies of this article/chapter may be purchased from The Haworth Document Delivery Center [1-800-3-HA-WORTH; 9:00 a.m. - 5:00 p.m. (EST)].

1

Stephen Grove, Clemson University
Larry D. Gustke, North Carolina State University
Mark Havitz, University of Waterloo
Stephen Holland, University of Florida
Claudia Jurowski, Virginia Polytechnic Institute and State University
Deborah Kerstetter, The Pennsylvania University
Francis Kwansa, Virginia Polytechnic Institute and State University
Patricia Maguire, Central Washington University
Stephen McCool, University of Montana
Cary D. McDonald, Clemson University
Robert McLellan, Clemson University
Brian Mihalik, Georgia State University
Ady Milman, University of Central Florida
Suzanne K. Murrmann, Virginia Polytechnic Institute and State University
Norma P. Nickerson, Black Hills State University
Joseph T. O'Leary, Purdue University
Richard Perdue, University of Colorado at Boulder
Laurel J. Reid, Brock University
Wesley Roehl, University of Nevada
Joseph W. Roggenbuck, Virginia Polytechnic Institute and State University
Steven Selin, University of Arkansas
Stowe Shoemaker, Cornell University
David Snepenger, Montana State University
Stephen L. J. Smith, University of Waterloo
Christine A. Vogt, Arizona State University
Alan Watson, Intermountain Research Station, U.S. Forest Service
Bruce E. Wicks, University of Illinois at Urbana-Champaign
Colleen M. Workman, Black Hills State University
Jeffrey B. Zeiger, Black Hills State University

Communicating Tourism Supplier Services: Building Repeat Visitor Relationships

Laurel J. Reid
Stanley D. Reid

SUMMARY. This paper views three marketing communication elements as critical in building and retaining repeat visitors: external, internal and word-of-mouth messages. The paper provides a conceptual model that links these communications elements to the phenomenon of repeat travel purchase behavior. The authors emphasize the importance of repeat customers to tourism services and explore why and how each type of marketing communication has an impact on these visitors. Finally the paper suggests ways tourism supplier services can attempt to strategically manage these functions.

INTRODUCTION

Quality service and client satisfaction are regarded as prerequisites for organizational success and for building a base of repeat customers. Repeat visitors not only represent a stable source of tourist revenues, they also act as information channels that informally link networks of friends, relatives and other potential travelers to a destination. If satisfied with service

Dr. Laurel J. Reid is Assistant Professor in the Department of Recreation and Leisure Studies, Brock University, St. Catharines, Ontario, Canada L2S 3A1. Dr. Stanley D. Reid is Professor of Management, University of West Indies, Barbados and Executive Director of the Centre for Management Development (Eastern Caribbean), University of the West Indies, P. O. Box 64, Bridgetown, Barbados.

[Haworth co-indexing entry note]: "Communicating Tourism Supplier Services: Building Repeat Visitor Relationships." Reid, Laurel J., and Stanley D. Reid. Co-published simultaneously in *Journal of Travel & Tourism Marketing* (The Haworth Press, Inc.) Vol. 2, No. 2/3, 1993, pp. 3-19; and: *Communication and Channel Systems in Tourism Marketing* (ed: Muzaffer Uysal, and Daniel R. Fesenmaier) The Haworth Press, Inc., 1993, pp. 3-19. Multiple copies of this article/chapter may be purchased from The Haworth Document Delivery Center [1-800-3-HAWORTH; 9:00 a.m. - 5:00 p.m. (EST)].

3

quality, repeat visitors effectively use word-of-mouth communications to promote destination awareness and encourage prospective travelers to become visitors. In addition, repeat clients can be more profitably served than new buyers. Consequently, it is surprising that the repeat visitor segment(s) has received so little attention in the tourism literature.

The potential for building repeat patrons as a marketing resource hinges on whether external communications (promised benefits) *match* the attributes that are communicated internally (experienced benefits) during the interactions that visitors have on-site at the destination. If this match occurs, the potential for visitor satisfaction with the tourism service is greater and suppliers have better opportunities to achieve higher repeat visitation levels. However, any communication strategies directed at increasing repeat visits must also take into account key service characteristics: intangibility, labor intensiveness and lack of standardization (cf. Chase, 1984; Berry, 1980). These features typify services provided by accommodations, transportations, attractions, food and beverage enterprises as well as travel intermediaries (tour operators and travel agents). In addition, these characteristics are tied to the interactions between visitors and employees. Consequently, effectively communicating the benefits offered by tourism supplier services, both off- and on-site, is of great import in obtaining repeat customers.

The above issues suggest that the topic of communications directed at repeat visitors merits specific conceptual and strategic treatment. This paper argues that repeat visitors represent a unique market segment(s) warranting special attention in both the external and internal communications extended by the tourism enterprise. The paper posits that these patrons are a valuable resource that should be managed to increase positive word-of-mouth communications. A conceptual model is presented which examines the importance of three communication dimensions: (1) formal external (promotion), (2) internal (on-site interactions), and (3) informal (word-of-mouth) communications. The accompanying discussion explores these communication elements in the context of serving repeat customers in tourism enterprises. Finally, the paper provides some implications and strategic recommendations for tourism service managers arising from this model.

IMPORTANCE OF REPEAT VISITORS
TO TOURISM SERVICE SUPPLIERS

Competition in the tourism industry is intense. This trend is increasingly evident as value-conscious consumers seek destinations that offer the *best* value. Particularly in times of economic downturn, strategies that can increase the efficiency of tourism enterprises are critically needed in order to effectively compete and maximize tourist revenues. One such approach involves a focus on repeat visitors, one of the most valuable marketing resources at a firm's disposal.

Although many tourism suppliers implicitly recognize this visitor segment, only recently have repeat customers been given an explicit focus in marketing strategies. Examples of the phenomenon include Frequent-Flyer (airlines) and Frequent-Stayer (hotel) programs. These programs give special inducements to frequent patrons in the hope that they will repeatedly patronize the same supplier. Frequent-stayer programs and other special incentives are often used by hotels to attract repeat patronage from business travelers who fly a great deal (Rivers, Toh and Alaoui, 1991; Lyke, 1989). Such programs are often offered by large tourism enterprises but small suppliers, who constitute the majority of firms and whose financial resources prohibit a mass market approach, can also profitably target repeat guests. These small businesses are in an advantageous position to adopt personalized marketing approaches aimed at attracting repeat visitors and developing the client base.

Specific attention to this visitor segment accrues many advantages. Building repeat visitation is a means by which tourism suppliers can increase revenues and decrease costs by reducing reliance on the much more difficult task of attracting new visitors (Gyte and Phelps, 1989; Gitelson and Crompton, 1984). A tourism enterprise can also depend on patronage from repeat patrons based on regular buying behavior patterns. Once repeat business volume is established and marketing programs are tracked, the task of forecasting becomes easier and more accurate. Repeat visitors also have the potential to be employed as a marketing resource, providing referrals and promoting positive images, which permits expansion of the firm's customer base.

Perhaps the greatest advantage outlined above is that repeat patrons are less expensive to target. They are easily accessible: names, addresses and other relevant data are known. This knowledge permits suppliers or intermediaries to precisely target the repeat segment and solicit direct responses to promotions, making it possible to more effectively measure promotional success. In addition, tourism supplier *awareness* is a step omitted from formal marketing communications (promotions) directed at repeat clients. Many marketers claim that it is five times more expensive to obtain a new customer than it is to retain a current customer (Haywood, 1989). Whether this figure is speculative or not, it is clear that if the potential exists for repeat buying behavior, it is cheaper to promote to these patrons than attempting to convert non-users to first-time trials. This feature, along with the previously outlined advantages argue for distinct marketing communication approaches, designed and targeted specifically at repeat visitors–as differentiated from communications targeted at prospective clients.

Although customer retention is widely acknowledged to be a favorable outcome of the firm's marketing efforts, it has received little attention in the tourism literature. Only a few studies have considered the pattern of repeat business at specific destinations (Fakeye and Crompton, 1991; Gyte and Phelps, 1989; Gitelson and Crompton, 1984). With the exception of Fakeye and Crompton (1991), these research efforts do not address the need to target repeat customers with specifically designed marketing communications.

Fakeye and Crompton (1991) examine destination image differences between prospective, first-time and repeat visitors to the Rio Grande Valley in Texas. The findings reveal that repeat visitors appear to have greater awareness of social opportunities, attractions and may have enhanced social networks, leading to a more "complex" image of the destination. These authors underline the need for three types of tourism promotion: (1) *informative*: to create awareness among prospective tourists, (2) *persuasive*: to persuade first-time visitors to buy again, and (3) *reminding*: to reinforce the destination so that travelers consider repeat visits and spread favorable word-of-mouth communications.

Gyte and Phelps (1989) also examine the role of destination image choice for first-time and repeat visitors to Spain. Not surprisingly, their findings indicate that travel intermediaries wishing to cultivate repeat business need to ensure that clients are able to: (a) visit the destination of first choice, and (b) have good holiday experiences.

In another marketing context, Gitelson and Crompton (1984) suggest that repeat travelers to Texas are older people visiting for either relaxation purposes and/or to see friends and relatives. Further qualitative interviews with a small sample reveal that repeat visitors returned to the destination for five major reasons: (1) risk reduction (dealing with "the known"), (2) meeting "like" people (socializing), (3) fulfilling an emotional attachment (grew up there), (4) finding new experiences, and (5) exposing others to the destination.

The research outlined above offers insights into the repeat customer phenomenon and underscores the important role that patrons play as: (a) informal and informed information sources used by prospective travelers, and (b) markets to be cultivated in their own right. Although Fakeye and Crompton (1991) briefly explore the need for different promotions directed at different users, this is done within the context of destination image. While offering some insights into repeat traveler behavior at the destination level, these studies do not address the role played by marketing communications at the micro (enterprise) level. In addition, these authors do not address the communication process within the firm that is responsible for the type, quality and persuasiveness of the information conveyed to and by patrons. Furthermore, the implications for improving marketing communications at the management level are sadly neglected.

MARKETING COMMUNICATIONS AND THE REPEAT CUSTOMER

Before exploring the process of marketing communications and how such messages affect repeat customer buying behavior, it is necessary to define the concept. Marketing communications are defined as, ". . . a mix of communications elements or message types which are designed to evoke certain thoughts, feelings or behaviors, within the context of a given marketing mix and situation" (Ray, 1982: 62). This dialogue with travelers involves externally directed formal and informal marketing communications that occur away from the tourism enterprise as well as internal communications that occur on-site. Formal external marketing communications (promotions) make promises, telling travelers about benefits offered by the tourism supplier. Internal marketing communications take place at the site during the interaction between the tourism service employees and clients when visitors actually experience the promised benefits. Informal marketing communications involve word-of-mouth information conveyed by: (a) visitors who return home and relay their experiences to others, and/or (b) employees who may discuss organizational issues with current and potential patrons. If inconsistencies arise between promised and expected benefits, dissatisfaction occurs and word-of-mouth promotion is likely to be negative.

These marketing communications elements are depicted in Figure 1. The model shows how tourism enterprises rely on external and internal marketing communications. Formal, externally directed communications (promotion), internal communications (visitor-employee interactions) and informal external communications (word-of-mouth) represent key components having an impact on the visitor's experience with the tourism enterprise, thus the decision to try the service or repeat the visit. The following discussion elaborates on the model's major elements and highlights the importance of differentiating messages targeted at repeat customers.

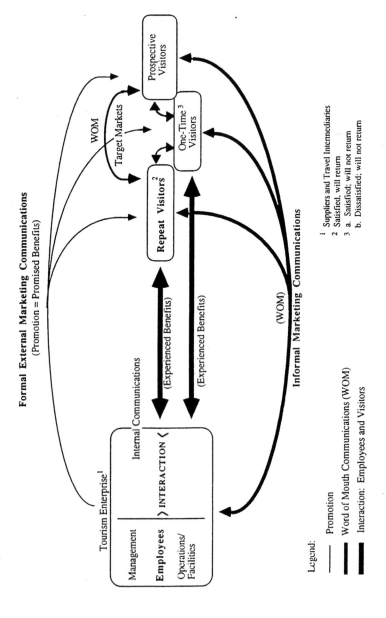

Figure 1: Marketing Communications
Critical to Repeat Visits

Formal External Marketing Communications
(Promotion = Promised Benefits)

WOM

Prospective Visitors

Target Markets

One-Time [3] Visitors

Repeat Visitors [2]

(Experienced Benefits)

(Experienced Benefits)

Internal Communications

Tourism Enterprise [1]

Management

Employees   ⟩ INTERACTION ⟨

Operations/ Facilities

Informal Marketing Communications

(WOM)

[1] Suppliers and Travel Intermediaries
[2] Satisfied, will return
[3] a. Satisfied; will not return
    b. Dissatisfied; will not return

Legend:

——— Promotion

▌▌ Word of Mouth Communications (WOM)

▐ Interaction: Employees and Visitors

8

Formal External Marketing Communications

Formal external marketing communications are represented by promotion in the form of intended messages directed at target markets. Management's task of communicating tourism service benefits and attributes to clients is extremely difficult due to service intangibility. The intangible aspect that characterizes tourism services designates them as *experiences,* with different notions of what constitutes a "good" or "bad" experience. This feature of services implies that their underlying benefits and attributes are more difficult to communicate than those of manufactured (tangible) goods.

This situation is compounded by the need to accurately specify which benefits or tourism service attributes are most critical to which markets. Repeat markets already have previous knowledge of the destination, the available services and amenities. Those who have never visited are likely to have more basic information needs due to their unfamiliarity with the site and offerings. Fakeye and Crompton (1991) suggest that repeat visitors have a more complex image since they have spent enough time on-site to be exposed to the different service dimensions available. These authors indicate that repeat patron information needs may revolve more around special social events and attractions since these visitors are more destination-familiar.

Promotion strategies directed at prospects are informational with the purpose of making them *aware* of the tourism service. However, persuasive approaches are more appropriate for one-time visitors to convert them to repeats. But, external communications directed at repeat customers should have an entirely different focus; promotions that remind these patrons about the destination are most relevant for these customers since they have previously experienced travel to a particular site. The latter promotional efforts are intended to keep the service uppermost in the minds of repeat prospects so that they consider return visits and are encouraged to spread favorable word-of-mouth communications.

Internal Marketing Communications: The On-Site Interaction

Just as external communications are important, internal communications also perform a fundamental role in maintaining repeat customers. Internal communications are those occurring on-site between visitors and employees. The critical nature of the interaction between consumers of services and contact personnel is widely acknowledged (Reid and Reid, 1986; Zeithaml, Parasuraman and Berry, 1985; Berry, 1984; Booms and Nyquist, 1981; Gronroos, 1981; Chase, 1984). Points of contact with personnel make up a substantial part of the communications side of tourism marketing; they dramatically affect how patrons view service supplier offerings by communicating the capabilities of the enterprise (Reid and Reid, 1986; Booms and Bitner, 1981). From a visitor perspective, this interaction embodies and represents the service and directly affects the benefits experienced by travelers.

Because employee-customer contact typifies tourism services, personnel represent a major component of the total experience realized. Employees directly affect how offerings are perceived by guests (George, Kelly and Marshall, 1983; Berry, 1980; Bateson, 1979; Eigler and Langeard, 1977). Contact personnel are in the unique position of influencing the outcome of service encounters. Once management recognizes that employees have considerable potential for managing these communications and can act as intervention agents, steps can be taken to ensure quality interactions. If appropriately managed, these interactions can lead to better service quality and the potential for increased return visits.

The concept of service quality is, at best, vague. The current quest to define service quality, (Fick and Ritchie, 1991; Berry, Parasuraman and Zeithaml, 1986; Zeithaml, Parasuraman and Berry, 1985; Chase, 1984) typically rests on dimensions that underline the key role played by employees in the service delivery process. Updating work initiated by Berry, Parasuraman and Zeithaml (1985), Fick and Ritchie (1991) argue for use of *Servqual,* a multiple-item scale that measures customer perceptions of service quality. The latter researchers propose a measure of service quality that incorporates five major dimensions: (1) *tangibles* (physical facilities, appearance of personnel), (2) *reliability* (performing the promised service dependably and accurately), (3) *responsiveness* (prompt service and willingness to service), (4) *assurance* (knowledge and courtesy; trust and confidence), and (5) *empathy* (caring, individual attention). Berry et al. (1985) also add competence, access (approachability), courtesy, communication (easy use of language and listening) and security (freedom from risk) dimensions. Each of these service quality measures emphasizes the importance of any communications in the visitor-employee encounter.

The Servqual approach implies that all patrons (first-time and repeat) evaluate services using the same framework. First time visitors, unlike repeat patrons, have no prior experience of the services being offered and thus have different expectations of the service being proffered. Consequently these buyers evaluate services based on information conveyed to them by tourism suppliers, destination marketing organizations (DMOs), travel intermediaries and informal sources (friends/relatives). In contrast, repeat users have previous experiences with suppliers that they expect to be repeated. These factors underline the necessity of having minimum performance standard levels that are consistently met.

While the attempts to standardize service quality measurement is admirable, the interaction between personnel and guests is subject to considerable variation due to the human factor. Since tourism service offerings are people based and labor intensive, it is difficult to guarantee replication of service delivery even if existing firm policy dictates this should occur. Consequently, service quality control becomes a challenge due to the potential for inconsistent performance levels. Although absolute standardization may not be desired by all visitors, a minimum quality standard is expected by both first time and repeat users alike. Service quality control thus becomes the challenge of offering a particular service level while maintaining sufficient flexibility to selectively offer higher performance levels where these can be consistently achieved.

Similar to other services, many tourism services have the added dimension of being produced and consumed at the same time. This issue is complicated by the fact that some repeat visitors may desire more familiar, informal encounters where interaction patterns have been previously established with some staff member(s). First-time visitors who are less familiar with the service may prefer a more formal interpersonal approach since they are relative newcomers. In either case, direct, face-to-face communications have a great deal of influence on the benefits experienced on-site. Employees have the responsibility of adjusting and tailoring encounters to suit visitors needs. As much as other marketing communication strategies may be designed to persuade or remind, the nature of the interaction with employees will solidify (or not) the potential for a repeat visit. In addition, the interaction on-site directly influences the informal marketing (word-of-mouth) communications transmitted regarding the service once the patron is off-site. Managing the internal marketing communications between customer contact employees and travelers thus becomes critical in: (1) ensuring a satisfied visit, (2) encouraging positive word-of-mouth communications, and (3) heightening the potential for repeat visits.

Informal Marketing Communications: Word-of-Mouth Messages

Influences on travel decisions extend far beyond formal communications. Travel inclinations are also affected by friends, relatives and acquaintances who have experienced services offered at a destination. Much of what is communicated to prospective travelers involves word-of-mouth information and whether it is positive or negative is a direct result of the degree of satisfaction derived from the visit. As Dichter (1966) so eloquently puts it, "To some degree (mass media) can influence public opinion, but in the final analysis they cannot shape or mold it. People mold opinion" (p. 166).

The importance of word-of-mouth in influencing travel-related decisions is well-documented, with friends and relatives often cited as the most used information sources. For example, information from this source is used in choosing: (1) travel destinations (Um and Crompton, 1990; Gitelson and Crompton, 1983; Nolan, 1976); (2) recreation environments (Uysal, McDonald and Reid, 1990; Raitz and Dakhil, 1989); and (3) leisure facilities/activity sites (Snepenger, Megad, Snelling and Worrall, 1990; Keown, 1989). There is therefore a need to expressly focus on repeat markets as a distinct category in strategic tourism market planning.

The model depicts word-of-mouth messages as a critical informal aspect of marketing communications. These messages are sent to prospective travelers by one-time and repeat visitors who have experienced the services offered. Employees who are either happy or disgruntled in their work also transmit these messages to current and potential visitors.

Two possible reasons for a negative travel experience resulting in poor word-of-mouth communications revolve around: (1) satisfaction levels that do not match expectations, and (2) dissatisfaction with amenities offered on-site and or the experiences with contact personnel (interaction). If visitors are satisfied in both categories, they will most likely positively promote the destination via word-of-mouth even if they do not return. Unsatisfied travelers, on the other hand, will send negative word-of-mouth messages, rendering the formal promotion efforts directed at prospective travelers negligible.

It is necessary to recognize that word-of-mouth activity is integral to the overall performance of the company. When making purchase decision for services, consumers generally rely more heavily on verbal messages (Davis, Guiltman and Jones, 1979). Because repeat visitors are satisfied patrons, they act as valuable information conduits who transmit verbal communications that informally link networks of friends, relatives and relevant others.

Although these communications are difficult to control and manage, there are strategies associated with repeat visitors that can facilitate this process. The Strategic Planning Institute at Cambridge (as cited in Haywood, 1989) suggests that the ability to manage word-of-mouth activity can give the firm a powerful competitive advantage, not only in lowering marketing costs but also in recovering hidden costs or off-setting negative verbal messages. Engel and Blackwell (1982) further advise that the potential exists for marketing-oriented firms to exert control over these communications by developing an integrated marketing program that allows mass media and personal influences to interact.

Haywood (1989) reinforces the notion that hospitality services can systematically manage word-of-mouth messages. He poses a model in which this activity is a function of: (1) "the people with whom the company and its employees come into contact (customers, suppliers, agents, competitors, the general public and other stakeholders), (2) its communications, and (3) the inherent interest in the company as a result of its actions" (p. 58).

Haywood's (1989) model focuses on people–the interactions the service firm has with various publics. The first steps in managing word-of-mouth communications involve developing positive relationships with employees and empowering these contact personnel to appropriately manage the communications between the traveler and the employee at the interaction stage. These precursors facilitate the next stage which involves systematically developing relationships with repeat visitors and actively soliciting and rewarding these individuals for providing referrals.

MARKETING COMMUNICATIONS AND MANAGEMENT CONTROL

The key to managing repeat business lies in using the control that management has over its marketing communications efforts (see Table 1). Formal external marketing communications directed at creating destination awareness or reminder promotions to repeat visitors are relatively easy to manage compared with those aimed at conveying the service benefits (attributes) offered by tourism suppliers. Irrespective of the target market, the challenge is not only one of identifying the benefits sought but also in designing promotional appeals that make the service tangible. These promotions are firm dominated and can be tailored so that they are directed at repeat, first-time and non-visitors, with benefit appeals designed for each group(s). The twin challenge is to identify the benefits sought by repeat visitors and design promotional appeals which effectively consider both elements. For example, promotions directed at first-time buyers are intended to create awareness, build favorable attitudes and perhaps encourage purchase. Consequently, these promotions focus on a variety of communication objectives. In contrast, repeat customers are familiar with product attributes and the communications objective is exclusively centered around encouraging repurchase activity. Promotion design and content features are explicitly within management's control and

---

TABLE 1

Communication Elements Relevant to
Obtaining Repeat Visitors and Degree of Management Control

Marketing Communication Type	Control Base
*Formal External Communications (Promotions; Promised Benefits)	*Management Control (Firm Dominated)
*Internal Communications (Employee/Visitor Interaction)	*Management Imposed Control (Firm/Visitor Dominated)
*Informal External Communications (Word-of-mouth; positive image promotion; information diffusion; referrals)	*Management Imposed Control (Visitor Dominated)

---

must ensure consistency between what is promised and what is actually delivered on-site.

Because tourists consume services at the same time they are produced by personnel, the visitor's evaluation of the travel experience is tied to communications occurring on-site and while participating in the use of the service. Arguably, the lack of standardization in human behavior is difficult to manage during the service encounter, but internal communications are still within management's control. However, concrete steps can be taken to encourage employees to consistently interact with customers in a positive manner. Lundberg (1991) suggests several motivating mechanisms, including: organizational and supervisor recognition, rewards, organization commitment to quality service, appropriate recruitment, hiring and selection as well as supporting technical systems.

Managers must also acknowledge expectation differences between repeat and first-time users. The first-time visitor has expectations built on promised benefits that are formally and informally communicated. The critical task here is to ensure that these promises are deliverable and expectations are satisfied during the first visit. On the other hand, expectations for repeat visitors are based on previous knowledge of the service arising from past experience and on-site interactions. Consequently, the thrust in service standardization should be on maintaining the attributes that attracted the repeat visitor in the first place. Management should also emphasize using visitor-employee communications as the strategy for building customer relationships and retention.

Word-of-mouth messages are the primary channel for information to flow between a service vendor and the market. In light of the dominant role played by visitors in sending these messages, managing informal communications should be viewed as a key issue by tourism supplier services. Two strategies can be used to control and manage informal communications to the tourism supplier's advantage. These are: (1) effectively managing the interaction or service encounter using policy and operational systems (cf. Lundberg, 1991) to maintain performance standards, as mentioned above, and (2) systematically using repeat visitors to: (a) promote positive images of the destination, and (b) recruit prospective customers. In the first instance, the tourism supplier manages operations and the physical plant in such a way that these systems are consistent (deliver promises) with the word-of-mouth messages communicated by trained employees. In the second instance, a conscious effort is made by service suppliers to develop a dialogue with repeat patrons, encourage them to promote a positive image and secure new visitor referrals by offering incentives. In summary, it is important to note that successfully managing word-of-mouth communications depends on consistent, satisfactory service encounters (interactions) between employees and visitors.

IMPLICATIONS AND RECOMMENDATIONS

The model and preceding propositions lead to several strategic considerations and recommendations for tourism service management personnel.

Explicit Focus on Building Repeat Visitor Base

- Establish the current volume of repeat visitors and set objectives for the future volume to be served.
- Identify the economic contribution (net of promotional costs) that is and can be realized by focusing on repeat visitor markets, in contrast to that obtainable from pursuing alternative markets.
- Set specific levels and rates of visitor retention as objectives of the tourism marketing strategy. Distinguish between promotional approaches that can be profitably "separated" and designed for repeat visitors as special markets versus those that should be combined with messages sent to prospective or one-time visitors.
- Profile repeat buyers and, at a minimum, track their buyer behavior patterns based on *Recency* (R) (of last visit), *Frequency* (F) (of visits) and *Monetary value* (M) (dollars spent on-site) (known as *RFM* criteria).

*Strategic Use of Formal External Marketing
Communications (Promotion)*

- Identify specific service and product attributes and cues that are salient to repeat visitors. Where profitable, design specifically tailored promotions to focus on these benefits.
- Explore the use of joint ventures with tourism suppliers who offer complementary products and services to offer augmented packages to attract the repeat market.
- Conduct continuous audits of promotional literature and communications to ensure consistency and integrity in attributes being offered and those that are actually delivered or deliverable.

*Strategic Use of Internal Marketing Communications
(the On-Site Interaction)*

- Integrate all personnel systematically into the internal communications system using both formal and informal methods to solicit employee feedback, encourage input and empower employees.
- Encourage continuous formal and informal feedback from visitors.
- Design personnel training and compensation systems to explicitly support employee feedback and initiative in areas that support service delivery.

*Strategic Use of Informal Marketing Communications
(Word-of-Mouth Messages)*

- Take advantage of the referral networks of friends, relatives and acquaintances that repeat visitors have by actively soliciting repeat visitors to refer the service. Reward repeaters for providing a specific number of referrals.
- Systematically determine from inquirers and first-time visitors, the individual sources of information used in making their patronage decision. Use this information, which will most likely contain previous patrons to build a data base for promotional purposes.
- Establish methods that can accurately track referrals made by repeat customers so this data can be factored into promotion conversation ratios.

The above recommendations offer a planned approach to ensure that tourism service suppliers can leverage the initial and costly investments made in their marketing communications in securing first time visitors to ensure the likelihood of obtaining repeat customers.

CONCLUSIONS

This paper suggests that repeat visitors to tourism establishments represent a unique segment that merits specific conceptual and strategic treatment. Although the paper briefly touches on the role of marketing communications aimed at one-time patrons, the authors are mindful of the fact that referrals and informal communications from previous users are still relied on for making most travel purchase and use decisions (Uysal, McDonald and Reid, 1990; Raitz and Dakhil, 1989). This feature suggests that businesses relying on one time patronage need to pay as much attention to using repeat patrons for cultivating new business as suppliers who focus predominantly on repeat patronage.

The paper argues that tourism supplier services should stress external and internal marketing communications directed at repeat visitor/user segments. These patrons represent a valuable resource which can be strategically managed for building profitable customer relationships. A conceptual model is presented which integrates three critical and significant dimensions of marketing communications: (1) formal external (promotion), (2) internal (on-site interactions), and (3) informal (word-of-mouth) communications. The paper shows that marketing communications used by tourism supplier services, when integrated with a focus on the repeat patron, has significant potential for building repeat visitor relationships that can ensure profitable growth.

REFERENCES

Bateson, J. (1979). Why we need services marketing. In J. Ferrell et al. (Eds.), *Conceptual and Theoretical Developments in Marketing* (pp. 131-146). Chicago, IL: AMA Proceedings Series.

Berry, L.L. (1984). The employee as customer. In C.H. Lovelock (Ed.), *Services Marketing* (pp. 271-278). Englewood Cliffs, N.J.: Prentice Hall.

Berry, L.L. (1980). Services marketing is different. *Business,* May-June: 24-29.

Berry, L.L., A. Parasuraman & V. Zeithaml (1986). *Servqual: A Multiple-Item Scale for Measuring Customer Perceptions of Service Quality.* Cambridge, MA: Marketing Science Institute #86-108: 5.

Booms, B.H. & M.J. Bitner (1981). Marketing strategies and organization structure for service firms. In J.H. Donnelly and W.R. George (Eds.), *Marketing of Services* (pp. 94-104). Chicago: American Marketing Association.

Booms B.H. & J. Nyquist (1981). Analyzing the customer/firm communication component of the services marketing mix. In J.H. Donnelly and W.R. George (Eds.), *Marketing of Services* (pp. 63-72). Chicago: American Marketing Association.

Chase, R.B.(1984). Where does the customer fit in a service operation. In C.H. Lovelock (Ed.), *Services Marketing* (pp. 400-407). Englewood Cliffs, N.J.: Prentice Hall.

Davis, D., J.P. Guiltman & W.H. Jones (1979). Service characteristics, consumer search and the classification of retail services. *Journal of Retailing*, Fall: 3-23.

Dichter, Ernest (1966). How word-of-mouth advertising works. *Harvard Business Review*, V. 44 (Nov-Dec), 147-166.

Eigler, P. & E. Langeard (1977). A new approach to service marketing. *Marketing of Consumer Services: New Insights*, 31-58.

Engel, J.F. & R.D. Blackwell (1982). *Consumer Behavior* (4th ed.) (pp. 371-372). New York: Holt, Rinehart and Winston.

Fakeye, Paul C. & J.L. Crompton (1991). Image differences between prospective, first-time, and repeat visitors to the Lower Rio Grande Valley. *Journal of Travel Research*, 30 (2): 10-15.

Fick, G.R. & J.R.B. Ritchie (1991). Measuring service quality in the travel and tourism industry. *Journal of Travel Research*, 30 (2) 2-9.

George W.R., J.P. Kelly & C.E. Marshall (1983). Personal selling of services. In L.L. Berry et al. (Eds.), *Emerging Perspectives in Services Marketing* (pp. 86-93). Chicago, IL: AMA Proceedings Series.

Gitelson, R.J. & J.L. Crompton (1984). Insights into the repeat vacation phenomena. *Annals of Tourism Research*, 11: 199-218.

Gronroos, C. (1981). Internal marketing–an integral part of marketing theory. In J.H. Donnelly and W.R. George (Eds.), *Marketing of Services* (pp. 63-72). Chicago: American Marketing Association.

Gyte, D.M. & A. Phelps (1989). Patterns of destination repeat business: British tourists in Mallorca, Spain. *Journal of Travel Research*. 28 (1): 24-28.

Haywood, K.M. (1989). Managing word-of-mouth communications. *Journal of Services Marketing*, 3 (2): 55-67.

Keown, C. (1989). A model of tourists' propensity to buy: the case of Japanese visitors to Hawaii. *Journal of Travel Research*, 27 (3): 31-34.

Lundberg, C.C. (1991). Productivity enhancement through managing the service encounter. *Hospitality Research Journal*, 30 (2): 63-71.

Lyke, Rick (1989). Amenities Key to Claiming Repeat Guests. *Hotel/Motel Management*, 204 (July 31): 34 and 48.

Nolan, S.D. (1976). Tourists' use and evaluation of travel information sources: summary and conclusions. *Journal of Travel Research*, 14 (1): 6-8.

Raitz, K. & M. Dakhil (1989). A note about information sources for preferred recreational environments. *Journal of Travel Research*, 27 (4): 45-49.

Ray, M.L. (1982). *Advertising and Communication Management*, Englewood Cliffs, NJ: Prentice Hall.

Reid, L.J. & S.D. Reid (1986). Communicating hospitality services: from the inside out. In S.B. Joseph, L. Moutinho and I.R. Vernon (Eds.), *Tourism Services Marketing: Advances in Theory and Practice* (pp. 190-200). Academy of Marketing Science and Cleveland State University. Special Conference Series, held in Cleveland, OH (September 24-26).

Rivers, M.J., R.S. Toh & M. Alaoui (1991). Frequent-stayer programs: the demographic, behavioral and attitudinal characteristics of hotel steady sleepers. *Journal of Travel Research*, 30 (2): 41-46.

Snepenger, D., K. Megad, M. Snelling & K. Worrall (1990). Information search strategies by destination-naive tourists. *Journal of Travel Research*, 29 (1): 13-16.

Um, S. & J. Crompton (1990). Attitude determinants in tourism destination choice. *Annals of Tourism Research*, 17 (3): 432-448.

Uysal, M., C. McDonald & L. Reid (1990). Sources of information used by international visitors to US parks and natural areas. *Journal of Park and Recreation Administration*, 8 (1): 51-59.

Zeithaml, V.A., A. Parasuraman & L.L. Berry (1985). Problems and strategies in services marketing. *Journal of Marketing*, 49 (2):33-46.

Market Structure Analysis
of Media Selection Practices
by Travel Services

David Snepenger
Mary Snepenger

SUMMARY. This paper examined media selection practices by tourism businesses competing in Alaska. Two media selection decisions, media use and media mix, were investigated. Media use decisions focused on the use/not use of television, national magazines, radio, newspapers, outdoor advertising, and a regional travel magazine. Media mix decisions explored what combinations of these six media firms utilized. A market structure analysis revealed that both media selection practices were affected by organizational, task, and demand characteristics facing firms. The market structure analysis also suggested that media mix decisions were likely to be more highly constrained than are individual media use decisions.

INTRODUCTION

When developing an advertising campaign a critical issue for the organization is the selection of media. Firms must decide on whether to adver-

Dr. David Snepenger is Associate Professor, College of Business, Montana State University, Bozeman, MT 59717. Mary Snepenger is Assistant Director, Office of Research Support, Sherrick Hall, Montana State University, Bozeman, MT 59717.

The authors gratefully acknowledge the financial support for the data collection provided by Dean Michael Rice, School of Management, University of Alaska-Fairbanks.

[Haworth co-indexing entry note]: "Market Structure Analysis of Media Selection Practices by Travel Services." Snepenger, David, and Mary Snepenger. Co-published simultaneously in *Journal of Travel & Tourism Marketing* (The Haworth Press, Inc.) Vol. 2, No. 2/3, 1993, pp. 21-36; and: *Communication and Channel Systems in Tourism Marketing* (ed: Muzaffer Uysal, and Daniel R. Fesenmaier) The Haworth Press, Inc., 1993, pp. 21-36. Multiple copies of this article/chapter may be purchased from The Haworth Document Delivery Center [1-800-3-HAWORTH; 9:00 a.m. - 5:00 p.m. (EST)].

tise in newspapers, radio, television, outdoor signs, magazines, and other forms of media. Media selection involves two critical decisions. The first decision focuses on deciding which media to use. The second decision involves what media best complement each other in order to develop a media mix which will effectively communicate to the firm's customers. This paper investigates these two decisions for firms competing in the Alaska tourism market.

THEORETICAL FRAMEWORK

The paper is exploratory in nature because the bulk of research in marketing and tourism has been on the consumer and not on producers of products and services (Lutz 1979; Wind and Robertson 1983; Day and Wensley 1983; Hunt 1983). A review of the advertising literature revealed no empirical studies or theoretical essays on the actual use of media by firms. It did, however, uncover two calls for research on the advertising practices of firms. An early 1980's review of the advertising literature identified understanding users of advertising as a priority research area (Schmalensee 1983). Later, Yale and Gilly (1988) in their content analysis of the advertising literature noted that the advertising literature continues to neglect firms as a unit of analysis for empirical studies and as a topical issue for advertising theorists.

Since the advertising literature did not provide direction regarding media selection by firms, the marketing and management literature on competition was utilized to provide a basis for the study. The theory of competition postulates that survival in a competitive market requires differentiation by firms (Henderson 1983). Differentiation stems from the firm's target market(s), competitors, and resources (Chaganti, Chaganti, and Mahajan 1989; Day and Wensley 1988; Keates and Bracker 1988; Vaccaro and Kassaye 1988). Both strategic and operational level decisions demonstrate differentiation actions by firms. Strategic issues typically deal with the firm's mission and its principal strategies, whereas operational decisions translate strategic plans into functional action. Operational decisions tend to be more specific, less comprehensive, involve smaller amounts of resources, are often repetitive in nature, and cover a time span of one year or less (Robinson, Logan, and Salem 1986). Operational level decisions, such as those involving media selection practices, may demonstrate differentiation patterns among competing firms more clearly than do strategic level issues because they are more observable, distinguishable, and thus easier to quantify.

Based on the above discussion it was hypothesized that firms competing in the Alaska tourism market would manifest differentiation in their media selection practices. Firms would differentiate themselves due to the markets they served, their geographical location, their resources, and their other promotional activities.

MARKET STRUCTURE ANALYSIS

Market structure analysis has received attention as a means of identifying differentiation activities by firms. Market structure analysis is similar to market segmentation in that data are used to form dependent variables which identify groupings of similar competitors (Kopp, Eng, and Tigert 1989; Grover and Srinivasan 1987; Day, Shocker, and Srivastava 1979). Market structure analysis then employs a variety of independent variables or correlates in an effort to understand organizational behaviors such as media selection.

The market structure analysis of media selection practices of Alaska travel services incorporated two dependent variables and three families of independent variables. The first dependent variable, media use, identified users and nonusers of newspapers, radio, television, magazines, outdoor advertising, and the *Milepost*, an Alaska travel magazine. The second dependent variable, media mix, examined the combinations of media used. In an effort to describe these two media selection activities organizational, task, and demand factors as suggested by d'Amboise and Muldowney (1988) were used as independent variables. The following paragraphs describe these families of independent variables.

Organizational variables serve a similar capacity in investigations of business practices as do demographics in consumer studies. They help to describe objective characteristics which may constrain or induce organizational management decisions (Zeithaml, Parasuraman, and Berry 1985; Blau 1974). The organizational characteristics utilized in this study are (1) age of the firm, (2) number of summer employees, (3) whether the firm is a corporation or not, (4) whether the firm was located in a major metropolitan area (urban) or not (rural), and (5) whether the mission of the firm is to provide a core travel service (lodging, transportation, or attractions) or a fringe travel service (retail or food and beverage services) (Gunn 1988).

Task specific factors offer information on issues closely related to the organizational behavior under investigation. For media selection these include the size of the advertising budget, the diversity of media desired, and the target(s) of the advertising message. These factors were quantified as the size of the advertising budget, the total number of media utilized, and the percent of advertising budget aimed at out-of-state travelers.

Demand factors play a major role in the goal attainment actions of firms, and in the case of advertising, the target audience directly influences which media best reaches and communicates to the customer (Schmalensee 1983). Important demand factors for tourism businesses include the origin of customers (out-of-state, in-state, or local), the timing of demand, and the relationship to wholesalers such as tour operators. The operationalization of these factors consisted of (1) percent out-of-state customers, (2) percent sales in summer, and (3) percent customers coming with tour groups.

DATA AND METHOD

Service firms competing in the Alaska tourism market furnished a geographical market to investigate media selection practices. The high involvement nature of travel purchases and the usual lack of knowledge about the destination makes advertising an important factor in the information search process of many travelers (Snepenger et al. 1990). Consequently, the selection of media plays a significant role in the marketing activities of Alaska travel services. The usual array of media available to advertising managers, namely, newspapers, outdoor advertising, radio, national magazines, and television, along with a regional travel guide, the *Milepost,* were considered when evaluating media selection practices (Schmalensee 1983; Shimp 1990).

During the winter of 1987 a sampling frame consisting of several thousand travel firms operating in Alaska was developed using industry directories and telephone books. Considerable effort was taken to include a cross section of businesses from the transportation, retail, food and beverage, lodging, attraction, travel agent, and tour operator sectors of the travel industry. Then a geographically stratified probability sample of 300 firms was drawn based on the historical volume of travel in the seven regions of the state.

The marketing manager or owner of the travel business was contacted by telephone during normal business hours in March 1987. Each of the contacted firms were screened to determine if at least 30 percent of their summer business was from travelers. Of the 212 qualified firms, 187 (88 percent) participated in the study. The high response rate was attributed to the length of the survey, the attention given to tourism practitioners from the University, and the confidentiality provided to respondents. In addition, the timing of the survey contributed to the response rate. Managers were preparing for the upcoming summer season so they were available, yet not too busy to respond because the summer season had not yet begun.

Of the 187 firms participating in the survey, two did not furnish information on media use and thus were excluded from the study.

Media use was measured with a use/not use format since it was the least obtrusive and most reliable measure of media use. Media mix was examined using a K-means cluster analysis algorithm. The K-means algorithm was selected because the procedure is often more robust than hierarchical methods, especially when there are firms which could potentially utilize an unusual media mix (Punj and Stewart 1983). Separate cluster analyses were undertaken dividing the sample of 185 firms into two, three, four, five, and six clusters. Five clusters resulted in groupings of firms which were large enough for statistical analysis and at the same time partitioned the sample of firms into groups with distinct media mixes. The stability of the five media mixes was evaluated using a split-half reliability procedure. The entire sample was randomly partitioned into two subsamples and then cluster analyses were performed on each subsample. The two subsequent cluster analyses again produced five clusters which were consistent with the results for the overall sample.

Similar to Zeithaml, Parasuraman, and Berry's (1985) investigation of service firms, parametric univariate statistical tests were considered for identifying relationships between media selection practices and the descriptor variables. However, examining the relationships proved problematic. Formal tests revealed that none of the continuous variables were normally distributed and most had a Poisson like distribution. Consequently, to test for relationships between the media selection variables and the descriptor variables, the following distribution free statistical procedures were employed: Chi-square test of homogeneity of proportions, Mann-Whitney U test, and the Kruskal-Wallis one-way analysis of variance (Gaither and Glorfeld 1985; Marascuilo and McSweeney 1977). For all statistical tests an alpha level of .05 was adopted. The tables report medians for the continuous distributions and percentages for the qualitative variables.

Multicolinearity existed among some of the descriptor variables with three relationships having Spearman correlation's of .5 or higher. First, the size of the firm covaries with the size of the advertising budget (rs = .606). Second, the demand variable, percent of out-of-state customers, related to the advertising variable, percent of advertising budget aimed at out-of-state travelers (rs = .696). Thirdly, the amount of out-of-state customers and the level of seasonality of demand correlated significantly (rs = .572). However, due to the paucity of published reports on the topic, the theoretically distinct purposes of the variables, and the use of univariate tests of significance all variables were retained for analysis.

FINDINGS

Media Use Decisions

The most frequently used medium was newspapers (85%) which was consistent with other reports which observe that newspapers are the leading advertising medium nationwide and important for promoting services (Shimp 1990; Zeithaml, Parasuraman, and Berry 1985). The second most often employed medium, outdoor advertising (71%), has often served as a primary communication channel for travel services and retailing even though it usually plays a lesser role for most advertisers (Kotler 1988; Shimp 1990). The third most cited medium, the *Milepost* (70%), is targeted at self-directed travelers to Alaska. Radio was adopted by slightly over half of the firms (57%) which paralleled national norms (Kotler 1988). National magazines (42%) and television (41%) provided a channel of communication for a minority of Alaskan travel firms. Magazine use by travel services mirrored national standards in terms of relative use. However, television use by travel services was less than national norms (Kotler 1988). This was consistent with Zeithaml, Parasuraman, and Berry's (1985) finding that television serves a lesser advertising role for services than for products.

Table 1 delineates the organizational, advertising, and demand characteristics of users and nonusers of the six media. Newspaper users tended to have more summer employees and a corporate structure, which suggested that they were larger more formal organizations. The advertising and demand relationships revealed that newspaper users tended to serve a customer base consisting of both locals and out-of-staters. Newspaper users probably utilized the medium as a low cost method to target local customers and travelers while in the vicinity of the business.

Outdoor advertisers differed from all other media users in that they generally had fewer summer employees than nonusers. They were also more urban and captured a larger portion of the tour operator business than nonusers. These findings implied that outdoor advertising was utilized by small establishments as an inexpensive means to advertise. Furthermore, the data supported the media literature which indicates that outdoor advertising is most useful in high traffic areas such as urban centers (Shimp 1990).

Users and nonusers of the travel guide, the *Milepost*, did not differ with respect to any of the variables under investigation except for the number of media used. *Milepost* users employed more media than nonusers. It should be noted that users of each media used significantly more media than nonusers of the media. Factors besides those examined here such as man-

TABLE 1. Organizational, Task and Demand Characteristics of Users and Nonusers of Advertising Media (1)

Characteristic	Newspaper Users N=158	Nonusers N=27	Outdoor Users N=132	Nonusers N=53	Milepost Users N=130	Nonusers N=55	Radio Users N=106	Nonusers N=79	Magazines Users N=77	Nonusers N=108	Television Users N=76	Nonusers N=109
Organizational												
Years in Business	9	8	9	8	9	8	10	7	9	8	9	8
Number of Summer Employees	10	5*	7	10*	10	7	13	4*	10	7*	12	6*
Percent Corporations	54	22*	52	42	48	51	62	32*	56	44	59	43*
Percent Core Travel Businesses	64	81	65	70	68	64	56	81*	79	58*	64	69
Percent Urban	44	48	50	30*	40	55	30	63*	40	47	30	54*
Task												
Advertising Budget ($ thousands)	6	3*	5	6	5	5	10	3*	7	5*	10	4*
Number of Media Used	4	3*	4	3*	4	3*	4	3*	4	3*	5	3*
Percent Aimed at Out-of-Staters	40	80*	40	50	50	40	30	60*	50	25*	40	45
Demand												
Percent Out-of-State Customers	50	65	50	60	50	50	50	60*	50	50	50	53
Percent Tour Customers	10	5*	15	5*	10	10	10	10	10	10*	10	10
Percent Sales in Summer	60	63	60	60	60	50	50	75*	70	50*	50	65*

(1) Chi-square test of homogeneity employed for percent corporations, percent core travel businesses, and percent urban variables. Mann-Whitney U test used for years in business, number of summer employees, advertising budget, number of media used, percent aimed at out-of-staters, percent out-of-state customers, percent tour customers, and percent sales in summer.
* Indicates a significant difference between users and nonusers at alpha = .05.

ager preferences, cost per viewer, and type of traveler reached may dictate selection of the *Milepost*.

Radio users and nonusers exhibited the most differences across the descriptor variables. Only age and percent tour companies did not significantly differentiate between users and nonusers of this medium. Radio users tended to consist of larger, more established, retail and restaurant establishments in rural locations with moderate to large advertising budgets who serve a more local clientele. These results corresponded to the advertising literature which suggested that radio was a favorite of local advertisers (Shimp 1990).

Magazine users also differed significantly from nonusers in many respects. Magazine advertisers were larger and more apt to be lodging, transportation, attraction, or other businesses centrally concerned with travelers. Consequently magazine users tended to have high seasonality of demand. They had larger advertising budgets than nonusers, but smaller budgets than radio and television users. They concentrated their advertising efforts on out-of-state travelers much more than nonusers of this medium. Magazines serve as a useful communication tool for travelers making purchase decisions at the origin of their trip rather than at the destination.

Television users tended to have more summer employees, a corporate structure, rural location, and large advertising budgets. They along with radio users had the largest advertising budgets. Television was the least used medium and was employed by firms who used the most media.

Media Mix Decisions

Table 2 presents the five media mixes identified by the cluster analysis. The media which were subscribed to more than the sample levels were used to characterize each media mix. Firms using the "All but Magazines" media mix utilized, newspapers, outdoor advertising, the *Milepost*, radio, and television more than the average and national magazines less. This media mix was employed by 72 of the 185 firms (39%). Compared to the other media mixes the "All but Magazines" media mix exhibits the greatest diversity of media use. The "TV, Radio and Newspapers" media mix is characterized by heavy use of radio, television, and newspapers with no use of outdoor and less than the average use of the *Milepost* and magazines. The third media mix, "Magazines, TV, Outdoor, and Newspapers," consists of firms that highly utilize all the media except radio and the *Milepost*. Those firms utilizing the fourth media mix, "Magazines and *Milepost*" concentrated their advertising budgets on only these two media, moderately used newspapers, and were less likely to use outdoor, televi-

TABLE 2. The Five Media Mixes Employed by Travel Firms in Alaska Reported by Percentage Use of Each Medium (1)

| Media | **Media Mixes** | | | | |
| | All but Magazines | TV, Radio and Newspaper | Magazines, TV, Outdoor, and Newspaper | Magazines and *Milepost* | Outdoor |
	N = 72	N = 25	N = 20	N = 32	N = 36
Newspapers	97%	88%	95%	53%	83%
Outdoor Adv.	100	0	95	31	86
Milepost	78	68	10	94	69
Radio	100	96	40	6	0
Magazines	33	32	85	88	0
Television	51	72	75	9	8

(1) For each media mix, the media which were subscribed to more than the sample norm; newspapers (85%), outdoor (71%), *Milepost* (70%), radio (57%), magazines (42%), and television (41%) were used to characterize each media mix.

sion, and radio. "Outdoor," the fifth media mix, displayed an over representation of outdoor advertising, slightly under representation of newspapers and the *Milepost*, and little or no use of radio, magazines and television.

As can be seen in Table 3, the five media mixes exhibited significant differences across the organizational, advertising, and demand characteristics. The only characteristics which were not significant were the age of the firm and the percent of customers coming with tour groups.

The firms using the "All but Magazines" media mix were generally older, larger corporations who were less likely to be solely concerned with tourism, and more rural (not located in Anchorage or Fairbanks). Of the five media mixes, they have average to high advertising budgets, use the most media, and aim very little of their advertising at out-of-staters. This corresponds to their relatively low number of out-of-state customers and low seasonality of demand.

The "TV, Radio, and Newspaper" media mix users had the most summer employees, were both corporations and non corporations, both core and fringe tourism businesses, and were predominantly rural. They had the highest advertising budgets, used about four media, and aimed very little of their advertising at out-of-staters. Firms using this media mix generated about half of their sales from out-of-state customers and had moderate

TABLE 3. Organizational, Task, and Demand Characteristics of Firms Employing the Five Media Mixes (1). N = 185

	Media Mixes				
	All but Magazines	TV, Radio and Newspaper	Magazines, TV, Outdoor and Newspaper	Magazines and *Milepost*	Outdoor
Characteristic	N = 72	N = 25	N = 20	N = 32	N = 36
Organizational					
Years in business	10	10	8	9	6
Number of summer employees	13	20	7	5	4*
Percent corporations	63	56	50	34	29*
Percent core travel businesses	56	52	75	88	75*
Percent urban	36	4	50	47	83*
Task					
Advertising budget	$8,000	$15,000	$7,000	$3,000	$3,000*
Number of media used	5	4	4	3	3*
Percent aimed at out-of-staters	28	20	63	70	45*
Demand					
Percent out-of-state customers	45	50	55	65	58*
Percent tour customers	18	10	13	5	10
Percent sales in summer	50	50	50	80	73*

(1) Chi-square test of Homogeneity employed for percent corporations, percent core travel businesses, and percent urban variables. Kruskal-Wallis one-way analysis of variance used for years in business, number of summer employees, advertising budget, number of media used, percent aimed at out-of-staters, percent out-of-stater customers, percent tour customers, and percent sales in summer.
* Indicates a significant difference between the five media mixes at alpha = .05.

seasonality of demand. These firms appear to serve the rural communities where they are located and secondarily provide services to tourists. The low percentage of firms using this media mix with an urban location probably explains the lack of outdoor advertising.

The media mix utilized by the fewest number of firms consisted of "Magazines, TV, Outdoor, and Newspapers." The media mix is typically associated with tourism oriented businesses that are slightly bigger, older and more corporate in structure than the firms utilizing either the "Magazines and *Milepost"* or "Outdoor" media mix. They have moderate advertising budgets, use about four media, and aim a large amount of their advertising at out-of-state travelers (63%). The amount of advertising aimed at out-of-staters contrasts with the amount of out-of-state customers generated (55%) and their relatively low seasonality of demand.

The "Magazines and *Milepost"* media mix users were similar in organizational characteristics to those relying heavily on outdoor advertising ("Outdoor") and dissimilar to those using the "All but Magazines" and "TV, Radio, and Newspaper" media mixes. They had few summer employees, were largely noncorporate, mostly core tourism businesses, and both urban and rural. They had small advertising budgets like the outdoor users, yet they aimed most of their budget at out-of-state travelers. They also differed from the firms using the other media mixes in their large number of out-of-state travelers, few tour customers, and high seasonality of demand. These firms demonstrated a distinct media mix designed to target out-of-state travelers, their primary market.

The firms using the "Outdoor" media mix use outdoor advertising, newspapers, and the *Milepost* almost exclusively, relying very little on the other advertising media to communicate to their customers. They consisted of younger, smaller, sole proprietorships or partnerships. These firms were mostly core tourism businesses residing mainly in urban areas. They had small advertising budgets and aimed less than half of their advertising at out-of-staters even though they had a large portion of out-of-state travelers as customers and high seasonality of demand. They may have used outdoor advertising due to their urban locations and low advertising budgets.

DISCUSSION

The market structure analysis revealed that media use decisions were affected by organizational, task, and demand characteristics. The number of summer employees, ownership structure, location, size of the advertising budget, number of media employed, target audience, and seasonality of demand all played a role in media use. For example, the size of the advertising budget affected the use of more expensive media like radio, national magazines, and television, while it did not influence selection of newspapers, outdoor advertising, or the *Milepost*. Furthermore, the findings indicated that radio and newspapers served as local media, while national magazines allowed the firm to focus on out-of-state travelers. The other media did not demonstrate such clear division as to their use for local or out-of-state markets. They may be used to target both local customers and also to attract tourists at the destination. For each medium, users employed more media than did nonusers demonstrating there was a core of firms who utilized three or fewer media and another group of firms which engaged four or more media.

Collectively the composition of the media mixes revealed complex media use patterns. The media mixes did not demonstrate unidimensionality such as found in a Guttman scale. For example, the clusters did not have an underlying unidimension based on frequency of use. If this was the case, then the clusters would have ordered by the inclusion of newspapers, followed by outdoor, *Milepost*, radio, magazines, and television. Instead outdoor advertising was part of the media mix which used the most media and another media mix in which it was the only highly used medium. The market structure analysis with the organization, task, and demand factors collaborated the lack of unidimensionality. These independent variables were not monitonically correlated, but more likely to demonstrate a checkerboard or nonlinear relationship.

Overall the media mix findings suggest that tourism businesses in Alaska employ one of five media mix strategies to advertise their services. Those businesses who were centrally concerned with travel like lodging, attractions, transportation, and travel agents chose any one of the five media mixes depending on other organizational, advertising, or demand factors. The fringe tourism businesses concerned with retail or food and beverage services, however, predominantly selected either the "All but Magazines" or the "TV, Radio, and Newspaper" media mixes.

The findings from the market structure analysis also demonstrated that firms will structurally differentiate themselves in an effort to survive and compete using operational decisions such as those associated with media selection practices. Media appear to serve as a tool to assist in establishing competitive niches. The examination of media selection using market structure analysis revealed five distinct competitive niches in the Alaska travel market. It has been argued that organizations with similar technological and competitive environments exhibit similar behavior. In essence, patterns emerge due to the constraints the environment imposes on the organization such as clientele, competitors, and available communication technologies (Thompson 1967).

The market structure analysis also suggested that media mix decisions were likely to be more highly differentiated then are individual media use decisions. The choice of whether to use a particular medium and the decision of what media to employ in concert was shaped by organizational, task specific and demand factors. The use or nonuse of a particular medium tended to not be as correlated (31 of 66 tests significant) by these factors as was the media mix decision (9 of 11 tests significant). This suggests that managerial discretion may be greater at the use/not use level than at the media mix level. Parsons (1960) has observed that the manager mediates between the organization and the constraints imposed by the environment. The constraints imposed by the environment, thus, appear to be more binding at the media mix decision than the decisions for individual media. Furthermore, to discuss media selection solely in terms of individual media does not reflect the use of media mixes as competitive tools. Few businesses rely on only one medium at a time. Most utilize a combination of media to achieve their advertising objectives.

Most of what is known about advertising is based on products sold by large firms, yet there is a need to understand the advertising practices of smaller service firms (Tauber 1986). What is currently known about small service firms is restricted to specific professions or industries. Zeithaml, Parasuraman, and Berry (1985) indicate that a research priority in services marketing is empirical study that transcends specific services and tests service marketing concepts. This study found differences in advertising practices among travel service firms. Travel service firms with different organization, demand and advertising characteristics utilized different media mixes. The rational, patterned media selection practices of the firms suggests that firms facing similar environments react in similar ways.

A definitive statement on whether or not media selection poses a problem to services requires additional research on the relationship between media selection and effectiveness. Effectiveness can be examined either as an advertising effectiveness issue which examines reach, frequency, and recall or as a business effectiveness issue which relates to profit and return on investment. Vaccaro and Kassaye (1988) indicate that different media are effective at reaching different target audiences, but that many small retailers routinely use newspapers without examining its effectiveness. The small business literature suggests that information on overall business effectiveness would also be useful for understanding marketing management practices of firms (d'Amboise and Muldowney 1988). The business effectiveness issue is difficult because it requires collecting financial data and/or the opinion of owner/managers (Fiorito and LaForge 1986). Many small businesses have different and less aggressive objectives than larger businesses. Defining success or effectiveness and measuring it may require different methods than used for large firms. For example some small owner operated firms may have lifestyle objectives, while others may have more focused economic and growth objectives.

CONCLUSION

Marketing theorists view the exchange relationship and the attendant actions of both buyers and sellers as the fundamental area of study for the field (Henderson 1983; Hunt 1983; Houston and Gassenheimer 1987). Yet, the vast bulk of theory-based behavioral research in marketing has been on the consumer, while the behavior of the parties selling to the consumer has been virtually ignored (Lutz 1979; Wind and Robertson 1983; Day and Wensley 1983; Hunt 1983). The advertising and tourism literatures reflect this perspective in that much attention has been given to the receiver in the communication process at the expense of understanding the sender. Examining media selection from the senders' perspective contributed to an understanding of media selection and its role as a competitive tool. The receiver in the communication channel, as measured by the demand variables did not exclusively correlate with media selection decisions. Organizational and task specific factors also influenced media selection behavior. Therefore to ignore organizational and task specific factors limits understanding of media selection and competitive behaviors of firms within the tourism sector of the economy.

REFERENCES

Blau, Peter M. (1974). *Inequality and Heterogeneity*. New York: The Free Press.

Chaganti, Radha, Rajeswararao Chaganti, & Vijay Mahajan (1989). Profitable Small Business Strategies Under Different Types of Competition. *Entrepreneurship Theory and Practice*, (Spring): 21-35.

d'Amboise, Gerald & Marie Muldowney (1988). Management Theory for Small Business: Attempts and Requirements. *Academy of Management Review*, 13(2): 226-240.

Day, George, S., Allan D. Shocker, & Rajendra K. Srivastava (1979). Customer-Oriented Approaches to Identifying Product-Markets. *Journal of Marketing*, 43(Fall): 8-19.

_____ & Robin Wensley (1983). Marketing Theory with a Strategic Orientation. *Journal of Marketing*, 47(Fall): 79-89.

Evanson, Donald (1984). Media Mix–Do We Practice What We Preach? *Journal of Advertising Research*, 24(5): 13-14.

Fiorito, Susan S. & Raymond W. LaForge (1986). A Marketing Strategy Analysis of Small Retailers. *American Journal of Small Business*, (Spring): 7-17.

Gaither, Norman & Louis Glorfeld (1985). An Evaluation of the Use of Tests of Significance in Organizational Behavior Research. *Academy of Management Review*, 10(4): 787-793.

Grover, Rajiv & V. Srinivasan (1987). A Simultaneous Approach to Market Segmentation and Market Structuring. *Journal of Marketing Research*, 24(May): 139-153.

Gunn, Clare A. (1988). *Tourism Planning*, Second Edition. New York: Taylor and Francis.

Henderson, Bruce D. (1983). The Anatomy of Competition. *Journal of Marketing*, 47(Spring): 7-11.

Houston, Franklin S. & Jule B. Gassenheimer (1987). Marketing and Exchange. *Journal of Marketing*, 51(October): 3-18.

Hunt, Shelby D. (1983). General Theories and the Fundamental Explanada of Marketing. *Journal of Marketing*, 47(Fall): 9-17.

Keates, Barbara W. & Jeffrey S. Bracker (1988). Toward a Theory of Small Firm Performance: A Conceptual Model. *American Journal of Small Business*, (Spring): 41-58.

Kopp, Robert J., Robert J. Eng, & Douglas J. Tigert (1989). A Competitive Structure and Segmentation Analysis of the Chicago Fashion Market. *Journal of Retailing*, 65(4): 496-515.

Kotler, Philip (1988). *Marketing Management: Analysis, Planning, Implementation, and Control*. Englewood Cliffs, New Jersey: Prentice Hall.

Lutz, R.J. (1979). Opening Statement. In O.C. Ferrell, S.W. Brown, & C.W. Lamb, (Eds.), *Conceptual and Theoretical Developments in Marketing* (pp. 3-6). Chicago: American Marketing.

Marascuilo, Leonard A. & Maryellen McSweeney (1977). *Nonparametric and Distribution-Free Methods for the Social Sciences*. Monterey, California: Brooks/Cole Publishing Company.

Parsons, Talcot (1960). *Structure and Process in Modern Societies*. New York: The Free Press of Glencoe.

Punj, Girish & David W. Stewart (1983). Cluster Analysis in Marketing Research: Review and Suggestions for Application. *Journal of Marketing Research*, 20(May): 134-148.

Robinson, Richard B., Jr., John E. Logan, & Moragea Y. Salem (1986). Strategic Versus Operational Planning In Small Retail Firms. *American Journal of Small Business*, (Winter):7-16.

Schmalensee, Diane H. (1983). Today's Top Priority Advertising Research Questions. *Journal of Advertising Research*, 23(April-May): 49-60.

Shimp, Terence A. (1990). *Promotion Management and Marketing Communications*. Chicago: The Dryden Press.

Snepenger, David, Kelli Meged, Mary Snelling, & Kelly Worrall (1990). Information Search Strategies by Destination-Naive Tourists. *Journal of Travel Research*, 29(1): 13-16.

Tauber, Edward M. (1986). Advertising in a Service Economy. *Journal of Advertising Research*, (April-May): 9.

Thompson, James D. (1967). *Organizations in Action*. New York: McGraw-Hill Book Company.

Vaccaro, Joseph P. & W. Wossen Kassaye (1988). Increasing the Advertising Effectiveness of Small Retail Businesses. *Entrepreneurship Theory and Practice*, (Fall): 41-47.

Wind, Yoram & Thomas S. Robertson (1983). Marketing Strategy: New Directions for Theory and Research. *Journal of Marketing*, (Spring): 12-24.

Yale, Laura & Mary C. Gilly (1988). Trends in Advertising Research: A Look at the Content of Marketing Oriented Journals from 1976-1985. *Journal of Advertising*, 17(1): 12-22.

Zeithaml, Valarie A., A. Parasuraman, & Leonard L. Berry (1985). Problems and Strategies in Services Marketing. *Journal of Marketing*, 49(Spring): 33-46.

Effects of Distribution Channel Level on Tour Purchasing Attributes and Information Sources

Charles R. Duke
Margaret A. Persia

SUMMARY. Attributes important to escorted tour participants were used to explore the differences between clients of tour operators and clients of travel agents. Customers purchasing directly from operators valued experience with the tour company and personal recommendations. Agency clients valued the ease of booking through agents along with information from guidebooks and tourist bureaus. Domestic travelers were more often operator clients, and foreign travelers were more often agency clients. Differences are discussed in terms of different segments of customers within the channel of distribution.

INTRODUCTION

Purchasers of tours, similar to other customer groups, differ in the benefits that they seek from tours. Companies within the tourism industry

Dr. Charles R. Duke is Assistant Professor, Department of Marketing, Clemson University, Box 341325, Clemson, SC 29634-1325. Margaret A. Persia is a doctoral candidate in the Department of Parks, Recreation, and Tourism Management, Clemson University, Clemson, SC 29634.

Data collection assistance for this project was provided by the member firms of the American Society of Travel Agents and the National Tour Association.

[Haworth co-indexing entry note]: "Effects of Distribution Channel Level on Tour Purchasing Attributes and Information Sources." Duke, Charles R., and Margaret A. Persia. Co-published simultaneously in *Journal of Travel & Tourism Marketing* (The Haworth Press, Inc.) Vol. 2, No. 2/3, 1993, pp. 37-55; and: *Communication and Channel Systems in Tourism Marketing* (ed: Muzaffer Uysal, and Daniel R. Fesenmaier) The Haworth Press, Inc., 1993, pp. 37-55. Multiple copies of this article/chapter may be purchased from The Haworth Document Delivery Center [1-800-3-HAWORTH; 9:00 a.m. - 5:00 p.m. (EST)].

attempt to meet these different needs by offering varying levels of services. This study investigates characteristics among consumers who choose to purchase tours from different levels within the tourism industry's channel of distribution. Specifically explored are the differences in customer purchasing decision attributes and information needs based on two channels of distribution available to tour operators: (1) sales made direct-to-consumer and (2) sales made through travel agents.

TOURISM SERVICES AND CHANNELS OF DISTRIBUTION

Even though promotional techniques have been researched and applied, other parts of the marketing mix have not received similar attention in the tourism industry (cf. Ryan 1991). Exploring the consumers' use of distribution channels will add to the information needed to provide more comprehensive tourism marketing programs (cf. Calantone and Mazanec 1991).

For many managers and academics, the issue of "channels of distribution" evokes concepts of distributors, warehouses, and transportation which are typical of hard goods marketing. The ideas of product flow, ownership flow, and title transfer are not always obvious or applicable where intangible services are marketed. In services marketing, consumers must come in contact with the firm to receive the service, but there is often little tangible evidence of ownership or title which removes much of the conventional concept of a "channel of distribution" (Bateson 1992). For example, package holidays can be wholesaled or retailed in terms of the right-to-use the package instead of transferring ownership of the package. The vacation itself is the *experience* of the resort, cruise, or tour. Rather than debate theoretical positions of whether services should or should not be described as channels of distribution, this study accepts that channels are appropriate and investigates channels within tourism to examine the type of customer served at different distribution channel levels (cf. Bateson 1992).

Consumers and Tourism Channels

Operators design tours and offer packages to the public. One channel of distribution for operators is direct sales to customers. Alternatively, operators offer tour packages through intermediaries by allowing travel agents to book purchases for travelers. Using agents as intermediaries allows a parallel or alternative channel of distribution for operators to reach customers. These intermediaries provide different types of services for consumers and add value to justify their function to not only the consumer but also the rest of the channel. Therefore, travelers who purchase these added services from intermediaries differ from those who purchase directly from operators.

Since traveler attitudes toward added services differ, the consumers' perceptions of the role of the travel agent is quite variable (cf. Michie and Sullivan 1990; Kendall and Booms 1989; Bellur, McNamara, and Prokop 1988; Gitelson and Crompton 1983). Consumers generally accept the idea that travel agents provide information regarding arrangements and act as facilitators; but consumers do not agree on the necessity for agents to provide such physical services as ticket delivery, pleasing office decor, or airport parking (Kendall and Booms 1989). With varying ideas of service requirements, consumers may choose to purchase directly from the tour provider if the value added by the agent does not meet their expectations. For example, a common assertion by tour operators is that agents know their clients and offer more personalized service to meet their individual needs (Kendall and Booms 1989). However, Michie and Sullivan (1990) found that travel agents dealing with international travelers were unfamiliar with the travel behavior of their clients and were less effective as market intermediaries. For this investigation, these differing opinions toward agents point toward characteristic differences between customers who purchase from agents and those who purchase directly from the tour operators. However, no prior research has attempted to distinguish these consumers.

Further descriptive information is needed to understand more about the consumers in tourism channels of distribution who either (1) purchase directly from operators or (2) use travel agent intermediaries. The descriptive research approach is appropriate in this situation since a substantial body of knowledge has not been built to suggest formal channel relationships. This approach is consistent with procedures recommended for theory development (cf. Deshpande 1983; Zeithaml, Berry, and Parasuraman 1988).

Channels and Tourism Communications

Little attention has been directed to the riskier nature of purchasing services and the appropriate information needs of service consumers (Murray and Schlacter 1990). Because more evaluation occurs during consumption and after purchase (Young 1981), more pre-purchase information is needed for services (cf. Deshpande and Krishnan 1977). The general marketing services literature indicates that more search for decision-making information occurs when risk rises (cf. Murray 1991). Additionally, more informal (personal) and independent sources of information are used instead of formal (company-sponsored) sources as risk becomes an important issue (cf. Gitelson and Crompton 1983). Those with personal experience seem to prefer internal information and then give credence to the advise of others who have experience. However, an alternative approach might suggest that personal information may be required instead of (not after) formal sources. Additionally, opinion leaders and reference groups play a more prominent role in services since the adoption process for each individual and the time required for diffusion of a service through a consumer population takes longer than the adoption and diffusion of products (Murray 1991). For example, if foreign travel is assumed to be higher risk, then more personal information and dependency on experienced travelers or independent agents (as opinion leaders and reference groups) might be expected. These personal sources may be used by the consumer because company-sponsored sources do not provide the persuasive information needed for purchase (Murray 1991).

Differences in information needs suggest distinct market segments. Segmentation based on communication needs have been discussed, especially for elderly (cf. McGuire, Uysal, and McDonald 1988). Different sources of information can be used to appeal to younger travelers as opposed to older travelers. For example, the elderly prefer family, experienced travelers, and friends over travel agents, formal communications, or printed material when gathering tour information.

Although differing information needs may be evident, not all communications methods have been effective throughout the channel of distribution. Communications such as ads and brochures differ for operators and agents. The consumer's use of these ads and brochures has received some attention but has not been developed as an issue within channels of distribution. Formal communications through advertising is an effective means of creating image and attitude toward destinations (Bojanic 1991) which are emphasized in operator communications. However, ads for travel agents are not as effective as these destination-oriented ads more often used by operators (Kendall and Booms 1990). Brochures as formal communications are a popular and tangible source of information in the tourism industry. However, when brochures were tested from both agency and consumer perspectives, they were not used to maximum potential by consumers in their travel decisions (Wicks and Schuett 1991). To understand more about communications, various methods of effectiveness testing, such as awareness and persuasion, have been suggested for separate travel periods including leaving home, enroute to destination, and arrival at destination (cf. Perdue and Pitegoff 1990). Understanding the differences between basic uses of communications between operator clients and agency clients will provide a starting point for this continuing communications research.

Channel Differences Between Domestic and Foreign Travelers

Along with many similarities, differences exist in the expectations of American travelers to foreign destinations compared with domestic travelers including comfort, value, adventure, and education (Duke and Persia, in press). Group travel is a major force in the tourism industry (cf. Sheldon 1986) with the escorted tour segment expected to grow modestly through the mid-1990's creating a highly competitive market in which both agencies and operators need to provide excellence in service (Ostrowski 1990). Cross-boundary tourism marketing is increasing (cf. Ziff-Levine 1990) creating a necessity for informed business and marketing decisions on the part of those involved in the distribution of tour services both domestic and foreign. To meet the consumer need for service and information prior to purchasing, both operators and agents must understand the differences among consumers who use each of these two levels in the channel of distribution.

Study Objectives

This study explored the similarities and differences in purchasing decision attributes and the sources of information used by customers purchasing directly from tour operators and customers purchasing through travel agents. The investigation concentrated on escorted tours with a national sample from a large number of agencies and operators within the United States. The specific objectives were (1) to determine the similarities and differences for purchasing decision parameters within each of the two levels in the channel of distribution, (2) to investigate differing information sources used by customers, and (3) to explore differences in decision parameters and information sources between domestic and foreign travellers.

METHOD

Design

Purchase decision attributes and communications use information were compared for tour operator clients and agency clients preparing to go on escorted tours. This simple design emphasizes the descriptive nature of this study. Comparisons were also made for domestic versus foreign purchasers on both decision attributes and information sources.

Sampling Procedure

Travel agencies were selected from a list of those approved by the Airline Reporting Corporation, the widest sample frame available. Tour operators were selected from a list of members of the National Tour Association (NTA). Firms were asked to distribute surveys to escorted tour clients booked on upcoming tours. To maintain confidentiality, responses were not associated with the distributing firm. Responses were obtained from 133 tour participants (response rate of 25%). Agency clients provided 52% of the responses and operator clients provided 48%.

The Airline Reporting Corporation list contained approximately 30,000 firms. The NTA membership list contained 570 firms. From these sample frames, a random selection of 909 firms (272 operators and 635 agencies) were invited to participate. Of those, 111 firms (41 operators = 15% response; 70 agencies = 11% response) requested questionnaires to distribute. Participating firms were given 5 questionnaires each (total 555), distributed a total of 248, and returned any that were not given to clients. Useable responses were obtained from a total of 133 tour participants (response rate of 23.9% of distributed questionnaires, or 53.6% of questionnaires distributed by the participating firms) which represented an appropriate sample size for Longwoods' (1990) estimate of America's touring market (2,975,200 customers) at a confidence interval of 99% and a tolerance of 10% given the widest standard deviation resulting from the questionnaire's scale responses (cf. Tull and Hawkins 1991, Lehmann 1989).

Respondent characteristics (Table 1) are similar to those for domestic escorted tours (Longwoods 1990). These demographics are also similar to findings from previous escorted tour studies (cf. Quiroga 1990). The majority of respondents were female, and most participants were between the ages of 61 and 75 years. Education level was relatively high, and respondents reported that they were experienced group travelers having participated in previous escorted tours. Thirty-seven respondents (27.2%) indicated they had visited their tour destination before. Tours occurred in every month of the year except January. Respondents resided in 29 states in the U.S. indicating geographic dispersion.

Instrument

Respondents were asked to provide information on the importance of decision-making attributes and information sources as a part of a larger

TABLE 1. <u>Respondent Characteristics.</u>

Variables		Number	Percent
Gender:	Male	49	36.8
	Female	84	63.2
Age:	20-40	8	6.0
	41-60	21	15.8
	61-65	27	20.3
	66-70	40	30.1
	71-75	23	17.3
	76-85	14	10.5
Education:	Less than High School	12	9.0
	High School Diploma	37	27.8
	Technical/Vocational	9	6.8
	Associate Degree/Some College	31	23.3
	Bachelor's Degree	27	20.3
	Graduate Degree	17	12.8
Tour Experience:	Never on Tour Before	5	3.7
	1-3 Tours	32	24.1
	4 or More Tours	96	72.2
Destination:			
Domestic:	United States	62	46.6
Foreign:	Canada/Mexico	18	13.5
	Europe	27	20.3
	Other "Overseas"	<u>26</u>	<u>19.6</u>
Total Foreign:		71	53.4
Month of Tour:	January	0	0.0
	February	3	2.3
	March	4	3.0
	April	1	.8
	May	5	3.7
	June	32	24.0
	July	19	14.3
	August	7	5.3
	September	33	24.8
	October	16	12.0
	November	4	3.0
	December	9	6.8

project investigating pre-trip escorted tour expectations. Along with purchasing decision attributes, sources of information used, and expectations of the upcoming trip, respondents provided information on their tours and traveling companions as well as other basic demographics. Printed questionnaires, mailed to the participants, included purchasing decision attributes and information sources which were developed from a prior study of escorted tours (Persia and Duke 1991) and were reviewed by tourism trade association research professionals (see Table 2). No prior research has attempted such a broad sampling of clients from multiple tour operators and travel agencies. Printed, mailed questionnaires were considered the best compromise to obtain such a wide response given resource constraints.

Instructions asked participants to indicate the importance of the list of 12 purchasing decision attributes on a scale from very important (scaled as +2) to unimportant (scaled as −1). An unbalanced scale was developed from the prior study (Persia and Duke 1991) and from pretests which matched the distribution of responses expected in the population (cf. Tull and Hawkins 1991). Additionally, respondents identified the sources of information used in the purchase decision. A list of 8 information sources (Table 2) was developed from an earlier study (Persia and Duke 1991). Respondents were asked to indicate all of the sources that they used in making a tour decision. Respondents returned completed questionnaires in pre-paid mailers.

RESULTS

This analysis examined differences in the importance of tour purchasing decision attributes and the frequency of information sources usage at two different levels in the channel of distribution: tour operator (as service provider) and travel agent (as the only intermediary). The analysis compared means between these two groups. Given the potential for variation based on destination, similar comparisons were made for domestic versus foreign purchasers.

Tour Operators versus Travel Agents

Purchase decision parameters were ranked from highest to lowest mean importance score among travelers who purchased from operators and those who purchased from agents (Table 3). To those purchasing through operators, the tour provider's reputation ranked highest in importance. Travelers purchasing through travel agents considered destination as most important. Tour company reputation, experience with the tour company, and ability to meet new friends were more influential factors for operator clients. Ease of booking and agent recommendations were more influential for agency clients.

TABLE 2. Survey Questions for Purchasing Attributes and Information Sources.

Purchasing Attributes

"Circle the response which indicates the importance of each statement in deciding which tour to purchase. If the statement was very important to you in deciding which tour to purchase, circle 'Very.' If the statement was moderately important, circle 'Mod.' If the statement was neither important nor unimportant, circle 'Neutral.' If the statement was unimportant, circle 'Unimp.'"

1. Reputation of the tour company.	Very	Mod	Neutral	Unimp
2. Brochure or other advertisements.	Very	Mod	Neutral	Unimp
3. Travel agent recommendation.	Very	Mod	Neutral	Unimp
4. Recommendation of friends and/or relatives.	Very	Mod	Neutral	Unimp
5. Destination.	Very	Mod	Neutral	Unimp
6. The time the tour was scheduled.	Very	Mod	Neutral	Unimp
7. Previous experience with the tour company.	Very	Mod	Neutral	Unimp
8. Ease of booking through a travel agent.	Very	Mod	Neutral	Unimp
9. Safety within a group setting.	Very	Mod	Neutral	Unimp
10. Potential to make new friends.	Very	Mod	Neutral	Unimp
11. Elimination of financial risk.	Very	Mod	Neutral	Unimp
12. Inclusion of a tour guide.	Very	Mod	Neutral	Unimp

Information Sources

"What are all of the sources of information you consulted before purchasing your escorted tour?"

___ Newspaper/Magazines	___ Guidebooks	___ Travel Agent
___ Tourist Bureaus	___ Travel Clubs	___ Tour Company
___ Radio/Television	___ Friends/Relatives	

___ Other (please specify) _____

TABLE 3. Importance of Escorted Tour Purchasing Attributes: Operator Clients versus Agency Clients.

Attribute	Operator (n = 61)			Agency (n = 72)			t-Value	p
	Rank	Mean	SD	Rank	Mean	SD		
Tour Company Reputation	1	1.83	.51	2	1.59	.75	2.38	.02 [1]
Tour Guide	2	1.62	.69	3	1.46	.86	1.33	.18
Destination	3	1.61	.75	1	1.69	.64	.64	.52
Experience with Tour Company	4	1.49	.93	8	1.16	.99	2.14	.03 [1]
Time Scheduled	5	1.39	.86	5	1.30	.78	.68	.50
Safety in Group	6	1.24	1.05	6	1.24	.97	.01	.99
Brochure/Ads	7	1.20	.84	7	1.17	.85	.20	.84
Eliminate Financial Risk	8	1.12	.99	11	.98	1.16	.83	.41
Ease of Booking	9	1.08	1.13	4	1.37	.87	1.77	.08 [2]
Friends/Family Recommendation	10	.77	1.06	10	.99	1.05	1.23	.22
Travel Agent Recommendation	11	.73	1.14	9	1.04	1.05	1.70	.09 [2]
Potential to Make New Friends	12	.61	1.15	12	.25	1.08	1.91	.06 [2]

[1] Significant (alpha = .05).

[2] Marginally significant (alpha = .10).

Note: Scale = (−1 = unimportant, 0 = no opinion, 1 = moderately important, 2 = very important).

Sources of information were also ranked by frequency of mention for operators versus agents (Table 4). Not surprisingly, tour operators more often provided information for those purchasing directly, whereas agents more often provided information for those purchasing from these intermediaries. Guidebooks were ranked higher for those purchasing from opera-

TABLE 4. Sources of Tour Purchasing Information: Operator versus Agency.

Source	Operators (n=61)			Agencies (n=72)			Chi-Sq	p
	Rank	Number Operator Clients	Percent Operator Clients	Rank	Number Agency Clients	Percent Agency Clients		
Tour Company	1	39	58.2	2	34	40.5	3.60	.05[1]
Travel Agents	2	26	38.8	1	56	66.7	13.65	<.01[1]
Guidebooks	3	19	28.4	4	26	31.0	.24	.62
Friends or Relatives	4	18	26.9	3	28	33.3	1.02	.31
Newspaper or Magazines	5	14	20.9	5	14	16.7	.31	.58
Travel Club	6	6	9.0	8	4	4.8	.94	.33
Tourist Bureaus	7	5	7.5	6	12	14.3	1.95	.16
Radio or Television	8	3	4.5	7	6	7.1	.55	.46

[1] Significant (alpha = .05).

tors, and personal information from friends and relatives was ranked higher by those purchasing from agents. Periodicals were used moderately by both groups. In general, this sample did not often use travel clubs, tourist bureaus, or mass media to obtain information. Agency clients used more total sources of information (2.22 sources) than did operator clients (1.94 sources).

Domestic versus Foreign Travelers

Purchase decision parameters were also ranked from highest to lowest mean importance score for domestic and foreign travelers (Table 5). For comparison, domestic rankings are shown in order along with foreign rankings for the same purchasing decision attribute. The attributes ranked first and second are reversed for the two groups with tour company reputa-

TABLE 5. Importance of Escorted Tour Purchasing Attributes: Foreign versus Domestic.

Attribute	Domestic (n = 62)			Foreign (n = 71)			t-Value	p
	Rank	Mean	SD	Rank	Mean	SD		
Tour Company Reputation	1	1.82	.46	2	1.59	.79	2.10	.04 [1]
Destination	2	1.65	.68	1	1.68	.71	.26	.80
Tour Guide	3	1.48	.84	3	1.52	.79	.26	.79
Experience with Tour Company	4	1.44	.95	10	1.14	1.03	1.71	.09 [2]
Time Scheduled	5	1.34	.81	5	1.32	.84	.14	.89
Safety in Group	6	1.10	1.08	6	1.31	.98	1.17	.24
Brochure/Ads	7	1.08	.78	7	1.24	.89	1.09	.28
Ease of Booking	8	.93	1.14	4	1.49	.77	3.24	<.01 [1]
Eliminate Financial Risk	9	.82	1.09	9	1.14	1.11	1.67	.10 [2]
Friend/Family Recommendation	10	.77	1.12	11	.88	1.05	.62	.54
Travel Agent Recommendation	11	.52	1.18	8	1.21	.97	3.62	<.01 [1]
Potential to Make New Friends	12	.33	1.16	12	.38	1.07	.27	.79

[1] Significant (alpha = .05).

[2] Marginally significant (alpha = .10).

Note: Source = (−1 = unimportant, 0 = no opinion, 1 = moderately important, 2 = very important).

tion being most important for domestic travelers and destination being most important for foreign travelers. Lowest ranked attributes were making new friends, agent recommendations, as well as recommendations of friends and family. Experience with the tour company was also important for domestic travelers but not relatively important for foreign travelers.

Ease of booking, agent recommendations, and elimination of financial risk were more influential for foreign travelers. Tour company reputations and experience with the tour company were more influential for domestic travelers.

Rankings of information sources indicated that domestic travelers used tour companies most often whereas foreign travelers used travel agents most often (Table 6). Foreign travelers used travel agents, guidebooks, tourists bureaus, and mass media more often than did domestic travelers. Foreign travelers used more total sources of information (2.27 sources) than domestic travelers (1.86 sources).

Post-Hoc Analysis of Variance

A review of the results revealed that tour company reputation was significantly more important for both operator clients and domestic travel-

TABLE 6. Sources of Tour Purchasing Information: Domestic versus Foreign.

Source	Domestic Travelers (n = 62)			Foreign Travelers (n = 71)			Chi-Sq	p
	Rank	Number Domestic	Percent Domestic	Rank	Number Foreign	Percent Foreign		
Tour Company	1	34	54.8	2	30	41.7	1.95	.16
Travel Agents	2	29	46.8	1	46	63.9	4.40	.04 [1]
Friends or Relatives	3	18	29.0	4	23	31.9	.17	.68
Newspaper or Magazine	4	14	22.6	6	11	15.3	1.11	.29
Guidebooks	5	13	21.0	3	27	37.5	4.58	.03 [1]
Travel Club	6	4	6.5	8	4	5.6	.04	.84
Tourist Bureaus	7	2	3.2	5	12	16.7	6.56	.01 [1]
Radio or Television	8	1	1.6	7	8	11.1	4.88	.03 [1]

[1] Significant (alpha = .05).

ers. Additionally, destination was ranked highest by agency clients and foreign travelers. These differences suggested potential interactions between distribution channel level and destination. A 2×2 analysis of variance was accomplished for each of the purchasing factors to evaluate any potential interactions. Evidence found in this post hoc analysis should be helpful in developing future research studies. Because main effect results duplicated the planned comparisons of means, only significant interactions are reported.

Elimination of financial risk was significantly more important for foreign-agency customers (Table 7). The significant interaction derives primarily from the lower mean for domestic-agency customers for whom

TABLE 7. Selected Purchasing Attributes ANOVA Results: Operator/Agency Clients versus Domestic/Foreign Travelers.

A. Purchasing Attribute:
Importance Means for "Elimination of financial risk."

Destination	Level in Channel Operator	Agencies	ANOVA			
			Source	df	M S	F	p
Domestic	1.08	.36	Main Effects:				
	(n = 40)	(n = 22)					
Foreign	1.09	1.16	Destination	1	5.20	4.43	.04
	(n = 21)	(n = 50)	Channel Level	1	2.73	2.32	.13
			Interaction:	1	4.51	3.84	.05
			Error:	128	1.17		

B: Purchasing Attribute:
Importance Means for "Time the tour was scheduled."

Destination	Level in Channel Operator	Agencies	ANOVA			
			Source	df	M S	F	p
Domestic	1.26	1.50	Main Effects:				
	(n = 40)	(n = 22)					
Foreign	1.50	1.24	Destination	1	<.01	.02	.99
	(n = 21)	(n = 50)	Channel Level	1	.01	.01	.92
			Interaction:	1	1.82	2.66	.10
			Error:	128	.68		

financial risk did not appear to be important. In the only other interesting interaction, tour timing was marginally more important with foreign-operator customers and domestic-agency customers (Table 7). Although this attribute should be considered in further research, caution with using this marginal result is emphasized by the lack of ANOVA main effects.

DISCUSSION

Purchasing Factors

Travelers who purchase directly through tour providers demonstrated stronger ties with these operators, especially domestic travelers. Reputation with the tour company ranked even higher than destination in purchasing choice. Good experiences with operators indicated that this experienced group of tour-goers tended to return to tour companies meeting their expectations. Although not highly ranked in importance, it is interesting to note that operator clients placed a marginally higher importance on risk reduction than did agency clients. Tour providers might appeal to their satisfied customers to return for another trip by promoting reputation and lower financial risk.

Travelers who use agencies indicated much higher importance for ease of booking, especially foreign travelers. The use of agencies for this administrative function appealed to those who wanted convenience but also insisted on good tour providers who served the desired destination.

Communications Use

Communications issues did not appear high in overall purchasing importance but shed some light on differences within the channel. Although no differences were given between levels in the channel, formal communications such as brochures and ads were the highest rated in overall importance. Operator clients and domestic travelers showed slight preference for friends and family over agent recommendations. However, travelers who purchased from agencies and took foreign tours valued agent recommendations over personal recommendations of friends. In contrast to some previous findings, high risk (foreign) travelers used more company-controlled sources (brochures, guidebooks, tourist bureaus) and formal sources (agents) than did lower risk (domestic) travelers.

Sources of information indicated that all travelers use both operators and agencies as major information sources. The only significant difference between clients of operators and agencies was which is used most often (Table 4). However, more differences existed when the destination was considered. Domestic travelers were more likely to use periodicals and ranked personal information sources (friends and family) slightly higher (Table 6). Foreign travelers were more likely to use information from guidebooks and tourist bureaus while placing slightly more emphasis on broadcast media.

These results suggest that foreign travelers do more total information search using different types of information. This may follow from the presumed higher risk (financial as well as uncertainty in arrangements and accommodations) associated with foreign tour selection. Although the rankings indicated some differences in the use of personal information sources (friends and family), these sources need to be further researched to determine the relative importance of each for both destination as well as channel of distribution level.

Agents appeared to be more important as information sources for international customers, perhaps because foreign travel is thought to be higher risk. The ease of making the purchase transaction was critical, along with the ability to simply provide information even though the agent's recommendation may not be uppermost in the decision process.

Limitations

Several restrictions must be acknowledged which limit the generalizability of this study. Primarily, this research was used to gain insight into consumer decision parameters and information sources at different levels in the channel of distribution. The generalizability of this study is limited by the specific characteristics of the sample. Most notably, these travelers were mature, experienced escorted tour-goers. Mature travelers may have different purchasing attitudes from younger travelers. Mature travelers may want less risk, suggesting an increase in agent dependency. Younger travelers may want more convenience in purchasing (using agents more) or may desire more "hands-on control" of the purchasing situation (favoring direct purchases from operators). Experienced travelers may have more confidence in their purchasing abilities, which favors direct operator purchases. Additionally, experienced travelers may be more prone to foreign travel which would increase the level of risk that they are likely to take. Style of touring also may contribute to some differences. This group of escorted tours involved motorcoach participants who may not respond in the same manner as, for example, airline-based travelers. Whereas motorcoach participants may be more interested in sight-seeing, other tours may attract travelers with interests in multi-day stays at a given location who have different attitudes toward purchasing parameters.

In this study, the sample demographics were similar to prior expectations (Longwoods 1990, Quiroga 1990) providing some confidence in the validity of the results. However as with many extensive projects, non-response bias is a major consideration. Operators and agents who did not participate perceived that the study would take too much of their time. Among those firms participating, operators and agents held customer lists as confidential which eliminated the possibility of contacting travelers who refused to complete the questionnaires. Therefore, calculation of differences in responses from those who did not participate was not possible. Additionally, tour operator and travel agent firm participation was low (as expected) because companies are hesitant to risk the loss of confidential client lists which are critical to their strategic positioning and success. Continued confidence building is needed to assuage professional skepticism of academic attempts to gain internal company information in broad studies such as this research. Bias may also have been introduced by the lack of control over the choice of participants made by the operators and agents. However, firms reported that they attempted to follow distribution instructions which emphasized the need for objective participants. Finally, higher numbers of planned comparisons tend to increase risk of Type II errors which can be reduced by focusing future studies on narrower questions. In this study, the risk of multiple planned comparisons and post hoc comparisons, well below the number of degrees of freedom, was accepted in favor of avoiding Type I errors which would have hidden potential important factor differences (cf. Keppel 1982).

CONCLUSION

Applying the channel concept to tourism services provides both academic or managerial insights into consumer characteristics. This research suggests that tour operators must strive to obtain and reinforce high quality reputations with their clients, especially for those domestic travelers who do not use travel agents. On the other hand, agencies must strive to maintain contact with operators providing high quality tours to desirable locations. In this way, travel agents can provide the information desired by travelers. In addition, agencies should continue to streamline booking procedures and added services to make tour purchasing easy, especially for foreign travelers. Domestic escorted tours have the opportunity to build clientele and repeat business independent of travel agencies. However, the higher risks of international travel, possibly financial costs and uncertainty of arrangements and accommodations, may encourage foreign travelers to seek out more information and to use agents as a method of ensuring that the arrangements are properly made.

Using this information, continued research can provide more information on the approaches that might be taken to identify, segment, and attract consumers within each level of the distribution channel. Prescriptives can be tested to provide managers with insight into the attitudes, interests, or life-styles of consumers purchasing directly from operators versus those purchasing from agents. Additionally, quality measures can be devised to provide specific attributes critical to satisfying customers at each of these two distribution levels. Because customer offerings may overlap between segments, areas of potential conflict between operators and agents can be identified along with solutions which can optimize the success of the entire channel. Each of these areas should help the escorted tour industry to remain competitive during difficult economic times and flourish during periods of economic growth.

REFERENCES

Bateson, J.E.G. (1992). *Managing Services Marketing,* Chicago: Dryden.

Bellur, V.V., McNamara, B. and Prokop, D.R. (1988). Factors Perceived as Important by Package Tourists: A Multivariate Analysis. In *Proceedings of the International Conference on Services Marketing,* E.G. Thomas and S.R. Rao, eds., 31-45.

Berry, L.L. and Parasuraman, A. (1991). *Marketing Services: Competing Through Time.* New York: Free Press. 57-73.

Bojanic, D.C. (1991). The use of Advertising in Managing Destination Image. *Tourism Management,* 12 (4, December), 352-355.

Calantone, R.J. and Mazanec, J.A. (1991). Marketing Management and Tourism. *Annals of Tourism Research,* 18, 101-119.

Deshpande, R. (1983). "Paradigms Lost": On Theory and Method in Research in Marketing. *Journal of Marketing,* 47 (4, Fall), 101-110.

_____ and Krishnan, S. (1977). A Consumer-Based Approach for Establishing Priorities in Consumer Information Programs: Implications for Public Policy. In *Contemporary Marketing Thought, 1977 Educators' Proceedings,* B.A. Greenberg and D.N. Bellenger, eds. Chicago: American Marketing Association, 338-343.

Duke, C.R. and Persia, M.A. (in press). Foreign and Domestic Escorted Tour Expectations of American Travelers. *Journal of International Consumer Marketing.*

Gitelson, R.J. and Crompton, J.L. (1983). The Planning Horizons and Sources of Information Used by Pleasure Vacationers. *Journal of Travel Research,* 21 (3, Winter), 2-7.

Kendall, K.W. and Booms, B.H. (1989). Consumer Perceptions of Travel Agencies: Communications, Images, Needs, and Expectations. *Journal of Travel Research,* 27 (4, Spring), 29-37.

Keppel, G. (1982). *Design and Analysis: A Researcher's Handbook,* 2nd Edition. Englewood Cliffs, NJ: Prentice Hall.

Lehmann, D.R. (1989). *Market Research and Analysis,* 3rd Edition. Boston: Irwin.
Longwoods Travel (1990). *National Tour Foundation Group Travel Report.* Longwoods International, USA.
McGuire, F., Uysal, M. and McDonald, C. (1988). Attracting the Older Traveller. *Tourism Management,* 19 (2, June), 161-165.
Michie, D.A. and Sullivan, G.L. (1990). The Role(s) of the International Travel Agent in the Travel Decision Process of Client Families. *Journal of Travel Research,* 29 (2, Fall), 30-38.
Murray, K.B. (1991). A Test of Services Marketing Theory: Consumer Information Acquisition Activities. *Journal of Marketing,* 55 (1, January), 10-25.
_____ and Schlacter, J.L. (1990). The Impact of Services Versus Goods on Consumers' Assessment of Perceived Risk and Variability. *Journal of the Academy of Marketing Science,* 18 (1), 51-65.
Ostrowski, P.L. (1990). Constant Turmoil and Sleepless Nights: Welcome to Travel Marketing in the 1990's. *Travel & Tourism Executive Report,* Association of Travel Marketing Executives, 11 (September).
Perdue, R.R. and Pitegoff, B.E. (1990). Methods of Accountability Research for Destination Marketing. *Journal of Travel Research,* 28 (4, Spring), 45-49.
Persia, M.A. and Duke, C.R. (1991). Expectations of Escorted Tour Participants, in *Interface: 1991.* Council on Hotel, Restaurant, and Institutional Education, 1991 Annual Conference Proceedings, D. Hayes, ed. Houston, TX: CHRIE.
Quiroga, I. (1990). Characteristics of Package Tours in Europe. *Annals of Tourism Research,* 17 (1), 185-207.
Ryan, C. (1991). Tourism and Marketing: A Symbiotic Relationship? *Tourism Management,* 12 (2, June), 101-111.
Sheldon, P.J. (1986). The Tour Operator Industry: An Analysis. *Annals of Tourism Research,* 13 (3), 349-365.
Tull, D.S. and Hawkins, D.I. (1991). *Marketing Research: Measurement and Method,* 5th Edition. New York: Macmillan.
Wicks, B.E. and Schuett, M.A. (1991). Examining the Role of Tourism Promotion Through the Use of Brochures. *Tourism Management,* 12 (4, December) 301-312.
Young, R.F. (1981). The Advertising of Consumer Services and the Hierarchy of Effects. In *Marketing of Services,* J.H. Donnelly and W.R. George, eds. Chicago: American Marketing Association, 196-199.
Zeithaml, V.A., Berry, L.L., and Parasuraman, A. (1988). Communication and Control Processes in the Delivery of Service Quality. *Journal of Marketing,* 52 (2, April), 35-48.
Ziff-Levine, W. (1990). The Cultural Logic Gap: A Japanese Tourism Research Experience. *Tourism Management* 11 (June), 105-110.

Communication Channels
to Segment Pleasure Travelers

Sheauhsing Hsieh
Joseph T. O'Leary

SUMMARY. Communication channels as a segmentation base provide a way to understand what kind of information sources travelers use, and whether potential travelers in different groups vary in terms of sociodemographics, travel characteristics, media habits, and psychographic behavior. Using cluster analysis, four groups of communication channels are identified for United Kingdom long haul pleasure travelers: word-of-mouth, brochures/pamphlets, travel agents, and combination packages. Results show that this segmentation is viable and that implications exist for promotional strategies, distribution channels, and market positioning.

INTRODUCTION

Communication channels are important in tourism planning and marketing strategies as the link between the hospitality industry and the target market. Based on a communication model developed by Schiffman and Kanuk (1991), the hospitality industry (sender) sends messages that impart

Sheauhsing Hsieh is a graduate student of International Travel and Tourism, Forestry & Natural Resources Department, Purdue University, West Lafayette, IN. Dr. Joseph T. O'Leary is Professor, Recreation Participation and Behavior, Forestry & Natural Resources Department, Purdue University, West Lafayette, IN.

[Haworth co-indexing entry note]: "Communication Channels to Segment Pleasure Travelers." Hsieh, Sheauhsing, and Joseph T. O'Leary. Co-published simultaneously in *Journal of Travel & Tourism Marketing* (The Haworth Press, Inc.) Vol. 2, No. 2/3, 1993, pp. 57-75; and: *Communication and Channel Systems in Tourism Marketing* (ed: Muzaffer Uysal, and Daniel R. Fesenmaier) The Haworth Press, Inc., 1993, pp. 57-75. Multiple copies of this article/chapter may be purchased from The Haworth Document Delivery Center [1-800-3-HAWORTH; 9:00 a.m. - 5:00 p.m. (EST)].

a belief, an attitude, or a fact to the target market (receiver) through communication channels. After receiving it, the receiver decodes the message and provides positive or negative feedback to the sender by purchasing a tour, booking air fare, renting a car, or reserving a hotel. Thus, examining communication channels can involve many questions such as who is the target market to reach and how the message is constructed and received. For consumers, effective communication channels and messages may affect their vacation choices. For marketing managers, travel opportunities and products can be promoted and positioned through effective communication choices to attract more travelers to the destination.

Communication channels can be categorized into interpersonal communication and impersonal (or mass) communication (Schiffman & Kanuk, 1991). Interpersonal communication occurs on a personal level between two or more people. For example, the formal interpersonal communication is planned by an organization such as a travel agency or takes place between a salesperson and a prospect. In addition, informal interpersonal communication such as word-of-mouth is the message related by the organization but uncontrolled and unmanaged by that organization. In contrast, communication directed to a large and diffuse audience is called impersonal or mass communication. It is carried out through nonpersonal types of impersonal communication by channels such as television, radio, newspapers, magazines, or printed materials (McDonough, 1987; Schiffman & Kanuk, 1991). Since travel is intangible and an experience, it may involve more risk than other consumer decisions (Morrison, 1989). Therefore, people may consult a greater variety of information sources to make travel decisions. Thus, the study of communication becomes an important concern to travel and tourism related organizations.

Many studies have been conducted to understand the relationship between travel related decisions and communication channels. The results of these investigations suggest that travelers often rely on interpersonal communication channels in making travel decisions (Donough, 1984, 1986; Stynes & Mahoney, 1986). In addition, the use of communication channels may be related to individual characteristics. Darden and Perrault (1975) found that media exposure groups were significantly different in terms of vacation duration, innovativeness, and distance. People with low media exposure tend to take shorter and closer to home vacations. On the other hand, persons in higher social classes consult more mass media.

Moreover, the use of information sources may be different not only in terms of sociodemographics and travel characteristics but also in the context of travel orientations (e.g., desire for excitement, relaxation, or well-planned trip) (Gitelson & Crompton, 1983). Schul & Crompton (1983) suggested that information search behavior is better explained by travel-specific psychographics than by demographics. Further, Vogt and Fesenmaier (1991) suggested that the effectiveness of a promotion strategy also depends on understanding ordinary media habits of target markets such as using a daily/Sunday newspaper or weekly/monthly magazines. Overall, these studies have focused attention on information search patterns of tourists to identify ways to communicate with tourists. Thus, understanding the sociodemographics, travel characteristics, media habits, and psychographic behavior of target markets can be an effective strategy to address target markets.

Market segmentation which adjusts a product or service and its price, promotion and distribution to meet the needs and wants of discrete target segments has been considered as a viable approach to understand consumers (Frank, Massy & Wind, 1972; Morrison, 1989; Stynes, 1985). Market segmentation is a management strategy based upon assumptions about the homogeneous behavior within and heterogeneous behavior between population subgroups. In general, a market can be segmented in many ways with a variety of variables. These variables are usually classified into seven broad categories: geography, demographics, purpose of trip, psychographics, behavior, product-related, and channels of distribution (Morrison, 1989).

Communication channels as a segmentation base may provide a new orientation to understand whether potential travelers using different communication channels vary in terms of sociodemographics, travel characteristics, and psychographic behavior. It is important to identify the type of information sources used by particular types of travelers. Gitelson and Crompton (1983) found that there are five information sources (i.e., friends and relatives, print media, broadcast media, consultants, destination specific literature) used by visitors traveling in (or through) Texas. The results suggested that tourist suppliers may distribute the promotion effort to potential travelers according to their media preference. For example, the type or print media are useful for the better educated market. McDonough (1987) concluded that the user groups are different in information preference. The characteristics of travel groups such as group size, experience level, and repeat visitation influence the effectiveness of information sources. Thus, sociodemographics and travel characteristic information can help marketing managers identify target markets and how to develop and plan for them. In addition, understanding media habits and psychographic behavior such as travel philosophy and the travel product choice of potential travelers as well as benefits sought can assist the development of more effective media promotion themes to attract additional travelers. Travelers' preferences and benefits sought can change in different information channel segments. Promotion themes and advertising strategies ought to vary by user groups. A tour operator, for example, could decide which information channel was the most appropriate to use. Then, the operator could develop an advertising campaign according to a traveler's specific philosophy, benefit sought, or product preference.

Therefore, the objectives of this study are to conduct analysis to: (a) understand the travel market through the use of communication channels; (b) segment the travel market by using communication channel segmentation; (c) identify significant variables which can differentiate groups using different communication channels; (d) explore this in terms of an international travel group.

METHODS

Background and Survey

Data from the Pleasure Travel Markets Survey for the United Kingdom were used to segment the market by communication sources. A total of 1,209 personal, in-home interviews were conducted from May 9 to June 6, 1989. All respondents were 18 years of age or older who took an overseas vacation in the past three years or intended to take such a trip in the next two years (Market Facts of Canada Limited, 1989). In this study, only the respondents who took an overseas vacation in the past three years were selected for further analysis because those people who actually took overseas trips may have different media habits than others. Thus, the total sample size is 851.

The sample was from England, Scotland and Wales, excluding only the most sparsely populated rural areas and council estates. Northern Ireland was not included in the survey. Households were screened by interviewers who followed a pre-determined walk pattern from a total of 126 computer-selected starting points. In households with more than one qualified respondent, a random selection was made using the next birthday method. The incidence of qualified respondents was determined by recording the results of these screening procedures (Market Facts of Canada Limited, 1989).

In the data-processing stage, weights were applied to correct for an apparent female bias. The survey collected information on: (a) socioeconomic and demographic variables–age, gender, income, education, occupation, life cycle, and region; (b) travel characteristics–party size, length of stay, trip description, travel season, and travel with whom; (c) travel philosophy, benefit, and product; (d) the most important information sources used to plan a trip; and, (e) the places visited on most recent and second most recent trips, etc.

Data Analysis

Segmentation is a multivariate technique where the task is not to predict or explain but rather to describe groups (Smith, 1989). Cluster analysis, as a segmentation tool, is a useful method to separate objects or respondents into groups such that homogeneity is maximized within the groups and heterogeneity is maximized between the groups (Beane & Ennis, 1987; Klastorin, 1983). That is, clustering segmentation design decides on a basis according to a clustering of respondents on a set of "relevant" variables (Smith, 1989; Wind, 1978). Cluster analysis has been found to be effective (Myers & Tauber, 1987) and has been used in various travel and tourism studies by Calantone and Johar (1984), Mazanec (1984), and Davis and Sternquist (1987). Thus, in this study, cluster analysis is used to segment British overseas travelers on a base of information sources.

Of the several different types of clustering analysis used, Ward's minimum variance was the particular method employed in this study. Ward's method is one of the better procedures for correctly placing observations in the right cluster (Kuiper & Fisher 1975; Bryant & Morrison, 1980; Blashfield & Morey, 1980). There are no satisfactory methods for determining the number of population clusters (Everitt, 1980). The actual decision concerning the number of clusters to be used in a classification scheme is left largely up to the researcher. However, the guideline is based on the cluster history and three decision rules: (a) the cubic clustering criterion (the CCC statistic), (b) the pseudo F and (c) the pseudo t-square (SAS, 1990). Thus, using these three statistics, it is advisable to examine the increase/decrease of these three statistics to identify the number of cluster to select.

Variable Identification

Cluster Variables

The cluster variables examined were the most important communication sources used by respondents. Respondents were asked to indicate whether they used each of 14 communication sources (i.e., travel agent, friends/family, printed materials, advertisement, etc.) to plan their trips in the past 3 years (Table 1). From this table, the travel agent was the most frequently used communication channel, followed by consulting friends/ family and reading brochures/pamphlets. Information sources such as books/library, airline, advertisements, and automobile association also were used to plan overseas trips. Then, four communication channels segments (word-of-mouth, brochures/pamphlets, travel agents, and a combination package) were identified by cluster analysis.

Sociodemographic and Situational Variables

The variables selected to describe the types of communication channels were: (1) socioeconomics and demographics (i.e., household income per year, age, education, occupation, sex, marital status); (2) travel characteristics (i.e., length of trip, party size, travel type, and destination); (3) travel

TABLE 1. The Communication Sources for British Travelers

Information Sources	Percent [a]
Travel agent	38.3
Brochures/pamphlets	10.2
Friends/family	24.8
Airline	3.0
Tour operator/cooperation	2.5
Newspaper/magazine/article	1.7
Books/library	3.3
Automobile Association	2.8
Government tourism office	0.3
Embassy/consulate	1.9
Clubs/associations	1.9
Advertisements	2.8

[a] Percentages were based on multiple responses. Respondents could indicate more than one information source.

philosophy (i.e, package travelers, independent travelers, and guarded travelers), benefit sought (i.e., adventure, social safety, getaway), and product (i.e., culture and nature, beach, developed resort, comfort and culture, sports and entertainment, outdoors and native culture) segmentation. These three sets of variables were identified using a K-means cluster analysis (Market Facts of Canada Limited Co., 1989). The travel philosophy was based on a series of 25 agree-disagree statements relating to how people think about travel in an overall sense as well as how they prefer to travel. The statements took in a variety of issues ranging from making travel arrangements to preferences for different kinds of trips. In addition, benefit sought was identified based on the importance rating of a series of 30 items relating to reasons people might want to go on vacation and experiences they might be looking for. The product preference was based on the importance ratings of 53 different activity features, and amenities that are important in the selection of a vacation destination.

Statistical Analysis

Once information channel segments have been formed by cluster analysis, the travelers comprising each segment have to be examined. A profile which includes all sociodemographic and situation variables for each type of communication channel was developed. Chi-square tests of homogeneity of proportions for categorical variables were used to examine whether difference existed across different type of communication channels.

RESULTS

The Use of Communication Channels

By communication channel segmentation, four distinct clusters emerged representing the groups of British travelers who used the different communication channels to plan their trips. For purpose of identification, each of the four clusters was given a name. They are: cluster 1: word-of-mouth (informal interpersonal communication); cluster 2: brochures/pamphlets (impersonal communication); cluster 3: travel agent (interpersonal communication), and cluster 4: the combination package (Table 2).

People in the word-of-mouth channel consulted travel information from friends and relatives. Over 24% of travelers made up this cluster. Reading brochures and pamphlets to search travel information was another communication channel for British travelers. People in this cluster comprised

TABLE 2. The Communication Segmentation for British Travelers

Cluster	Information Sources	Cluster Size	Percent
Word-of-mouth	Friends/family	205	24.1
Brochures/pamphlets	Brochures/pamphlets	80	9.4
Travel agents	Travel agents Brochures/pamphlets Friends/relatives	321	37.7
Combination package	Travel agents Brochures/pamphlets Airline Tour operator/cooperation Newspaper/mag./art. Books/library Auto. association Gov't. tourism office Embassy/consulate Clubs/association Advertisements	245	28.8

9.4% of the British travel market. Travel agents represented the major communication channel for the third group of British travelers and comprised the largest share (37.7%). Finally, travelers in the combination package channel used a variety of different kinds of tools (i.e., airline, books/library, advertisements, tour operator/company, etc.) to plan their trips. This combination package group accounted for almost 29% of British overseas travelers (Table 2).

British Travel Market Profile
by Communication Channel Segment

The profile of British travel market is presented by media habits, socio-demographics, destination choice, travel characteristics, and travel philosophy/benefit sought/product.

Media Habits

The *Daily Express, Daily Mirror* and *Daily Mail* were the most popular daily newspapers for British travelers. More travelers in the combination package segment read *The Independent* and "other" daily newspapers. In terms of Sunday papers, most British travelers liked to read the *Sunday Times, News of the World, Sunday Express, Sunday Mirror* and *Mail on Sunday*. Travelers who used brochures and pamphlets to plan their trips read *Mail On Sunday*. People in the word-of-mouth cluster were more likely to read *The Observer* than other groups. It is relevant to note that about 15% of British travelers reported they did not read any daily or Sunday newspapers.

Of the specific magazine titles, *TV Times* and *Radio Times* were the most popular weekly magazines for the British travel market. Travelers who searched for travel information from brochures/pamphlets tended to read weekly magazines such as *TV Times, Radio Times, Woman,* and *Woman's Own*. In terms of monthly magazines, *Reader's Digest* was read by most British travelers. As noted earlier, almost half of the British travelers did not read any weekly or Sunday magazines.

Sociodemographic Variables

Sociodemographic variables did not vary significantly among the different clusters. Generally speaking, travelers who read brochures and pamphlets were married (76.6%) and skilled workers (25.0%). Travelers who used the combination package communication channel had a higher education level. Females represented a higher percentage (58.1%) of travelers in the word-of-mouth cluster. Older people over 55 years old preferred to consult with travel agents to plan their trips. Additionally, word-of-mouth (38.0%) and the combination package communication channels (39.4%) tended to have more younger people. Over 38% of respondents in the word-of-mouth cluster were from Greater London and the South East. Travelers who used the combination package communication channel for trip planning were from the South East and North West regions (Table 3).

Destinations

Respondents who got travel information from a travel agent liked to travel to Mainland U.S.A. and Australia/New Zealand. Almost 20% of brochure/pamphlet users traveled to the West Indies/Caribbean. In addition, travelers who liked to consult friends/relatives or read brochures/pamphlets tended to go to Far/East Asia. The Chi-square tests for destination choice showed significant differences for the Mainland U.S.A., the West Indies/Caribbean and Australia/New Zealand destinations (Table 4).

TABLE 3. The Sociodemographics Segmentation of British Travelers

Sociodemographics	cls1	cls2	cls3	cls4	Chi2
Marital Status					0.12
Single	24.2%	16.3%	22.1%	23.8%	
Married	60.0%	76.6%	58.6%	61.2%	
Living together	1.7%	1.6%	3.3%	4.2%	
Div./sep./Widowed	14.1%	5.9%	16.1%	10.8%	
Occupation					0.07
Owner/manager	3.4%	4.4%	2.3%	2.4%	
Professional/technical	5.6%	10.0%	8.5%	7.6%	
Clerical sales	21.3%	15.2%	23.1%	23.5%	
Skilled worker	18.9%	16.0%	16.0%	18.4%	
Unskilled worker	13.3%	19.7%	16.5%	14.3%	
Farming/fishing/forestry	7.8%	2.8%	6.9%	6.6%	
Military	0.0%	3.2%	0.0%	0.5%	
Student	8.3%	0.0%	4.1%	7.0%	
Retired	3.0%	6.8%	6.0%	4.1%	
Homemaker	18.5%	13.0%	16.6%	15.7%	
Education					0.06
No qualifications	30.7%	33.0%	37.4%	23.4%	
CSE/CGSE/"O" levels	27.8%	27.1%	24.2%	27.6%	
"A" levels	13.4%	3.4%	9.7%	13.3%	
OND/ONC/HND/HNC/ business/commercial	11.0%	24.4%	13.2%	16.4%	
University	17.2%	12.2%	15.6%	19.3%	

Sociodemographics	cls1	cls2	cls3	cls4	Chi2
Income (£)					0.12
8,000 or less	25.9%	7.7%	24.9%	21.2%	
8,001-11,000	13.1%	5.3%	12.2%	15.1%	
11,001-15,000	13.4%	10.7%	14.6%	11.6%	
15,001-20,000	19.5%	26.2%	19.2%	19.2%	
20,001-30,000	18.7%	36.0%	14.7%	16.7%	
30,001-40,000	4.1%	8.3%	9.5%	10.1%	
40,001-50,000	2.8%	5.9%	4.0%	3.3%	
Over 50,000	2.6%	0.0%	0.9%	2.9%	
Sex					0.37
Male	41.9%	51.6%	48.4%	48.6%	
Female	58.1%	48.4%	51.6%	51.4%	
Age Group					0.12
18-24	22.2%	8.0%	11.8%	17.1%	
25-34	15.8%	24.7%	18.8%	22.3%	
35-44	17.9%	21.2%	19.3%	17.9%	
45-54	13.1%	17.9%	15.5%	12.7%	
55-64	12.2%	17.9%	15.3%	15.0%	
65 years or more	18.7%	10.4%	19.4%	15.0%	
Region					0.11
Greater London	17.8%	9.9%	7.2%	15.0%	
South East	20.5%	20.7%	18.8%	15.8%	
South West	7.8%	11.2%	11.1%	11.6%	
Wales	2.0%	3.2%	1.0%	4.0%	
Midlands	14.2%	17.6%	18.8%	14.1%	
Anglia	9.0%	8.0%	10.6%	5.2%	
North East	9.2%	6.3%	12.0%	11.9%	
North West	13.9%	14.0%	14.5%	16.8%	
Scotland	5.7%	9.1%	6.1%	5.6%	

Note: cls1: word-of-mouth, cls2: brochures/pamphlets, cls3: travel agents, cls4: the combination channel.
*: P<= 0.05, **P<= 0.01.

TABLE 4. The Travel Destinations Segmentation of British Travelers

Destinations	cls1	cls2	cls3	cls4	Chi^2
Mainland U.S.A.					0.01**
Yes	42.7%	50.5%	57.1%	47.5%	
No	57.3%	49.5%	42.9%	52.5%	
Canada					0.60
Yes	19.9%	13.9%	17.6%	20.2%	
No	80.1%	86.1%	82.4%	79.8%	
Mexico					0.24
Yes	1.3%	0.0%	3.1%	1.5%	
No	98.7%	100.0%	96.9%	98.5%	
Central/South America					0.62
Yes	1.5%	1.2%	1.9%	3.1%	
No	98.5%	98.8%	98.1%	96.9%	
The West Indies/Caribbean					0.00**
Yes	5.9%	19.1%	6.0%	7.0%	
No	94.1%	80.9%	94.0%	93.0%	
Central/S. Africa					0.26
Yes	10.9%	6.3%	6.4%	9.7%	
No	89.1%	93.7%	93.6%	90.3%	
Far/East Asia					0.06
Yes	24.4%	22.3%	16.2%	15.6%	
No	75.6%	77.7%	83.8%	84.4%	
Hawaii/Guam/American Samoa					0.66
Yes	3.4%	2.8%	3.0%	1.5%	
No	96.6%	97.2%	97.0%	98.5%	
Other South Pacific					0.09
Yes	0.0%	0.0%	2.4%	2.4%	
No	100.0%	100.0%	97.6%	97.6%	
Australia/New Zealand					0.03*
Yes	16.7%	4.0%	17.3%	13.7%	
No	83.3%	96.0%	82.7%	86.3%	

Note: cls1: word-of-mouth channel, cls2: brochures/pamphlets, cls3: travel agents, cls4: combination channel.
   *: $P <= 0.05$, **$P <= 0.01$.

Travel Characteristics

Travelers who got travel information from their friends/relatives and travel agents were more likely to visit friends/relatives during the trip. The brochure and pamphlet users tended to take touring and resort vacations. Travelers who used the combination package channel preferred trips that combined business and pleasure. The vacation type differences between communication channels are statistically significant for visiting friends/ relatives, touring, resort, exhibit/special event/theme parks, and business/ pleasure trips (Table 5).

Most British travelers liked to travel alone or with a spouse and/or a significant other. Respondents who used brochures and pamphlets as the information source were more likely to travel with a spouse and/or a significant other. They also preferred to take package tours when compared with other clusters. The variables "people with whom traveled on trip" and "whether took a package tour vacation" were significantly different among four clusters (Table 5).

People in the brochures/pamphlets cluster liked to travel in small parties (two people together) and took trips between 10-16 nights. On the other hand, 12.3 % of the respondents who used the combination package communication channel tended to travel with more than six people. People who consulted information from friends/relatives usually took longer trips (39% of them traveled more than one month). Both "party size" and "length of trip" were different across communication channel segments. In terms of travel decisions, respondents who used travel information from the word-of-mouth channel had shorter decision times (22% of them made their decisions within one month). Thus, almost 41% of them booked vacations late (one month before the trip.) Over 51% of the travelers who read brochures/pamphlets as a major information source booked their trips earlier (more than 6 months ago) (Table 5).

Travel Philosophy, Benefit Sought
and Product

In terms of travel philosophy, 64.1% of the respondents who used brochures/pamphlets preferred to take package tours. The travel philosophy of travelers who got the information from friends/relatives seemed to emphasize guided tours (38.3%), followed by independent tours (37.3%), and package tours (24.5%). In addition, almost 50% of the benefit segment who consulted information from travel agents were social safety travelers. Social safety travelers have a strong social orientation in terms of the benefits they seek. They enjoyed meeting people with similar interests from outside their family. They also prefer travel to places where they feel safe and secure, and are generally not interested in adventure and new experiences. In addition, 40% of people who were in the brochure/pamphlet information cluster were get away travelers. They want to escape from the demands of home and work and unwind. The combination package information cluster had more adventure travelers who wanted to be daring and adventuresome and look for thrills and excitement (36.6%),

TABLE 5. Travel Characteristics Segmentation of British Travelers

Travel Characteristics	cls1	cls2	cls3	cls4	Chi^2
Most recent and Second Most Recent Trip Description					
Visit to friends and relatives					0.00**
Yes	64.7%	13.5%	55.3%	44.6%	
No	35.3%	86.5%	44.7%	55.4%	
Touring Trip					0.00**
Yes	24.2%	48.6%	21.1%	29.1%	
No	75.8%	52.4%	78.9%	70.9%	
City Trip					0.30
Yes	5.0%	2.8%	2.1%	2.4%	
No	95.0%	97.2%	97.9%	97.6%	
Outdoor Trip					0.07
Yes	1.7%	1.2%	0.7%	3.8%	
No	98.3%	98.8%	99.3%	96.2%	
Resort Trip					0.00**
Yes	10.2%	33.9%	12.3%	10.0%	
No	89.8%	66.1%	87.7%	90.0%	
Trip to Exhibition, special event or theme parks.					0.04*
Yes	2.5%	9.5%	8.0%	4.9%	
No	97.5%	90.5%	92.0%	95.1%	
Trip that combined business and pleasure.					0.00**
Yes	4.8%	2.8%	9.8%	13.6%	
No	95.2%	97.2%	90.2%	86.4%	
Persons with whom traveled on trip					0.00**
Traveled alone	28.1%	4.4%	28.3%	21.7%	
Wife/Husband/sig. others	28.7%	55.4%	35.1%	35.4%	
Child(ren)	18.6%	12.4%	13.1%	11.0%	
Father/Mother	2.5%	1.2%	1.4%	2.2%	
Other relatives	9.6%	9.1%	9.1%	8.0%	
Friends	11.3%	14.7%	9.6%	10.9%	
Organized group/club etc.	1.3%	0.0%	1.9%	7.5%	
Business asso./colleagues	0.0%	2.8%	1.6%	3.4%	
Whether a Package Tour Vacation					0.00**
Yes	17.2%	65.6%	28.0%	30.3%	
No	82.8%	34.4%	72.0%	69.7%	

Note: cls1: word-of-mouth channel, cls2: brochures/pamphlets, cls3: travel agents, cls4: combination channel.
*: P<=0.05, **P<=0.01.

TABLE 5 (continued)

Travel Characteristics	cls1	cls2	cls3	cls4	Chi^2
Party Size					0.00**
One	27.9%	4.5%	28.5%	21.9%	
Two	38.1%	62.5%	45.4%	42.7%	
Three	12.2%	10.9%	6.6%	10.9%	
Four	15.4%	15.3%	13.0%	8.9%	
Five	3.1%	2.4%	3.2%	3.4%	
Six	1.8%	1.6%	1.2%	0.8%	
Seven	0.9%	0.0%	0.3%	0.9%	
Eight	0.0%	0.0%	0.6%	0.0%	
Nine or more	0.6%	2.8%	1.2%	10.6%	
Length of Trip (Nights)					0.00**
4-6 nights	3.1%	0.0%	0.3%	2.6%	
7-9 nights	2.9%	2.4%	4.9%	4.6%	
10-16 nights	18.9%	60.0%	31.6%	28.0%	
17-29 nights	36.1%	31.5%	33.2%	36.5%	
30-59 nights	21.6%	6.1%	14.6%	13.2%	
60 or more	17.4%	0.0%	15.4%	15.2%	
Decision Time for Trip					0.08
1 month or less	17.7%	2.8%	19.8%	15.0%	
1 + months - 2 months	14.2%	11.5%	12.6%	12.9%	
2 + months - 3 months	19.1%	14.4%	14.9%	13.8%	
3 + months - 4 months	6.6%	10.7%	5.0%	6.7%	
4 + months - 5 months	4.3%	5.6%	6.9%	4.8%	
5 + months - 6 months	14.7%	24.0%	19.2%	20.5%	
6 + months - 7 months	2.5%	5.6%	1.4%	1.8%	
7 + months - 8 months	1.4%	4.7%	1.9%	1.7%	
8 + months - 9 months	5.8%	4.0%	3.2%	3.8%	
9 + months - 12 months	12.4%	16.8%	10.5%	15.0%	
Over 12 months	1.4%	0.0%	4.7%	4.0%	
Booking Time for Trip					0.00**
1/2 month or less	14.6%	1.6%	13.7%	14.2%	
1/2 month - 1 month	22.9%	1.2%	17.6%	15.8%	
1 + month - 2 months	16.6%	21.5%	21.0%	14.6%	
2 + month - 3 months	14.7%	13.5%	14.2%	12.4%	
3 + month - 4 months	9.5%	15.6%	6.9%	8.6%	
4 + month - 5 months	4.5%	4.0%	6.4%	6.4%	
5 + month - 6 months	10.1%	24.0%	11.4%	13.9%	
6 + month - 7 months	1.6%	5.2%	1.7%	1.7%	
7 + month - 8 months	0.9%	1.2%	1.1%	2.7%	
8 + month - 9 months	2.6%	3.5%	0.7%	4.0%	
9 + month - 12 months	2.2%	8.8%	4.4%	5.6%	
Over 12 months	0.0%	0.0%	1.0%	0.0%	

when compared to other groups. In the product segment area, respondents in the brochure/pamphlet cluster had more interest in beach, developed resort, and entertainment trips. On the other hand, respondents who used the combination package channel preferred the comfort and culture type of vacation. In addition, the word-of-mouth cluster had more travelers who were likely to choose sports/entertainment as well as beach travel activities. Finally, British travelers who liked to consult with travel agents tended to choose sports/entertainment and culture/nature travel products. The Chi-square tests for travel philosophy, benefits sought and travel product choice were significantly different across the four groups (Table 6).

CONCLUSIONS AND IMPLICATIONS

The results of this study provide a profile of British travelers by communication channels. Through cluster analysis, four communication chan-

TABLE 6. Travel Philosophy, Benefit Sought, and Product of British Travelers' Segmentation

Segments	cls1	cls2	cls3	cls4	Chi^2
Travel Philosophy					0.00**
Guarded	38.3%	17.9%	32.2%	33.7%	
Independent	37.3%	17.9%	32.3%	31.8%	
Package	24.5%	64.1%	35.5%	34.5%	
Travel Benefit Sought					0.01**
Getaway	27.7%	40.6%	28.2%	25.7%	
Social Safety	44.0%	35.1%	48.9%	37.8%	
Adventure	28.3%	24.3%	22.9%	36.6%	
Travel Product					0.00**
Sports/entertainment	22.0%	22.3%	21.4%	20.5%	
Outdoors/native cultures	6.9%	0.0%	7.4%	14.8%	
Comfort/culture	17.6%	16.8%	18.5%	22.9%	
Beach	21.7%	23.1%	15.0%	16.9%	
Developed resort	15.3%	23.1%	18.3%	8.4%	
Culture/Nature	16.4%	14.7%	19.5%	16.5%	

Note: cls1: word-of-mouth channel, cls2: brochures/pamphlets, cls3: travel agents, cls4: combination channel.
*: $P<=0.05$, **$P<=0.01$.

nel segments were identified: word-of-mouth, brochures/pamphlets, travel agents, and the combination package channel. The results suggest that travel agents and the combination package are the major communication channels for British overseas travelers. In contrast to other studies, socio-demographic variables did not vary among different clusters. However, travel characteristics, destination choice, psychographics (travel philosophy and travel benefit sought), and product preference were significantly different. These findings, particularly the lack of sociodemographic difference, could result from the nature of long haul pleasure trips. Since international travel may involve more deliberative factors than domestic travel, the search for travel information is more related to the trip itself. For example, respondents who got information from travel agents tended to travel to Mainland U.S.A. and Australia/New Zealand. People who used brochures/pamphlets as an information source preferred to take package tours and planned their trips earlier. In order to design promotional themes and identify a more precise marketing position, psychographic variables are important in the study of communication channels. For example, analysis of the results point out that social safety travelers tended to consult information from travel agents and getaway travelers liked to use brochures/pamphlets. Finally, understanding travelers' product preference can assist in efficiently targeting major markets by helping to provide proper activities and services.

The choice to look at communication channels as a way to understand and segment British travelers was based on literature suggesting that these channels could be divided into two parts–interpersonal and impersonal–each of which had specific ways in which contact was initiated. The results of the cluster analysis suggest that: (a) the international, long haul pleasure travelers in this study can be separated into distinct groups that appear to fit the models proposed by McDonough (1987) and Schiffman and Kanuk (1991), and (b) statistical and substantive differences exist that warrant attention from the travel industry. For at least some of the results, the suggestion by Schul and Crompton (1983) that psychographics might better explain search behavior appears to have merit. However, the limited ability of media habits to differentiate between groups was somewhat surprising. This must be examined in the context of almost half of those responding not reading any of the material at all. In fact, with changes taking place in reading habits by younger people in many countries, exploring this issue in relation to travel planning and decision making in greater detail could represent a challenge for marketing of products.

Implications

This research study should provide useful marketing information for those interested in outbound travel from the United Kingdom. In the case of the British travel market, there is a heavy reliance on travel agents. Any destination interested in this market should develop a close liaison with selected British travel agents and tour wholesalers, and with the airlines who service the United Kingdom. The selection of these agents and wholesalers should be most effective by carefully matching the destination's characteristics to the key client profile of each agency or wholesaler.

The group who sought travel information from friends and relatives was also important. These people tended to travel longer, visit the places where family came from, and enjoyed meeting people with similar interests. This profile suggests that an emphasis be placed on mentioning and/or illustrating family ties in advertising copy and photography. Another approach may be to appeal to the friends and relatives of those living in the United Kingdom. Developing information for and with the family for use by visitors could improve the experience of these visitors and address the needs that they may have on their repeat visits to find new things to do and see, particularly if it involves family.

Separate product and advertising strategies may be appropriate for influencing travelers who used different communication channels. Certain promotional messages that are appropriate to send to adventure travelers may not be effective if sent to other persons who seek a more safe opportunity during a trip. Travelers could be targeted with different promotional strategies through an identified communication channel. For example, for respondents who used travel information from friends/relatives, the personal messages that "Family is together!" and "Have fun with your family on our beautiful beach!" might emphasize position themes. For travelers who usually used the brochure/pamphlet information and sought get- away benefits during their trips, "Rest and relaxation in our comfortable resorts!" might be used. For the travelers who used the combination package channel and pursued adventure and excitement during trips, "Visiting adventure land!" is an appropriate position strategy. In concert with promotional themes, host countries may place more emphasis on new or improved product development with the design of activity packages such as sports/entertainment packages for people in the word-of-mouth set or resort activity packages for travelers in the brochure/pamphlet cluster. In addition, host countries may develop special programs and events to attract travelers.

The results also showed that certain daily and Sunday newspapers were popular or read by different groups of travelers. Promoters or marketing personnel may link advertisement and promotional themes to their target markets on their favorite newspapers. It is relevant to note that there is a large proportion of travelers in each segment who did not read any newspaper or magazine. It is important to find out why this is the case and identify alternative information channels in order to send advertisements and promotion to them.

Certainly one of the concerns with the results presented in this paper is that only travelers from one country are examined. If an analysis was done with travelers from another country would the same clusters emerge? We know from the series of international reports that have come from Tourism Canada and the U.S. Travel and Tourism Administration that the relative ranking of communication channel use is similar for many travelers around the world. But would the combinations or proportions remain the same if the clustering techniques used here were applied? Does the use of communication channels change if we look at shorter or longer domestic travel opportunities? Do sociodemographic variables emerge as significant for investigations of other countries or in domestic studies? The results here would indicate that there is value in proceeding with other research using the communication models that have been proposed in the literature. However, there is still much be done.

NOTE

The data utilized in this paper were made available by Tourism Canada. The data for the United Kingdom Pleasure Travel Market Study, 1989, was originally collected by Market Facts of Canada. Neither the collector of the original data nor Tourism Canada bear any responsibility for the analysis or interpretations presented here.

REFERENCE

Beane, T. P. and Ennis, D. M. (1987). Market segmentation: a review. *European Journal of Marketing, 21*(5), 20-42.

Blashfield, R.K. and Morey, L.C. (1980). A comparison of four clustering methods using MMPI Monte Carlo data. *Applied Psychological Measurement, 4,* 57-64.

Bryant, B.E. and Morrison, A.J. (1980). Travel market segmentation and the implementation of market strategies. *Journal of Travel Research, 18*(3), 2-8.

Calantone, R. J. & Johar, J. S. (1984). Seasonal segmentation of the tourism market using a benefit segmentation framework. *Journal of Travel Research, 23*(2), 14-24.

Darden, W.R. and Perrault, W. D. (1975). A multivariate analysis of media exposure and vacation behavior with life style covariates. *Journal of Consumer Research, 2*: 93-103.

Davis, B. D. & Sternquist, B. (1987). Appealing to the elusive tourist: an attribute cluster strategy. *Journal of Travel Research, 25*(4), 25-31.

Everitt, B. (1980). *Cluster Analysis.* New York, N.Y.: John Wiley & Sons, Inc.

Frank, R.E., Massy, W. F. & Wind, Y. (1978). *Marketing Segmentation.* New Jersey: Prentice Hall.

Gitelson, R.J. and Crompton, J. L. (1983). The planning horizons and sources of information used by pleasure vacationers. *Journal of Travel Research, 21*(3), 2-7.

Klastorin, T. D. (1983). Assessing cluster analysis results. *Journal of Marketing Research, 20,* 92-98.

Kuiper, F.K. and Fisher, L.A. (1975). A Monte Carlo comparison of six clustering procedures. *Biometrics, 31,* 777-783.

McDonough, M. H. (1984). *Information Networks and Great Lakes Recreation: Implications for Increasing Tourism in Michigan.* Unpublished Final Report. Department of Park & Recreation Resources, Michigan State University.

_____ (1986). Information and traveler decision making. *Cooperative Extension Bulletin.* Michigan State University.

_____ (1987). Communication channels in recreation research. In *A Literature Review: The President's Commission on Americans Outdoors.*

Market Facts Of Canada Limited (1989, November). *Pleasure Travel Markets To North America: United Kingdom.* A report prepared for Tourism Canada. Montreal: Toronto.

Mazanec, J. A. (1984). How to direct travel market segments: a clustering approach. *Journal of Travel Research, 23*(1), 17-21.

Myers, J. H. and Tauber, E. (1977). Market Structure Analysis. Chicago, Illinois: American Marketing Association, 68-90.

Morrison, M. A. (1989). *Hospitality and Travel Marketing.* Albany, N.Y.: Delmar Publishers Inc.

SAS (1990). *SAS/STAT User's Guide.* Version 6, Fourth Edition, Volume 2. Cary, N.C.: SAS Institute Inc.

Schiffman, L.G. and Kanuk, L. L. (1991). *Consumer Behavior.* Englewood Cliffs, N.J.: Prentice Hall.

Schul, P. and Crompton, J. L. (1983). Search behavior of international vacationers: travel-specific lifestyle and sociodemographic variables. *Journal of Travel Research. 2*: 93-103.

Smith, S.L.J. (1989). *Tourism System.* New York: John Wiley & Sons, Inc.

Stynes, D.J. (1985). Marketing tourism. *Journal of Physical Education and Dance, 54*(4), 21-23.

Stynes, D.J. and Mahoney, E. M. (1986). *1984 Michigan Commercial Campground Marketing Study.* Department Paper. Department of Park and Recreation Resources, Michigan State University.

Vogt, C.A. and Fesenmaier, D. R. (1991). Evaluating Tourism Marketing Communications and Mass Media. Proceedings of Research and Academic Papers, Volume III. The Society of Travel and Tourism Educators Annual Conference, Indianapolis, Indiana. October 24-27, 1991.

Wind, Y. (1978). Issues and advances in segmentation research. *Journal of Marketing Research, 15,* 317-321.

Using Travel Brochures
to Target Frequent Travellers
and "Big-Spenders"

Bruce E. Wicks
Michael A. Schuett

SUMMARY. Travel brochures are used throughout the industry to promote virtually all tourist destinations. This study examines how regional travellers request and use this material, specifically focusing on the relationships between brochure use and propensity to travel and travel expenditures. The results from a mail survey of 276 brochure requesters suggest that in general brochure requests are marginally related to high conversions, yet those marketing destinations can distinguish between how brochures are used and travel propensity and travel expenditures.

INTRODUCTION

Those marketing travel destinations use an array of print media for promotions (Etzel & Wahlers, 1985). Known as Destination Specific Travel Literature (DSTL) these publications are the tools used to help develop program images (Dilley, 1986) and respond to information requests gener-

---

Dr. Bruce E. Wicks is Assistant Professor, Department of Leisure Studies, University of Illinois, 1206 South Fourth Street, Champaign, IL 62820. Dr. Michael A. Schuett is Assistant Professor, Department of HPER, Southwest Texas State University, San Marcos, TX 78666-4616.

[Haworth co-indexing entry note]: "Using Travel Brochures to Target Frequent Travellers and "Big-Spenders." " Wicks, Bruce E., and Michael A. Schuett. Co-published simultaneously in *Journal of Travel & Tourism Marketing* (The Haworth Press, Inc.) Vol. 2, No. 2/3, 1993, pp. 77-90; and: *Communication and Channel Systems in Tourism Marketing* (ed: Muzaffer Uysal, and Daniel R. Fesenmaier) The Haworth Press, Inc., 1993, pp. 77-90. Multiple copies of this article/chapter may be purchased from The Haworth Document Delivery Center [1-800-3-HAWORTH; 9:00 a.m. - 5:00 p.m. (EST)].

77

ated by the consumer or potential client (Gartrell, 1988). Successful promotional campaigns are multi-phased processes that include an analysis of the market(s) and how they may be reached, and what communication method may most efficiently be employed (Gitelson & Crompton, 1983). Irrespective of how this analysis is conducted, e.g., as a result of sophisticated research or basic intuition, the brochure continues to be a mainstay for those promoting travel destinations (Holloway & Plant, 1988). From local Bed and Breakfasts to entire nations, brochures are produced and disseminated widely.

The effectiveness of brochures, or almost any communication technique, in attracting visitors or promoting a destination is largely unknown. Common knowledge suggests that some written promotional piece is required for each destination. Yet blanketing potential markets or haphazardly distributing any promotion, no matter how inexpensive each piece is, may suggest an efficient marketing and promotional campaign has not been implemented. It's not surprising that all too often such approaches result in poor results and lead to comments such as: "We sent out over 10,000 brochures–I can't understand why our event drew so few people."

To make the use of travel brochures more efficient and effective, promoters would benefit by knowing which distributional techniques were related to high conversions (visits) and who those visitors were. The more sophisticated destination marketer might wish to target only those persons that are likely to spend the most money when travelling (Fitzgibbon, 1987). With such information, inefficient practices could be discontinued in favor of those with a higher probability of generating a visit and increased return on promotional investments.

Targeting markets for destinations with local or regional draw may be difficult because the distinguishing characteristics of visitors and non-visitors are either unknown or unmeasurable at this time. Whereas a very specific market segment flies on the Concord or visits world renowned spas, the potential market for local special events or attractions are largely undifferentiated due to the general appeal of the destination and a lack of sophisticated market analysis. One segment of the market that is identifiable are those persons who have visited similar attractions and/or travel frequently. By understanding the travel patterns of existing markets, new opportunities to tag advertisements, co-promote and reach the clientele of other destinations may be realized (Witt & Moutinho, 1989).

There may be many reasons why destinations do not attract the audiences they might. The brochure is only one part of the complex process of destination marketing and travel decision-making (Gitelson & Crompton, 1983). This study examined a group of individuals that have requested destination specific travel literature (DSTL) from six travel brochure producers to uncover relationships between those requesting such information and their: (1) likelihood to visit the site; (2) propensity to travel, and (3) the amount of money they spent when visiting the site. This research is not about brochure design, lay-out or artistic content. Rather, it seeks to provide a better understanding of how travellers use this promotional material. Admittedly, there may be a relationship between design and use that should not be ignored. To control for the possibility of such bias, each brochure used in this study was evaluated to insure they were of comparable quality. Specific criteria used were: artistic quality, color, size, completeness of information, and print quality.

The data generated by this study will be valuable to those disseminating DSTL as it will be helping them segment and target markets most likely to visit and effect their profitability.

METHODS

The population for this study consisted of individuals that had requested travel information from six brochure producers in a mid-western U.S. state. To help ensure that the individuals surveyed would be representative of the travelling public, the cross section of brochures studied were selected because they represented very different markets and destinations. Criteria for their selection were: geographic representation, use of secondary mailing lists, scope of promotion, specificity of message, and size and type of sponsoring agency. The sample was stratified on the basis of sub-population size, and a sample of 530 was drawn from a total of 24,000+ addresses the six producers provided. To insure that respondents' recall of the brochure and site visit(s) was as accurate as possible, the front panel of each brochure was reproduced on the cover of the survey instrument. A response rate of 52% was achieved after an initial mailing, a post card reminder and two more mailings. The net usable returned responses numbered 276.

Various descriptive statistics have been employed to summarize the data collected (Wicks & Schuett, 1991). In this report that data has been subject to more sophisticated analysis to discover the relationships between brochure type and selected travel variables, expenditures patterns, and propensity to travel. Methods of analysis include chi-square, correlations, t-tests, one-way analysis of variance with Scheffe's tests and factor analysis.

RESULTS AND DISCUSSION

Site Specific or General Purpose Brochure

Brochure requesters may use site or destination specific brochures differently than they do general purpose or multi-destination guides. For example, it may be suggested that travellers requesting a specific brochure might be more likely to visit that destination than one receiving a brochure that was less descriptive of the site. To determine if such a difference did occur, respondents were assigned to one of two groups relating to the type of brochure they requested (site specific or general purpose). In this case, the general purpose brochures were a regional antique shopping guide and a multi-county festival calendar. A series of chi-square tests were completed for brochure type and nine travel related variables.

Table 1 summarizes the results of the chi-square tests and shows that in only one case was there a difference between brochure type. As might be expected there was a significant difference between the accuracy of describing destinations and the type of brochure. Those receiving general purpose brochures felt it less accurately portrayed the destination than those who had requested site specific brochures. Surprisingly there was no difference between the other eight variables and brochures type. One possible explanation of this finding may be that brochures or DSTL play

---

TABLE 1. Chi-Square Analysis of Brochure Type (Site Specific or General Purpose) and Nine Travel Related Variables

Variable	Probability
1. Site visitation (yes or no)	NS
2. Likelihood of visiting the site if respondent had not already	NS
3. Method of requesting brochure (phone, mail, coupon)	NS
4. How respondents learned about the brochures	NS
5. Did brochure depict the site accurately	0.5
6. Was brochure brought to site	NS
7. Length of trip planning horizon	NS
8. Type of travel group	NS
9. Travel group decision maker	NS

Note: NS=Not Significant

such a small role in the overall travel decision-making process that those requesting it see no discernable difference between types.

Travel Expenditures

An index of travel expenditures for those visiting the site described in the brochure they requested was created by summing expenses across eight categories (lodging, meals, vehicle, groceries, entertainment, entrance fees, shopping and other) for each respondent. These values were then compared to the methods of requesting brochures, other promotional methods used, travel expenses and demographic factors. Table 2 shows the mean total trip expenditures and t-test probabilities for five variables. The mean amounts vary considerably across variables due to the occurrence of missing values found in the expenditure data. Higher missing values reduce the "n" in the divisor when calculating the mean resulting in higher values. Thus caution should be exhibited when making cross-variable comparisons.

For all the variables reported in Table 2, the mean trip expenditures were significantly different. Those respondents indicating they had planned their trip within three weeks of going showed significantly higher expenditures than those with longer planning horizons. This occurrence may be due to increasing time constraints faced by most families, and the growing tendency to take more frequent and spontaneous short trips which require less pre-planning. This finding may indicate that time constraints rather than financial concerns are more important to many of today's harried travellers. For the destination marketer this suggests there is a need to respond quickly to the large number (46%) of requesters with relatively short planning horizons or to explore ways of increasing retention of travel information that was previously collected.

The findings shown for item one on Table 2 may be related to trip planning, as those indicating they received the brochure more quickly than expected (16%) had expenditures more than twice the amount of those who were not so favorably impressed. Respondents bringing the brochure to the site also reported significantly higher average expenditures suggesting that there may be a relationship between the ability to refer to destination information and expenditures. However, the data also shows that the average expenditure for those requesting site-specific brochures was less than general purpose offerings. This finding may be attributed to travellers spending less on single purpose or site-specific trips.

Additionally, there may be a relationship between positive trip experiences, travel expenditures and retention of DSTL. Those no longer possessing the brochure were shown to spend significantly less than those that kept this promotional material. Also, the group of brochure requesters that

TABLE 2. Mean Trip Expenditures and the t-Test Probabilities for Selected Factors of Travel Brochures Use

	Mean Expenditures	t-test Probability
1. Reasonableness of wait of brochure		
As expected or longer	$57.81	
Shorter than expected	$129.93	0.000
2. Trip planning horizon		
Less than 3 weeks	$203.00	
3 weeks or longer	$117.70	0.000
3. Bring brochure to site		
Yes	$215.07	
No	$66.42	0.000
4. Still have brochure		
Yes	$80.91	
No	$30.91	0.000
5. Number of brochures possessed		
Less than nine	$79.89	
Nine or more	$52.59	0.000
6. Type of brochure		
General	$80.65	
Specific	$39.35	0.000

may be described as "collectors," i.e., those with 9 or more, who are a majority (59%) of the respondents, spent significantly less than those possessing less DSTL. This group may also be very value conscious travellers.

For variables with multiple and mutually exclusive nominal level values an analysis of variance procedures with a means separation test (Scheffe's) was employed to test if average expenditure levels differed. The results of those procedures are shown in Table 3 and indicate that no significant differences were present in four of the five variables tested. Differences in trip expenditures for the four travel groups and the four types

TABLE 3. Analysis of Variance and Scheffe's Multiple Range Test for Expenditures and Selected Variables

	1	2	3
1. Knowledge of the destination			
1. Knew nothing			
2. Knew little			
3. Was knowledgeable	*		
2. Description of travel group			
1. Tour Group			
2. Parents with children			
3. Adults with children	NS		
4. Group of friends or relatives			
3. Method of requesting brochure			
1. Phoned site			
2. Mailed coupon			
3. Individual request			
4. Other request	NS		
4. Group decision maker	NS		
1. Tour group			
2. Parents with children			
3. Adult(s) or couple with child(ren)			
4. Group of friends or relatives			
5. Other			
5. Income	NS		
1. < $20,000			
2. $20,001-40,000			
3. $40,001-60,000			
4. $60,001-80,000			
5. > $80,000			
6. Brochure	NS		
1. Festival guide			
2. Developed attraction			
3. Antique guide			
4. Architecture tour			
5. Special event			
6. Recreation guide			

TABLE 3 (continued)	
7. Evaluation of visit	NS
1. Greatly exceeded expectations	
2. Moderately exceeded expectations	
3. Met expectations	
4. Fell somewhat below expectations	
5. Fell greatly below expectations	

$*p = .05$
Note: NS = Not Significant

of decision makers were insignificant, as was the respondents' household income levels. Taken together these findings suggest that the more personal characteristics of the traveller (group, decision-making and income) may be less likely to effect travel expenditures for short trips to local destinations.

The fact that these data show no statistically significant differences between income and travel expenditures contradicts common knowledge about travel behavior, namely that the more resources one has the more one can and does spend when vacationing. An explanation of this finding may be related to the regional nature of the travellers surveyed and the destinations examined. That is, the destinations depicted in the brochures studied appeal to local and regional markets that visited them during a day or perhaps overnight trip. Unlike long and distant vacations which are very expensive, this type and scale of travel is not restricted to upper income persons and there is a relative narrow range of expenditures possible. For example, with the possible exception of some extraordinary purchases of expensive items there is likely to be little difference in total trip expenditures for visitors to a one-day special event no matter what their income. Both use similar amounts of fuel to get there, pay equal admission and probably eat equal amounts.

A significant difference was found to occur between knowledge about the destination and trip expenditures. Respondents that were knowledgeable about the destination were found to have spent more when visiting that attraction than those reporting that they knew nothing about it. Perhaps those new visitors were participating on a trial basis and were not prepared to spend much, whereas repeat visitors were more familiar with destination offerings and travelled to the site with pre-existing notions of how much they would spend.

If persons knowledgeable about the attraction spent more on their visit than others, promoters would benefit from targeting those with greater awareness. Awareness or knowledge of the attraction may be further segmented by the sources of information used. Table 4 lists mean expenditures levels for the five most frequently reported sources of information (other than the brochure) used by those travelling to the sites examined in this study. The data indicate a generally positive relationship between greater information and greater spending. The differences between average expenditures of persons with prior personal knowledge of the site, or those who had received a recommendation by a friend or family member were substantial. This finding was expected as such sources of information are highly credible and widely reported. The difference found for newspaper advertisements and spending levels was the largest for any information source and not initially expected. There is little direct evidence to suggest why this is so, but it may reflect the importance of targeting audiences for day and weekend trips through their local newspaper. Radio advertisements showed the opposite relationship. If respondents reported this in-

TABLE 4. Sources of Travel Information by Amount Spent on Site

	Mean	t-test Probability
Knowledge from previous visit		
Yes	$239.72	
No	$125.57	0.000
Friends/family recommendation		
Yes	$244.40	
No	$126.88	0.000
Newspaper ad		
Yes	$298.72	
No	$120.90	0.000
News story		
Yes	$198.47	
No	$160.01	0.000
Radio ad		
Yes	$77.25	
No	$170.73	0.010

formation source influenced their decision to visit, expenditures were significantly lower than those who did not. A possible explanation for this finding is that the radio ads were broadcast in communities where the site was located and attracted local residents who were less likely to have high total travel expenditures.

Travel Propensity and Brochure Use

Those surveyed were asked to indicate how many times in the past year they had participated in sixteen travel activities. An index of travel propensity for each respondent was then developed by summing participation across all activities. This index was subsequently used to determine if relationships existed between the use of travel brochures and frequency of travel. Table 5 shows the results of seven t-tests for selected variables and trips taken. In summary, the most frequent travellers are in the upper income brackets, possess 10 or more brochures, have shorter rather than longer trip planning horizons, and bring their brochure to the destination with them. This profile of travellers suggests that for those requesting brochures this form of DSTL is an important component of their travel planning. They report having many brochures in their possession and tend to be spontaneous in their decision making. It is quite possible the group discovers an opportunity to take a day trip or overnight jaunt, reviews the material they have collected and uses the brochure as a reference when travelling.

The travel market is large and comprised of individuals with wide arrays of interests. Vacationers often seek diversity in their travel experiences yet are likely to fall within categories or clusters of destinations they will visit (Plog, 1991). Using factor analysis survey, respondents were grouped on the basis of their travel activities. Five very "clear" factor groupings, e.g., those exhibiting high loadings and low cross-over, were produced. Table 6 shows the structure of trip types which are characterized as: (1) the weekend traveller and day tripper, (2) the outdoor recreator, (3) the cultural and business traveller, (4) the up-scale traveller and (5) the motorcoach tourer. When combined, the variance explained by these five factors was 62.5%.

The grouping of destinations by survey respondents may help marketers place advertisements for their respective destination(s). For example, those promoting historic sites might wish to place brochures at museums, national parks or at convention facilities. Similarly, those promoting Bed and Breakfasts might find it valuable to target persons that had made foreign trips.

TABLE 5. Propensity to Travel by Selected Variables

	Mean Trips/Year	t-test Probability
1. Bring brochure to site		
Yes	43	
No	25	0.001
2. Type of brochures		
Site specific	31	
General	33	NS
3. Trip planning horizon		
Less than 3 weeks	39	0.050
More than 3 weeks	26	
4. Waiting period for brochures		
As expected and shorter	32	NS
Longer	38	
5. Number of brochures possessed		
Less than 10	27	0.030
10 or more	38	
6. Age		
Under 45	33	
45 and over	32	NS
7. Income		
Low (< $40,000)	31	0.012
High (> $40,000)	40	

CONCLUDING COMMENTS

The effectiveness of travel promotions and their role in the public's decision to vacation are not well known. This study examined the use of travel brochures by those requesting them with the goal of assisting marketers in more efficiently and effectively promoting their travel destinations.

	Factor Loadings
TABLE 6. Travel Pattern Factor Groupings	
Factor 1. "Weekend Traveller and Day Tripper"	
A. Visit festivals and events	0.8139
B. Take overnight trips to state	0.6355
C. Take overnight trips in other states	0.7079
D. Attend ethnic events	0.7259
E. Take day trips	0.6478
Percent of Variance 23.1	
Factor 2. "Outdoor Recreator"	
A. Visited a state park	0.8009
B. Went hunting	0.9168
C. Went fishing	0.9320
Percent of Variance 14.1	
Factor 3. "Cultural and Business Traveller"	
A. Extended business trip	0.6156
B. Visited historic sites	0.7988
C. Visited a national park	0.6278
D. Went to a museum	0.7352
Percent of Variance 11.1	
Factor 4. "Up-Scale Traveller"	
A. Took a foreign trip	0.7271
B. Stayed at a bed and breakfast	0.7052
Percent of Variance 7.4	
Factor 5. "Travel Tour"	
A. Took a coach tour	0.8562
Percent of Variance 6.7	
Total Variance of 62.5%	

To improve the efficiency of distributing travel brochures, promoters should learn more about their markets and target those most likely to visit with the travel information they need. Those surveyed showed little evidence of distinguishing between site specific and general purpose brochures. In general, travellers appear familiar with brochures, generally accept them, and use them to help plan travel and as references when travelling. The degree to which this promotional tool creates travel demand may singularly be small yet such information appears to be widely used. This "supporting role" for brochures does appear to be related to frequency of travel. For example, respondents who travelled most were likely to bring the brochures with them when vacationing, be more spontaneous in making travel decisions and have higher incomes.

Travel patterns of brochure requesters were found to be grouped into five segments: (1) weekend travellers and day trippers, (2) outdoor recreators, (3) cultural and business travellers, (4) up-scale travellers and (5) motorcoach travellers. These clusters of travel preferences may help those distributing brochures target markets likely to be interested in their destination and eliminate other less productive markets. Additionally, this data provides strong evidence for the use of co-promotions among related activities rather than the diversity of attractions in one community or region.

Attracting additional visitors to a destination will most likely have a positive effect on tourism revenues for that locale. However, it is widely recognized that certain groups of visitors spend far more money than others, and for many destinations attracting this group may mean its survival. Different patterns of brochures requests and use were found to be related to travel expenditures. The causality of this relationship is not known at this time but persons that were knowledgeable about the destination, took the brochure to the site, made more spontaneous travel decisions and received the brochure in a shorter time than expected reported spending more.

Evidence collected in this study does not strongly support the thesis that brochures have a decisive impact upon an individual's decision to travel. What the data does suggest is that brochures are an integral, albeit small, part of the decision making process for individuals using them. Marketers wishing to more efficiently and effectively use brochures should focus on more sophisticated target marketing strategies. Expenditures and the travel patterns of potential and actual markets may prove to be useful means of segmenting travellers.

REFERENCES

Dilley, R. S. (1986). Tourist Brochures and Tourist Images. *The Canadian Geographer*, 30(1), 59-65.

Etzel, M. J. & Wahlers, R. G. (1985). The Use of Requested Promotional Materials by Pleasure Vacationers. *Journal of Travel Research*, 24(1), 2-6.

Fitzgibbon, J. R. (1987). Market Segmentation Research in Tourism and Travel.

In J. R. B. Ritchie and C. R. Goeldner (Eds.), *Travel, Tourism, and Hospitality Research*, (489-496). New York: John Wiley & Sons.

Gartrell, R. B. 1988. *Destination Marketing*. Dubuque, Iowa: Kendall/Hunt Publishing Co.

Gitelson, R. J. & Crompton, J. L. (1983). The Planning Horizons and Sources of Information Used by Pleasure Vacationers. *The Journal of Travel Research*, 22(3), 2-7.

Holloway, J. C. & Plant, R. V. (1988). *Marketing For Tourism*. London: Pitman.

Plog, S. C. (1991). *Leisure Travel*. New York: John Wiley & Sons.

Wicks, B. E. & Schuett, M. A. (1991). Examining the role of tourism promotion through the use of brochures. *Tourism Management*, 12(4), 301-312.

Witt, S. F. & Moutinho, L. (1989). *Tourism Marketing and Management Handbook*. New York: Prentice Hall.

State Slogans:
The Case of the Missing USP

John Richardson
Judy Cohen

SUMMARY. State tourism advertising slogans fail to communicate Unique Selling Propositions (USP). This is mostly due to the fact that states themselves are geologically and culturally diverse entities whose many and diverse appeals cannot be captured in a single slogan. We make two basic recommendations to remedy this. First, we recommend breaking states into smaller regions that can legitimately present a unique selling position to prospective tourists. Second, we recommend that geologically and culturally similar regions in adjoining states band together in strategic alliances in order to share advertising expenses and reduce unnecessary advertising clutter. Both suggestions require at least some decentralization of state tourism bureaus.

INTRODUCTION

In their quest to lure tourists, states rely heavily on advertising campaigns that involve what are clearly meant to be pithy and pleasing slogans, e.g., "Virginia is for lovers," "New Mexico–America's land of enchantment." In this paper, we will argue that these slogans fail to com-

---

John Richardson is a consultant with ALENJA, 47 Wallace Road, Princeton Junction, NJ 08550. Dr. Judy Cohen is Associate Professor, Marketing Department, Rider College, 2083 Lawrenceville Road, Lawrenceville, NJ 08648-3099.

[Haworth co-indexing entry note]: "State Slogans: The Case of the Missing USP." Richardson, John and Judy Cohen. Co-published simultaneously in *Journal of Travel & Tourism Marketing* (The Haworth Press, Inc.) Vol. 2, No. 2/3, 1993, pp. 91-109; and: *Communication and Channel Systems in Tourism Marketing* (ed: Muzaffer Uysal, and Daniel R. Fesenmaier) The Haworth Press, Inc., 1993, pp. 91-109. Multiple copies of this article/chapter may be purchased from The Haworth Document Delivery Center [1-800-3-HAWORTH; 9:00 a.m. - 5:00 p.m. (EST)].

municate unique selling propositions for the respective states. Such unique selling propositions are essential for effective advertising.

We will then, however, show that this problem is a reflection of a deeper problem. This problem is that, although there are many geographic areas for which tourism marketers could readily come up with unique selling propositions, the boundaries of these areas seldom, if ever, correspond to state boundaries. Within any one state, there will be several regions that have little in common with each other. For instance, New York State has the Long Island beaches, New York City, the Catskills, and Niagara Falls. On the other hand, two or more states often share a single coherent geographic region. For instance, the Lake Superior region is shared by Michigan, Wisconsin, and Minnesota, not to mention Ontario, Canada.

Because of these mismatches between genuine geographical and arbitrary political boundaries, future marketing strategies need to be developed that encourage maximum cooperation within coherent geographical regions, regardless of state boundaries. Once this is done, advertising slogans can be developed that pithily and pleasingly express genuine unique selling propositions.

A PRIMER ON USP ADVERTISING

The unique selling proposition (USP) approach to advertising was developed by Rosser Reeves (1961). Reeves divided advertising success into two components. The first component, which he called *penetration,* is simply a measure of the number of people who recall an advertising campaign. Obviously, the potential success of a campaign depends on that number being reasonably large. The second component, which Reeves called *pull,* is a somewhat more complex measure. One divides the entire population into those who do and those who do not recall the advertising campaign. One then determines for each of these two subpopulations the proportion of people who use the advertised product. One then compares these two proportions. Obviously, a successful advertising campaign will, by definition, induce greater usage among those who recall the campaign than already exists among those who do not recall the campaign. Reeves documents several cases of striking success and dramatic failure with respect to both penetration and pull. Reeves felt that success could be easily predicted: advertising campaigns using the USP approach would be successful with respect to both components, while those not using a USP approach would fail in one or both components.

The USP approach identifies four criteria. First, good advertising is propositional. That is, good advertisements make statements about products that are substantial enough to be true or false. Second, a well-focused advertisement will make either only one such proposition or, at the very least, will make only a few such propositions that share some thematic coherence. Third, the proposition or propositions must be "selling" in the sense that they inform the audience of genuine product benefits, where a product's benefits are defined as that product's ability to satisfy consumer needs and wants. Finally, the array of benefits claimed must be unique. That is, the benefits offered can not be claimed by competing products.

While the strongest version of uniqueness would entail that literally no other product in the world can offer the advertised benefits, a more reasonable (but still contentful) version would entail that no other product within the range of products offered to a certain market can offer the advertised benefits. For example, Sanibel, Florida can claim to have the best beaches for collecting seashells when advertising to U. S. residents who are interested in beach shelling but who do not wish to travel abroad. For more intrepid global travellers, there are beaches in Africa and Asia that provide better shelling opportunities. This sort of situation is highly typical of tourism.

This USP approach to advertising has been recognized as an "ancient, though time-honored axiom" (Kagan 1989, p. 32)) for creative people in advertising who realize the need for advertising to be part of a solid marketing strategy that contributes to sales. That a USP is a requirement of successful advertising is recognized in recent "primers" on effective advertising which have been written for marketers as diverse as accountants (Churchill 1989), fund rasiers (Hemmings 1990), catalog marketers (Rapp 1990), and grocery stores (Raphel 1991). But to fully recognize the fundamental importance of the USP approach, note that Kagan (1989) has gone so far as to argue that the modern concept of positioning "is little more than a gussied-up creative repackaging" (p. 32) of the USP approach to advertising. As the importance of positioning becomes more widely recognized in the hospitality and tourism industry (cf. Burdenski 1986 and Lewis 1990), the USP approach to advertising will be recognized as axiomatic.

In this paper, we apply the criteria of good USP advertising to the issue of state tourism advertising slogans. Slogans are widely acknowledged to play a crucial role in advertising. As Moriarity (1991, p. 400) put it, slogans are the "battle cries" of advertising campaigns. To play this role successfully, Moriarity (p. 401) continues, slogans must "hook or stick in the mind easily" and "should reflect the character or personality of the product and the tone and atmosphere of the campaign." Putting these considerations in USP terms, we can simply say a good slogan should pithily and pleasingly express the USP itself.

If a single benefit is claimed, the slogan should clearly but succinctly communicate this benefit. If more than one thematically coherent benefits are claimed, the slogan should clearly but succinctly communicate the coherent theme uniting these benefits. For example, if some coastal resort area can legitimately claim to be the best place in the world for windsurfing, an appropriate slogan might be "Westerland: Where wind meets surf." If, on the other hand, another coastal resort area wishes to position itself as a place where a uniquely wide variety of aquatic sports can be enjoyed, an appropriate slogan might be "Easterland: A thousand ways to be all wet."

USP ADVERTISING AND THE STATE OF STATE SLOGANS

In order to determine the extent to which USPs are present or missing in current state advertising, the tourism bureau for each state was called and tourist information was requested. The information was then scanned for state slogans. States which had not responded were telephoned and directly asked for their state's advertising slogan. A total of 46 slogans were identified. The authors then analyzed the content of the slogans and judged them by the four criteria of USP advertising described above. The slogans were taxonomized into seven groups that ranged from those which least met the criteria (Level 0) to those which most met the criteria (Level 4b) of USP advertising. Figure 1 shows the seven levels, and the slogans which belong to each level. We do not expect that every reader will agree with every detail of this taxonomy. However, we feel that we have been extremely liberal and have, if anything, generally erred in the direction of exaggerating the number of criteria any given slogan meets, in part or full. We will now define the seven levels and discuss a few examples of slogans from each of these levels. (See Appendix A for the results of an exploratory study which supplements and generally supports this discussion.)

Level 0: No Proposition. The first criterion of USP advertising is simply that good advertising is propositional. That is, it makes a statement about the product that is substantial enough to be true or false. There are two slogans that do not, by any stretch of the imagination, make a claim about the state they advertise. These are: "Yes! Michigan!" and "Utah!" These slogans make no claims whatsoever, let alone any claims substantial enough to be true or false. At best, these slogans express some generic and undefined sense of excitement.

Level 1: Proposition equivalent to "Buy our product." Slogans which

FIGURE 1. State Slogans by Category

Level 0: No Proposition
Yes! Michigan!
Utah!

Level 1: Proposition equivalent to "Buy our product"
You have a date to discover The Californias.
Discover Idaho.
Explore Minnesota.
Wake up to Missouri.
Send a postcard from Nebraska.
Destination Washington.
Find yourself in Wyoming.

Level 2: Proposition equivalent to "Our product is good"
Alabama! The state of surprises.
Georgia on my mind.
Come to life in Hawaii.
The time is right. Discover Iowa's treasures.
Kansas. The secret's out.
Maryland more than you can imagine.
The spirit of Massachusetts.
New Jersey and you. Perfect together.
It's right in New Hampshire.
I ♥ NY.
The best part of your vacation is where you go.
North Carolina.
Discover the spirit! North Dakota.
Vermont makes it special.
West Virginia. A welcome change.

Level 3a: Proposition gives a product attribute, but virtually any state could claim the same attribute
Arkansas. The natural state.
Illinois: The American renaissance.
Back home in Indiana.
The uncommon wealth of Kentucky.
Maine. The way life should be.
Picture it. Mississippi.
Oregon. Things look different here.
Virginia is for lovers.
Wisconsin. You're among friends.

Level 3b: Proposition gives a product attribute, but many states claim the same attribute
Classic Connecticut.
New Mexico. America's land of enchantment.
Ohio the heart of it all!
Oklahoma—Native America.
South Carolina. This is your day in the sun.
Texas. It's like a whole other country.

Level 4a: Proposition gives a unique product attribute which is not a product benefit (i.e., does not "sell")
Delaware. The first state.
Pennsylvania. America starts here.
Rhode Island. America's first resort.

Level 4b: Unique selling proposition
Arizona. The Grand Canyon state.
Florida coast to coast.
Louisiana. We're really cookin'!
South Dakota. Great faces. Great places.
Tennessee. We're playing your song.

95

state "Discover Idaho" or "Destination Washington" are in effect saying no more than "come here" or "buy our product." One could argue that slogans that express no more than this actually do not meet the criterion of propositionality, since they do not really make a claim about the product itself. At best, one can infer from them that the advertiser feels that there is some reason why the consumer should buy the product. The generous interpretation is that there is some good reason to buy (that is, from the consumer's point of view), but that reason is not spelled out.

Level 2: Proposition equivalent to "Our product is good." The slogans in this category follow the formula pioneered by undifferentiated mass-appeal products like Coke and Pepsi: (1) generate a phrase or sentence that expresses some generic "warm and fuzzy" good feeling; (2) insert your brand (i.e., state) name in the appropriate spot. For example, "_____ and you, perfect together," could refer to New Jersey. It could also refer to any other place in the world or, for that matter, any product. In short, these slogans do no more than assert that there is something good about the state, but once again do not identify what that is.

Two of the slogans in this category deserve special mention. The slogan "I [heart] NY" was very successful. However, it was also the slogan of the first major state tourism campaign. As such, it had high novelty content without actually saying anything novel or contentful about New York. Moreover, the use of the heart to express the verb "love" coupled with the conciseness of the pronoun "I" before the heart and the initials "NY" after it made this slogan graphically striking, once again despite the fact that the slogan said nothing striking about New York. Indeed, the subsequent proliferation of "I [heart] _____" slogans, such as "I [heart] my wire-haired fox terrier" and "I [heart] quantum uncertainty" testify on the one hand to the artistic attractiveness of the "I [heart]" symbol, but on the other hand to the generic applicability of the proposition it expresses.

Another special case which needs to be discussed is Georgia. One might argue that "Georgia on my mind" is uniquely appropriate to Georgia because there is a song of the same name which is obviously meant to be evoked by the slogan. While this might lead to good recall of the advertisement, it does not express a USP because it does not describe an attribute unique to Georgia. In fact, the proposition says little even by the meager standards of Level 2. For people familiar with the song, however, a positive sentiment, albeit a generic one, is undoubtedly evoked.

Level 3a: Proposition gives a product attribute, but any state could claim the same attribute. The slogans at Level 3a make a product claim appreciably more specific than "our product is good." Examples are "Maine. The way life should be" and "Wisconsin. You're among friends." The problem here, however, is that any of these claims could be made by any other state just as well. In fact, for certain claims, other states could make them better. For example, although Arkansas calls itself "the natural state," the considerably more pristine states of Alaska, Montana or Maine can make this claim more appropriately. Similar arguments can be made for "Illinois: The American Renaissance" (cf. Massachusetts and its colleges or California and its pacesetting lifestyles); "The Uncommon Wealth of Kentucky" (cf. the patrician state of Connecticut or the prestigious colonial commonwealth of Pennsylvania); and "Virginia is for Lovers" (cf. the honeymoon destination of Hawaii). Indeed, if any of these more appropriate states had made these claims, these slogans might have approached the status of being genuine USPs. This points up an important principle: a claim will become increasingly meaningless as it is made by those for whom the claim is least plausible.

Level 3b: Proposition gives a product attribute, but many states could claim the same attribute. Level 3b is similar to level 3a, but the claim is distinctive enough that not every state can make the same claim. "Not every" can, however, range from several to many. For example, Ohio's claim to be "the heart of it all!" could also be claimed by any of the heartland states of the Northern Great Plains. South Carolina's claim that "this is your day in the sun" could be claimed all year round by all of the sunbelt states, and during the summer months by all but the most northern states. These slogans do, however, at least begin to differentiate their states.

Level 4a: Proposition gives a unique product attribute which is not a product benefit (i.e., does not "sell"). Three slogans fit into this category: "Delaware. The First State," "Pennsylvania. America starts here," and "Rhode Island. America's first resort." Nothing can be more unique than being the first at something or the starting point for something. But it is difficult to imagine that anyone would plan a vacation on the basis of the order in which a state entered the union or which state has the oldest tourism industry. And while Philadelphia's role as the cradle of the nation has left behind several genuine tourist attractions, the state as a whole, from the Pocono Mountains to the western coal regions, are at best incidentally connected with this historical fact. Furthermore, by using the present tense "starts" instead of the past tense "started," the slogan is obviously intended as a play on words, with a coy interpretation something like "you haven't begun to see America until you've seen Pennsylvania." This interpretation, unlike the literal historical interpretation, belongs among the vacuous claims of Level 2.

There is a similar problem with Rhode Island's slogan. "First" can mean either "first in time" or "first in quality" or "first in popularity." On the temporal meaning, the claim is presumably true but of little interest. On the "quality" reading, the claim is questionable, and on the "popularity" reading, the claim is false. On either of these two readings, this slogan would sink at least to Level 3b, with the further demerit that it would belong among those slogans that are so inappropriate that they render themselves meaningless.

Level 4b: Unique selling proposition. Five slogans were judged as expressing USPs: "Arizona. The Grand Canyon State," "See Florida coast to coast," "Louisiana. We're really cookin'!" "South Dakota. Great faces. Great places," and "Tennessee. We're playing your song." South Dakota's slogan expresses a USP only in conjunction with its visual of Mount Rushmore. This limits its use to visual media (or reminder ads aimed at those already familiar with the slogan). More importantly, however, it is not a state slogan per se. Rather, it advertises one tourist destination within the state. The same problem exists for Arizona (which may be the reason why, at this writing, they are seeking a new slogan). The remaining three slogans do about as well as possible (see next section) in evoking a general feature of the state that is reasonably unique to that state and of interest to potential tourists.

In summary, only five of the forty-six slogans analyzed can be said to express a USP, and two of these expressed the USP for an attraction in the state, rather than for the state in general. The vast majority of slogans either made no meaningful claim at all or made a claim that could be made equally well by other states. As we will show in the next section, however, the problems with these slogans are at least in large measure a function of the difficulties in marketing an entire state, rather than a function of poor creative efforts by the authors of the slogans.

USP ADVERTISING AND THE STATE OF STATES

To be fair to state tourism marketers, for most states, it would be difficult to impossible to devise a unique selling proposition, let alone a slogan that concisely expresses it. Simply put, the powers that were who drew state boundaries during the colonial and manifest destiny periods of previous centuries did not worry themselves about the sorts of issues that are of current concern to state tourism marketers. This has resulted in two complementary problems.

On the one hand, states are internally heterogeneous with respect to tourist attractions. We mentioned the diversity of New York State's attractions at the beginning of the paper, including the Long Island beaches,

New York City, the Catskills and Niagara Falls. Other obvious examples include California (Los Angeles versus San Francisco, Yosemite Park versus Disneyland, the Pacific coast versus the mountains versus the desert) and Pennsylvania (historic Philadelphia, the Pocono Mountains, the Pennsylvania Dutch country, and the western small coal town regions). Even a small state like Massachusetts offers the variety of Boston, Cape Cod, and the Berkshires, attractions that are different enough to make the development of a USP a difficult task.

On the other hand, large regions like the Appalachians or the Atlantic barrier islands that are reasonably homogeneous with respect to tourist attractions are at least as likely to straddle two or more states as they are to be contained within one state's borders. Therefore, although it may be easy to devise a USP and associated slogan for these large homogeneous regions, the fact that they are broken up amongst different states entails that there is no one authority in charge of tourism marketing for the entire region. In many cases, this will mean that there will be no authority financially strong enough to be able to mount a major advertising campaign on behalf of the region.

For convenience, we will call the first problem the geographical heterogeneity of states. Please note that 'geographical' heterogeneity is meant to denote geological heterogeneity, e.g., mountains versus shorelines, cultural heterogeneity, e.g., cities versus rural areas, or any combination thereof. Since the second problem is due to the existence of arbitrary political boundaries that break up what are otherwise geographically homogeneous regions, we will call this problem the political heterogeneity of geographical regions.

STRATEGIES FOR DEALING WITH THE GEOGRAPHICAL HETEROGENEITY OF STATES

In spite of the obstacles to developing USP advertising due to the geographical heterogeneity of states, many states attempt to create a single advertising proposition for their state. Hawes, Taylor and Hampe (1991) found that 28 percent of the state marketing plans they analyzed included a strategy to "[d]evelop and promote a statewide 'theme' (and/or tag line) as a unifying coordinating and reinforcing mechanism" (p. 12). Nineteen percent of the plans included a strategy to "[s]trive for an overall consistent image of the state" (p. 13).

Some state marketers do seem to recognize the futility of trying to develop USP-based slogans. This is evidenced by the frequent changes in slogans. For example, when one of the authors called a particular state and asked their state slogan, the response was "do you want to suggest one?" This state was seeking a new slogan, as was another state which was called for slogan information. Another slogan which was included in the survey, "New Jersey and You. Perfect Together" was just replaced by "New Jersey. You should see us now." And even the greatly touted slogan "I can't wait!" which was developed for South Carolina as a result of in-depth consumer research (Kooyman 1991) is now "South Carolina. This is your day in the sun."

A further implicit recognition that states are too heterogeneous geographically to support a USP is the fact that most states' tourism bureaus break the state up into several geographic regions in their printed tourism literature (i.e., in the brochures that they mail to potential tourists and distribute at tourist information centers). Of the 42 packets of tourism literature which the authors received from U. S. states, 36 contained brochures that explicitly divided the state into smaller, geographically specific regions. For example, Pennsylvania is divided into eight regions: the Lake Erie Region, the Allegheny National Forest Region, the Valleys of the Susquehanna, the Pocono Mountains Region, the Philadelphia Country-side, the Hershey/Dutch Region, the Laurel Highlands Region, and the Pittsburgh Region. Each of these regions can far more readily support a USP, and therefore a USP-based slogan, than can the totality of Pennsylvania. (Recall that Pennsylvania's slogan, "America Starts Here" is really only appropriate to Philadelphia.)

However, the logic of USP advertising would dictate that dividing a state into smaller, geographically specific regions is a useful strategy only if each region has, or has the potential to acquire, a unique and interesting, i.e., "selling," image of its own. If, on the other hand, the only description which can be given of a region within a state is its compass location (e.g., "northeast," "central," "south"), the principles of USP advertising can not be successfully applied.

Of the 36 states that were divided into smaller regions, 22 of them gave descriptive names which evoked unique geological or cultural images to all or most of their regions. The other 14 states simply described the region's compass location. This may have resulted from an arbitrary compass point division of the state without regard for the geographical homogeneity of the resulting units. If this is so, the problems of advertising entire states have simply been reinvented on a more local level. On the other hand, if each region does have a unique and interesting image of its own, developing a USP for each area would demand first identifying that image and then replacing the compass location name with a name that evokes that image. Only then can USP advertising principles even be applied. One last possibility must be considered. It may be that after, say, three or four homogeneous geographical regions of genuine touristic interest are identified within a state, one or more regions of no particular touristic interest are, so to speak, left over. We suggest that funds not be used to market these areas as tourist sites. (We will presently discuss a solution to the potentially difficult political ramifications of cutting a region off from tourism development funds.)

Assuming that a state has been divided into smaller regions, each with its own unique image and descriptive name, our first advertising suggestion is to have each region develop and run its own advertising campaign. Because each such region will, by definition, have a unique image, it will be relatively easy to develop a USP-based slogan for that region. This proposal entails that state advertising campaigns per se should be more or less discontinued. This leads to certain obvious budgeting and related logistical questions. First, how are these regional campaigns to be funded? Second, who is in charge of gathering and spending the necessary funds? Third, what happens to those regions that do not receive funding for tourism development at all?

While we can not give definitive answers to these questions, we will offer some alternative approaches. One alternative is to maintain a centralized approach. Under this scheme, state taxing authorities would continue to allocate funds to a state tourism and development bureau. However, the state bureau would not develop campaigns but would in turn allocate funds to regional tourism and/or development bureaus. Another option would be to cut out the intermediary and have state taxing authorities directly allocate funds to regional tourism and/or development bureaus. The use of an intermediary may be preferable to the extent that the expertise and (relative) apoliticism of a centralized agency results in benefits that outweigh the added cost of an extra level of administration. A third option would be to decentralize entirely. Under this option, the taxing authorities of the counties and/or municipalities included in a region would contribute funds to a regional tourism and/or development bureau. Under each of these options, each region would decide how much of these funds to allocate to tourism development versus other types of economic development. Such local empowerment finesses the problem of regions being cut off from tourism development funds since all regions will receive general development funds.

We should note that under any of the above funding alternatives, regional budgets will be significantly smaller than state budgets. For this reason, there are limits to how finely a state can be divided into regions. If there are too many regions, the budget for each region will be too small to mount an effective advertising campaign. This financial constraint on how finely states can be divided dovetails with a "psycho-informational" constraint. If, for example, states divided into an average of four regions, there would be a fourfold increase in the number of campaigns competing for the attention of the same potential tourists. But if states divided into an average of ten regions, the number of competing advertising campaigns would multiply tenfold. In short, regional tourism marketers have a collective interest in keeping the babble of competing voices to a manageable minimum.

STRATEGIES FOR DEALING
WITH THE POLITICAL HETEROGENEITY OF REGIONS

We have just seen that there are financial and psycho-informational reasons for wanting to limit the number of regions both on the state and national levels. One further way to limit this number is for regions to form cross-border alliances with regions from other states which are contiguous and share or potentially share the same image. Consider the example in which two states straddle a single river. The riverfront region of State A could enter a strategic alliance with the riverfront region of State B. In so doing, the two regions would pool their financial resources, thereby increasing the potential reach and/or frequency of a combined campaign without sacrificing their USP. At the collective level, the more such strategic alliances there are, the fewer voices there will be competing for the attention of potential tourists. (See Hill and Shaw 1992 for a discussion of factors which affect the viability and desirability of strategic tourist marketing alliances on an international level.)

Some pioneering cases of such alliances are given by Bacas (1990). The Lake Superior Circle Tour has been promoted by shore regions in Wisconsin, Minnesota, Ontario and Michigan. Similar tours are being promoted by regions surrounding other bodies of water such as the other Great Lakes and the upper St. Lawrence River. These alliances have been successful because they are made up of smaller-than-state regions which share genuine commonalities with respect to the attractions offered. In contrast, an attempt by six entire states (Idaho, Montana, North and South Dakota, Washington and Wyoming) to form an alliance to promote the Northwest Centennial celebration has met with very little success (Gudridge 1989). This is only to be expected from the point of view of USP advertising. Lumping together groups of internally heterogeneous states will only create a larger and more heterogeneous entity that would be hard to manage and impossible to promote. Indeed, Montana's tourism director concluded "[t]he region is just too broad to market in this country as one unit" (Gudridge 1989, p. S-4).

Creating these alliances at the correct level poses certain logistical challenges. Since entire states should not be involved, the decision to enter an alliance can not be made by state tourism bureaus. On the other hand, a region within one state that could appropriately enter an alliance with a region within another state may not have the discretionary decision making power either in terms of funds or in terms of logistics to consummate such an alliance. This problem will be preempted if regional tourism bureaus are set up as autonomous units with their own budgets and discretionary spending powers. This is one more reason to adopt a moderately or radically decentralized strategy, as discussed above with respect to the problem of the geographical heterogeneity of states.

If none of the above government-initiated strategies are feasible, a grassroots approach will be necessary. Such a grassroots approach would be at least in part privately funded by those with a stake in joint tourism development, e.g., hotel and restaurant owners, tourist site operators, certain retailers and transportation providers. For any such grassroots effort to receive public funds, successful appeals would have to be made to the legislatures and/or tourism bureaus of more than one state, with no guarantee that any state will consider the project top priority. In the case of the Lake Superior tour, a grassroots group of five businesspersons from Lansing, Michigan were able to get small but crucial amounts of funding from the state legislature early on, including funds to coordinate the project with the other states involved.

We would like to end with a cautionary note. Regional cooperation is necessary but not sufficient for improving the success of tourism marketing strategies. That is, all things being equal, one will have more success marketing a geographically homogeneous region than one will have marketing a geographically heterogeneous region. How much actual success one has depends mostly on how inherently attractive the advertised region is to potential tourists. Recall that USP advertising presupposes the existence of a genuine product benefit. There is no form or style of advertising that can magically lure a large and continuous stream of tourists into regions that have little of interest to offer them.

CONCLUSION

Most state tourism advertising slogans fail to communicate unique selling propositions. This is mostly due to the fact that states themselves are geologically and culturally diverse entities whose many and diverse appeals cannot be captured in a single slogan. We make two basic recommendations to remedy this. First, we recommend breaking states into smaller regions that can legitimately present a unique selling proposition to prospective tourists. Second, we recommend that geologically and culturally similar regions in adjoining states band together in strategic alliances in order to share advertising expenses and reduce unnecessary advertising clutter. Both suggestions require at least some decentralization of state tourism bureaus.

REFERENCES

Bacas, Harry (1990). Allies for Growth. *Nation's Business* 78 (11), pp. 40-43.

Burdenski, Helen (1986). Tourism: America's Hottest Industry. In W. Joseph, L. Moutinho & I. Vernon (Eds.), *Tourism Services Marketing: Advances in Theory and Practice* (pp. 3-12). Proceedings of the Special Conference on Tourism Services Marketing Presented by the The Academy of Marketing Science and the Marketing Department of Cleveland State University, held at Cleveland, Ohio (September 24-26).

Churchill, Phil (1989). Uses and Abuses of Advertising. *Accountancy*, 104 (1154), pp. 130, 132.

Gudridge, Kevin (1989). Squabbling Mires Down Centennial. *Advertising Age*, (January 16) pp. S-4, S-6.

Hawes, Douglass K., Taylor, David T. & Hampe, Gary D. (1991). Destination Marketing by States. *Journal of Travel Research*, 30 (5), pp. 11-17.

Hemmings, Robert (1990). Think Before You Write. *Fund Raising Management*, 20 (February), pp. 23-24.

Hill, Tracey and Robin N. Shaw (1992). *Strategic Alliances in International Tourism Marketing*. Paper presented at the American Marketing Association Summer Educator's Conference, Chicago, Illinois.

Kagan, David S. (1989). Trout and Reis Bite the Hand that Feeds. *Advertising Age* (August 7), pp. 20, 32.

Kooyman, Mark E. (1990). Stress Busters. *Business and Economic Review* 36 (3), pp. 7-9.

Lewis, Robert C. (1990). Advertising Your Hotel's Position. *The Cornell Hotel and Restaurant Administration Quarterly*, 31 (August), pp. 84-91.

Mok, Henry M. K. (1990). A Quasi-Experimental Measure of the Effectiveness of Destinational Advertising: Some Evidence from Hawaii. *Journal of Travel Research* 29 (4), pp. 30-34.

Moriarty, Sandra E. (1991). *Creative Advertising: Theory and Practice*. Englewood Cliffs, N. J.: Prentice Hall.

Raphel, Murray (1991). 6 Ways to Carve Your Own Niche. *Progressive Grocer*, 70 (October), pp. 13-14.

Rapp, Stan (1990). New Challenge for Look-Alike Catalog Marketers. *Direct Marketing*, 52 (April), pp. 73, 75.

Reeves, Rosser (1961). *Reality in Advertising*. New York: Knopf.

APPENDIX A

SUPPLEMENTARY SURVEY

An exploratory study was also done to give further insight into the analysis of state slogans. A fill-in-the-blank (i.e., the appropriate state) survey was developed (Figure 2). Note that the survey asks respondents not only to fill in the blanks with state names, but also asks if each answer was based on prior familiarity with the slogan or was an educated guess.

In the context of this paper, the case of correct response through prior familiarity is relatively uninteresting. The interesting question is how many accurate educated guesses can be made. Only when a correct educated guess can be made, can the slogan be said to express a unique proposition about the state. Of course, even a unique proposition may not be a selling proposition, that is, it may not describe any product benefits (e.g., "California–come feel the earth quake!").

One shortcoming of the survey is that a correct educated guess is predicated on prior knowledge about a state. This survey was given to a small convenience sample (34 students in two MBA classes). While the sample was small, it did consist of well educated, upwardly mobile persons who are both likely to travel and to have some familiarity with regions other than the one they currently live in. However, since extensive knowledge of all states is not likely, even among this educated group, the results should not be considered conclusive in themselves. They can, however, offer potentially interesting insights to supplement the analysis of state slogans which was presented in the body of the paper.

Several categories of responses are of interest. As stated above, a correct educated guess at least indicates that the slogan offers a unique proposition. The state which was most often correctly identified was "Delaware. The first state," followed by "Arizona. The Grand Canyon State," "Georgia on my mind" "See Florida coast to coast," "Louisiana. We're really cookin' " and "Tennessee. We're playing your song." (See Table 1.) With the exception of Georgia (which was, as discussed above, a special case), these are all Level 4 slogans. It is interesting to note that in this small sample, at least, only 21 per cent of respondents were familiar with the song "Georgia on my mind." Since this slogan can be considered unique only to the extent that people are familiar with the song, Georgia tourism marketers should take note. While the song is certainly a classic, it is not widely known among younger people.

The two states which each received two correct guesses and the six that each received one correct guess may have been the result of the respondent hearing the slogan but not consciously remembering it. (The "Virginia is

FIGURE 2. Survey of State Slogans

Below you will find a listing of slogans for tourism advertising used by different states in the U.S. For each slogan, please write the name of the state which you think uses that slogan. Then indicate whether you chose that state because (1) you are familiar with the advertising, and are making an educated guess based on how the slogan describes the state itself. If you are not familiar with the slogan and feel you can not make a reasonable guess, please answer "do not know" in the space provided.

Slogan	Familiar with advertisement	Educated guess	Do not know
Send a post card from ___.			
Destination ___.			
___ the heart of it all.			
Discover ___.			
___ makes it special.			
___ More than you can imagine.			
___ Native America.			
The time is right. Discover ___ treasures.			
It's right in ___.			
You have a date to discover ___.			
___. Things look different here.			
___. We're playing your song.			
Picture it. ___.			
The best part of your vacation is where you go. ___.			
___. The natural state.			
___. The American renaissance.			
Discover the spirit! ___.			
___. America starts here.			
The uncommon wealth of ___.			
___. A Welcome Change.			
___! The state of surprises.			
___. America's first resort.			
Yes ___.			
Explore ___.			
___ is for lovers.			
___!			
___. The First State.			
___. You're among friends.			
The spirit of ___.			
Find yourself in ___.			
___ and you. Perfect together.			
See ___ coast to coast.			
___. America's land of enchantment.			
___. Great faces. Great places.			
___ on my mind.			

Slogan	Familiar with advertisement	Educated guess	Do not know
I ___.	_____	_____	_____
Come to life in ___.	_____	_____	_____
Classic ___.	_____	_____	_____
___. The way life should be.	_____	_____	_____
___. This is your day in the sun.	_____	_____	_____
___. We're really cookin'!	_____	_____	_____
Wake up to ___.	_____	_____	_____
Back home in ___.	_____	_____	_____
___. The secret's out.	_____	_____	_____
___. It's like a whole other country.	_____	_____	_____
___. The Grand Canyon state.	_____	_____	_____

TABLE 1. Correct Educated Guesses About State Slogans

State Slogans	Number of Responses (%)
Delaware. The First State.	10 (29%)
Arizona. The Grand Canyon State.	8 (24%)
Georgia on my mind.	7 (21%)
See Florida coast to coast.	6 (18%)
Louisiana. We're Really Cookin'!	4 (12%)
Tennessee. We're playing your song.	4 (12%)
Back home in Indiana.	2 (6%)
Virginia is for lovers.	2 (6%)
Classic Connecticut.	1 (3%)
The spirit of Massachusetts.	1 (3%)
Oregon. Things look different here.	1 (3%)
Pennsylvania. America starts here.	1 (3%)
South Dakota. Great faces. Great places.	1 (3%)
Texas. It's like a whole other country.	1 (3%)

for lovers" campaign is heavily promoted in the area where the survey was given.) The low level of educated guesses for South Dakota no doubt is due to the lack of an accompanying visual of Mount Rushmore. (This special case was discussed above.) The low number of correct responses for Pennsylvania ("America starts here") reflects the ambiguous nature of the slogan, also discussed in the analysis of the content of the slogans. With certain exceptions which were noted in the analysis of the content of the slogans themselves, the low numbers of correct responses for these slogans, as well as the content of these slogans themselves, do not seem to indicate the presence of truly unique appeals.

Incorrect guesses generally indicate a lack of USP advertising. Forty-five (of forty-six) slogans generated at least one incorrect response. Although space limitations preclude listing all of them, Table 2 includes those slogans for which at least five respondents made incorrect guesses. These results are especially unsurprising for those slogans which are Level 1 or 2 (e.g., "Send a postcard from ___"; "Discover ___"; "Discover the Spirit! ___").

Perhaps more disheartening for the tourism marketers in some states is the fact that several slogans evoked images of an "incorrect" state more than the state which had the slogan. For example, no respondents thought "Discover ___" meant "Discover Idaho," but four gave the educated guess of "Discover Alaska." Similarly, more respondents thought of sending a postcard from Alaska, California, Florida and Hawaii than from Nebraska, which uses that slogan.

While Level 3 slogan, "The uncommon wealth of ___" invokes images of the original thirteen states, no respondents thought it described Kentucky. Massachusetts is seen more as a state of "American Renaissance" than Illinois (although perhaps the fact that the survey was taken at a college in the northeast affected these responses). The high rate of incorrect guesses of Pennsylvania for the slogan "___. You're among friends" no doubt reflects the fact that Pennsylvania's former slogan was "You've got a friend in Pennsylvania."

TABLE 2. Incorrect Educated Guesses About State Slogans (Slogans with at least 5 incorrect guesses)

Slogan	States guesses (number respondents)
Back home in ___.	AL (1), KY (1), NM (1), WV (1)
Discover the Spirit! ___.	AK (1), MA (2), MO (3), PA (2), TX (3)
Discover ___.	AK (4), FL (1), WY (2)
Send a postcard from ___.	AK (1), CA (1), FL (1), HI (2)
___. The Grand Canyon State.	CO (1), NV (1), NM (2), OR (1), WY (1)
___. The Heart of it all!	AL (1), KS (2), NY (2)
___. You're among friends.	NJ (1), PA (5)*
___. The American renaissance.	LA (1), MA (4)
The uncommon wealth of ___.	NJ (2), MA (2), PA (5), VA (4)
___. America's first resort.	FL (4), VT (1)

* The high rate of incorrect guesses for PA no doubt reflects the fact that PA's former slogan was "You've got a friend in Pennsylvania."

Although "Rhode Island. America's first resort" is a USP slogan when "first resort" is understood in a historical context, more people think of Florida as "America's first resort," presumably thinking in terms of popularity rather than history. One unexpected result reminds us that even when a state has an unambiguous unique selling proposition, a certain amount of background knowledge or exposure to advertising is necessary. Six people identified states other than Arizona as "the Grand Canyon State."

In sum, even the most recognizable slogans were recognizable by only a minority of respondents. Overall, 81 percent of the responses were simply "don't know." This supports the notion that most slogans were too generic to inspire even a guess.

Design of Destination and Attraction-Specific Brochures

Donald Getz
Lisa Sailor

SUMMARY. The design of destination and attraction-specific brochures is examined, with particular reference to attributes of attractiveness and utility. Results from three focus groups are employed to generate hypotheses which can be tested. Implications are drawn on the design and use of brochures and their role in trip motivation and destination choice.

INTRODUCTION

This paper explores the design of attraction and destination-specific brochures, stressing their attractiveness and utility. A general discussion is presented of the design of brochures and their roles in tourism marketing. Results are then discussed from a specific contract research study conducted for a consortium of public and private-sector museums and heritage sites. The research focused on evaluation of exiting brochures, leading to recommendations for their improvement. More generically, the research led to the generation of testable hypotheses concerning

Dr. Donald Getz is Associate Professor of Tourism Management at the University of Calgary. Lisa Sailor is a graduate student in Recreation and Leisure Studies at the University of Waterloo.

Address correspondence to Dr. Getz, Faculty of Management, University of Calgary, 2500 University Drive N.W., Calgary, Alberta, Canada T2N 1N4.

[Haworth co-indexing entry note]: "Design of Destination and Attraction-Specific Brochures." Getz, Donald, and Lisa Sailor. Co-published simultaneously in *Journal of Travel & Tourism Marketing* (The Haworth Press, Inc.) Vol. 2, No. 2/3, 1993, pp. 111-131; and: *Communication and Channel Systems in Tourism Marketing* (ed: Muzaffer Uysal, and Daniel R. Fesenmaier) The Haworth Press, Inc., 1993, pp. 111-131. Multiple copies of this article/chapter may be purchased from The Haworth Document Delivery Center [1-800-3-HAWORTH; 9:00 a.m. - 5:00 p.m. (EST)].

111

brochure attractiveness and their utility for trip planning, and provided insights on how brochures might influence trip motivation and destination choice.

DESTINATION AND ATTRACTION-SPECIFIC BROCHURES

Within the tourism and hospitality industry, brochures are a standard communication tool. They are considered to be almost a necessity for destination areas and individual businesses or attractions, especially by the many public and not-for-profit agencies that wish to promote their facilities and sites as tourist attractions.

Wicks and Schuett (1991), based on research in Illinois, concluded that for many small attractions the brochure may be the only form of paid promotion used. Furthermore, brochures were distributed in an undifferentiated manner–aimed at the general public, rather than target segments–in 85 per cent of their sample. Accordingly, there is a real need for research to assist small agencies and attractions in designing and distributing their brochures for maximum impact.

According to the Economic Planning Group of Canada (n.d.) there are three distinct types of brochure: "informational" types are mostly descriptive, such as directories and travel guides; "promotional" brochures aim to sell an attraction or business; "lure" brochures promote a destination area. In fact, one brochure can encompass all three. They may also be aimed at potential customers or at intermediaries–particularly travel agents. Their use by consumers can include comparison shopping, trip planning, making bookings, and some can even be valued as souvenirs.

Considerable advice is available on the design and distribution of destination and attraction-specific brochures (e.g., Martin 1983; Yale 1986; Conroy 1987; Reid 1989; Nykiel 1989; Coltman 1989; Economic Planning Group of Canada n.d.; Wicks and Schuett 1991). And while a number of studies have been undertaken to assess consumers' use of advertising material in trip planning (e.g., Nolan 1976; Gitelson and Crompton 1983; Etzel and Wahlers 1985), very little research on the evaluation of brochure design effectiveness has been published. Examples of commissioned brochure evaluations include two studies for the Scottish Tourist Board (Hoffman Research Co. 1984 and 1986), and Hodgson reported on work by Thomson Holidays in the U.K. Gilbert and Houghton (1991) reported an evaluation of U.K. tour operators' brochures (results are discussed later in this paper). However, these studies all examined larger-format, informational brochures which featured destination attractions, listed accommodations and described tour packages, as opposed to the smaller lure and promotional brochures assessed in the research reported herein.

Conventional Wisdom on Brochure Design

A startling uniformity of design, shape, size and overall appearance was found when examining brochure displays at information centers during this research, at least with respect to small stapled or folded lure and promotional types. Whether this is due to the constraints imposed by the display cases, or by universal acceptance of common design guidelines is difficult to determine.

The advice being given, as exemplified by Coltman (1989), stresses adherence to the principle called AIDA (Attention, Interest, Desire, Action). The cover of a brochure is meant to grab the attention of brochure "browsers." This can be accomplished through the use of bright colors and the illusion or appearance of size (Martin 1983), or through a primary selling message or positioning statement (Reid 1989). Photographs are the norm on front panels, plus a name, logo and headline.

Interest in the product, and a desire to purchase the offer must be stimulated through text and illustrations which clearly depict consumer benefits and competitive advantage. Reid (1989) advises the brochure designer to use action photos to stimulate the reader's imagination (i.e., picture yourself here, doing this). Also, Reid suggests an attractive image must be fostered through illustration and information. Commonly recommended features of the middle portion of the brochure include: descriptive text; illustrations with succinct, informative headings; full presentation of available amenities, services and attractions.

Action should be facilitated through provision of the information necessary to make a decision and a purchase. Mostly this is the role of the back page (or flipside of the cover), where full details on the following are typically suggested: location (preferably a map); directions on how to get there, and available transportation; opening dates and hours; prices; contact persons with address and telephone number. Some authors advise against the use of information, such as times and price, which might become out of date. Instead, a replaceable insert can be more efficient.

There is also a creative element to the design of brochures, and the need to keep fresh and ahead of the competition (Martin 1983). Yale (1986) argues that most people are not really interested in any given brochure, so that clear, readable copy is necessary to instantly attract attention and convey the key message. Yale also provided advice on graphic design, print type and size, use of headlines and call-out boxes.

THE RESEARCH

Evaluative research was conducted on behalf of a region-wide consortium of museums and heritage sites, mostly in the public domain, whose goal was to market their properties more effectively to residents of the region and to tourists. With the assistance of a government grant, they had previously collaborated in the preparation and distribution of three brochures–two of which are discussed herein (the third was an events calendar).

Objectives of the evaluation were to determine the attractiveness and utility of the brochures from the perspective of potential users. Only residents of the region were consulted, in part because of the difficulty in contacting real or potential tourists, and partly because residents were a major target market. No attempt was made to determine the effectiveness of the brochures in attracting tourists to the region.

Description of the Brochures

The "lure" brochure was intended for widespread circulation within and outside the destination area. Its format was a fairly standard nine-inch by four-inch size, when folded, with a total of twelve $9'' \times 4''$ panels on the front and back. A scenery photograph, theme message, and the sponsor's name were on the cover. Inside, it consisted of a collage of photos from the region, including some of the consortium's sites and artifacts, but also general scenery and other attractions, and a large-scale map showing the destination area in a regional context. On the flipside (back page) was a directory of the ten sites, a list of visitor information centers in the area, a logo, and a portion of a detailed destination map. The concept, according to the client, was to foster an image of lots to see and do, with emphasis on heritage and culture.

The second brochure can be described as being more "promotional" in nature. It was intended to be distributed primarily within the destination area and at the various consortium sites, and to act as both a lure and a guide to the ten participating sites. Its size was slightly larger (ten inches by four), and it was stapled. The front and back cover showed a logo, the sponsor's name, a theme message, and the words: "visitor's guide." Inside was a page devoted to the theme message, a second page provided a general description of the area, and a third provided a directory of the sites. Each site had a separate page on which a photograph and information were displayed. The middle two pages of the brochure consisted of an area map. The last two internal pages were for "notes" and provided a pocket in which other brochures could be stored. Overall, this brochure had a more glossy and expensive look than the lure brochure.

RESEARCH METHODOLOGY

Given a limited budget for evaluation, only a small, qualitative study was possible. The brochures were evaluated in three ways: a subjective content and design appraisal by the research team; interviews with members of the client group and with local distributors of the brochures; three focus groups within the study area, each targeted to a distinct segment judged by the clients to be potential customers.

Results of the focus groups are discussed herein, as they led to a number of hypotheses concerning brochure design and use in general. With a larger budget it would have been desirable to conduct interviews and group discussions outside the region, and to undertake replications of focus groups.

Hodgson (1990) suggested that focus groups are very useful in evaluating brochure design and visual impact, especially where the material must catch the eye of browsers. The method offers the advantage of ensuring an in-depth evaluation of reactions, particularly as to whether the material creates the right impression of both product and the company or agency producing it. Group discussions can establish what potential customers see as being important, relevant and attractive in a brochure.

Focus Groups

Focus groups, according to Kinnear and Taylor (1991: 309) are "one of the most frequently used techniques in marketing research." Also called "group depth interviews," they are defined as "a loosely structured interview conducted by a trained moderator among a small number of respondents simultaneously" (p. 310). They are a relatively quick and cost-effective method for evaluating products and promotions, but their usefulness is somewhat constrained. Because they employ small groups not drawn randomly from whole target populations, they cannot be used to "prove" advertising effectiveness (Calder 1977; Morgan and Spanish 1984). Calder examined the theoretical bases of group discussions and stressed that their results cannot be generalized to entire populations–quantitative research must follow. Morgan and Spanish recommended the use of focus groups as an element in research triangulation–that is, approaching the same problem with multiple methods.

Many researchers therefore use them as a starting point, to generate ideas and hypotheses for more quantitative, follow-up research. However, Hodgson (1990) notes that practice in the United Kingdom is different from that in North America, as U.K. researchers tend to view qualitative research as being able to stand on its own.

Advice on the conduct of qualitative research, and focus groups in particular is easily found (e.g., Peterson 1987; Kinnear and Taylor 1991; Byers and Wilcox 1991). Although ten essential ingredients for a successful group interview have been postulated (referenced in Byers and Wilcox 1991), focus group design and practices vary widely (Fern 1982; Byers and Wilcox 1991). For example, Hodgson reported that U.K. practice favors smaller groups: 6 to 8 participants, versus 10-12 in the U.S.A. Kinnear and Taylor also suggested that 6 or 7 participants may be best for evaluation of nonconsumer goods, in order to maximize interaction. As well, U.K. group discussions tend to be less structured and use home venues rather than rooms with one-way mirrors. Clients rely more on the moderator's interpretations in the U.K., and view the qualitative results as being legitimate on their own. Morgan and Spanish (1984) also reported unorthodox focus group methods. They preferred smaller groups of four or five in ordinary seminar rooms, with recording devices, comfortable seating, and snacks provided. Acquaintances were not eliminated and the moderators had little involvement in the actual discussion. Participants were initially asked to complete a questionnaire on the topic of discussion, and completed a second questionnaire at the end of discussion. All were paid a small fee.

Description of the Three Focus Groups

While professional research firms would likely employ paid participants, or use random telephoning to obtain homogeneous groups, the researchers used personal contacts to arrange for three distinct discussion groups. Size of groups was restricted deliberately, as quick analysis of written notes was the goal. Participants were not paid, but for two of the groups a cash donation was made to a designated charity. Two of the discussions were held in private homes in a very relaxed setting, including refreshments and normal distractions. The student group was conducted in a comfortable board room, with a choice of refreshments.

The first group consisted of one male and six female university undergraduates, aged 20-29. This gender imbalance was inadvertent and ideally would have been corrected either by eliminating the one male or adding a balanced follow-up group. The six participants in the second focus group consisted of a mixture of 25-35 year old professionals and home-makers, half males and half females, all members of a church-related organization. The third focus group was made up of six older adults (55+ years), divided equally by gender, and also members of a church-related organization. It was found that none of the participants in the three groups had any knowledge of the subject brochures, but several had visited one or more of the subject sites. The sponsor of the research was not identified until well into the discussion.

In conducting the group interviews, the main lure brochure was first shown to participants as an unidentified component in a sample of nine lure or promotional brochures, from within and outside the region, which had been selected by the researchers to represent both a wide range of museums and heritage sites and a range of styles. All were similarly sized, and had been found in tourist information centers. Participants were given a questionnaire and asked: "Which three of the brochures do you think are most attractive? Write down the title . . . and your reasons for choosing it." After this step was completed, with discussion suppressed, the groups were then asked: "Which of the brochures are most useful to you in planning a visit to the place? Please write in their titles and give your reasons." Again, discussion was discouraged. Thirdly, the subject lure brochure was distributed to each participant and they were asked to study it and then complete (in writing) several evaluative questions. Only after completion of these steps was open discussion encouraged. Subsequently, the other two subject brochures were distributed, followed by both questionnaire responses and open discussion of all the previously mentioned points. Opinions expressed in the discussions were recorded (in writing) by the assistant. No taping was employed, and there were no representatives of the client group present.

This structure was employed in order to obtain spontaneous, unbiased input from each participant. By examining each brochure under quiet conditions, then writing down their initial impressions, the participants all had the opportunity to express first impressions. Later, when the discussion was completely opened, group interaction tended to shift some opinions and generate new ideas among the group, all of which were recorded to the extent possible. To avoid domination by a few "talkers," for a number of crucial questions each participant was polled individually and the answers were written down.

In this research project a combination of questionnaire and group discussion worked very well to elicit individual reactions to the brochures as well as to yield more in-depth discussion. Taping the conversations would have generated useful material for more detailed post-assessment, but because private homes were used in two cases it was felt that a more relaxed atmosphere should be retained and tapes not employed.

Whether or not this overall approach is better than others cannot be proved, but it did produce exactly the kind of reactions and advice the clients needed to evaluate and improve their brochures.

ANALYSIS AND DISCUSSION

Analysis of focus group discussions can take several forms (Byers and Wilcox 1991). If clients witness the discussions, they might formulate their own impressions and a formal analysis will not be needed. A qualitative summary of observations or conclusions by the moderator might suffice in some circumstances. More systematically, a content analysis of discussion points can be completed, involving coding and quantitative tabulations. Some researchers feel that a listing or ranking of points raised in discussion is inappropriate, and that themes should be extracted from the discussion, with verbalizations quoted as examples. The search for meanings underlying the discussion is the most difficult and important challenge for the researcher.

In this research each focus group yielded three types of data: written, individual responses to questions; discussion points recorded by the assistant and later tabulated; and general themes identified by the researchers. The data of greatest relevance to the generic theme of brochure design are discussed below, including hypotheses generated by the research.

Ranking Attributes of Attractiveness and Utility

Tables 1 and 2 list written responses from all three focus groups on the questions of what attributes of nine brochures were found to be most attractive and most useful in planning a trip. Respondents were asked to select the three most attractive brochures, write down their reasons, then do the same for the three most useful brochures. Open discussion was more useful in focusing on the clients' brochures, while these written answers are most pertinent to the generic issues of brochure design.

Regarding attractiveness, it can be seen that the most frequently mentioned items pertain to conciseness and readability (especially for older adults), color, pictures showing things to do, and uniqueness of design. Attractiveness was not defined for participants, so some of the derived attributes might also be placed in the utility list (e.g., "easy to open and read").

TABLE 1. Attractiveness Attributes Developed Through Three Focus Groups
(Number of mentions in descending order)

Attractiveness Attributes	Students n = 7	Young Adults n = 6	Older Adults n = 6
Easy to read; concise	3	3	6
Very colorful	4	5	2
Lots of pictures showing what you can do	7	4	–
Unique cover; catches the eye	4	3	3
Well composed; nice layout	5	3	2
Good, clear map	5	3	2
Unique shape	7	2	–
Beautiful, high quality photos	3	2	2
Informative; explanatory	3	1	3
Attractive scenery photos	3	2	–
Balance between pictures and words	2	2	–
Catchy slogan or title	–	2	2
Large poster–picture included	2	1	–
Comical; fun	1	2	–
Compact size	1	–	1
Easy to open and read	1	1	–
Attractive to children	–	1	1
Blend of color and black/white	1	–	–
Peaceful atmosphere	–	1	–
Historic flavor	–	1	–
Reflective; luring	–	1	–
Illustrates four seasons	–	1	–
Not too much writing	–	1	–
All details on flip side	–	1	–
Not too bulky	–	1	–
Sense of wonder	–	1	–

Table 2 lists the utility attributes, clearly showing a predominance of a small number of factors: an effective map and/or directions to the area or sites; good descriptions of what is offered; technical data on cost, times, contacts.

Because these lists emerged from an evaluation of potentially competitive destinations and sites, all with a heritage theme (i.e., museums, parks authorities, galleries, historic properties), it cannot be assumed that these attributes would apply to all destination-specific brochures. Another limitation is that gender differences cannot reliably be analyzed, due to the

TABLE 2. Utility Attributes Developed Through Three Focus Groups

(Number of mentions in descending order)

Attractiveness Attributes	Students n=7	Young Adults n=6	Older Adults n=6
Clear, easy to use map; directions	14	17	2
Clear, thorough descriptions of what is offered	12	9	6
Cost or price is listed	9	7	1
Dates and hours of operations	7	2	2
Sparks interest in what there is to do there	2	2	5
Phone number listed	4	3	–
Attractions, variety of things to do in the area (described)	7	–	–
Photos are enough in themselves to determine what is there	3	–	–
Appeals to families	2	–	1
All information on flip side	–	3	–
Concise	–	2	1
Answers all your questions	1	1	–
Lots of pictures on each site	–	1	1
Good layout; easy to access	–	2	–
Clarity of print; easy to read	1	–	1
Educational	–	–	1
Comparisons of sites	–	1	–
Photos show ideal seasons to visit	–	1	–
Insert map gives locational context	–	1	–
Includes application for membership	1	–	–
Visually stimulating map	1	–	–
Humor	1	–	–
Lists accommodations in area	1	–	–

small number of participants and the imbalance in one of the groups. However, the identified attributes seem to be quite generic, and because the respondents were comparing brochures for sites and areas both inside and outside their home region there is reason to expect that the attributes apply to tourists in general.

Although developing a list of generic attraction and utility attributes can assist in the brochure design process, some pre-testing among target market groups would be advantageous. Over time, systematic comparison of results might lead to validation of key attributes. To assist in both the design and validation process, a number of hypotheses have been generated regarding brochure attractiveness and utility, based on the qualitative evaluation of all the written and verbal responses obtained in the three focus groups.

Hypotheses Regarding Brochure Attractiveness

H1: Brochure attractiveness will prove to be a multi-dimensional construct.

The discussions revealed that two criteria dominated: aesthetics, such as color, photographs and layout, and interest-generating qualities, which can be interpreted as depictions of consumer benefits. An unexpected result was the mention of a number of abstract attributes such as "sense of wonder," "reflective" and "peaceful." These suggest that specific, quantifiable attributes of design and layout do not completely explain attractiveness, but that a more holistic image of the brochure is quickly formed by viewers.

This finding is similar to the conclusions of Um and Crompton (1990) on how consumers form a destination image. They describe the destination image as a holistic/gestalt construct, at least partially based on attitudes towards the destination's perceived attributes. With this in mind, brochure designers are challenged to display and feature desired destination/site attributes in a way which conveys an attractive overall theme and image.

H2: Older adults will have markedly different preferences from younger respondents.

Color, unique shape and attractions seemed to be less important, and readability more important to older respondents. This group also noted fewer attributes than the other two, despite the fact that the sessions and discussions were just as long. The meaning of this fact is uncertain, but because this focus group consisted of long-time residents of the subject region they seemed to be more interested in getting information than in being "lured" to travel within the area and visit specific sites. This observation also suggests that perceptions might vary by gender and age in general, but the focus group samples did not allow detailed analysis.

H3: Local and tourist target markets will display some different priorities.

Discussions suggested that locals, and especially long-term residents, are likely to be more impressed with hard information than by more subjective attributes. Brochures aimed at tourists on the road might also have to be designed differently from those intended for direct mailing or for circulation within remote target market areas, depending on the means of distribution, cost, and other factors.

H4: Attractiveness, and hence the actual selection and use of a lure brochure from among numerous choices, will be a partial function of the theme of the brochure.

Conversation revealed that some participants were more inclined to find attractive those brochures concerning a personally interesting theme, such as an aviation museum. A marketing implication is that brochures for attractions should make their theme clear on the top of the cover, or that brochures should be customized for special interest groups.

H5: Unusual shapes or cover designs will be more attractive, or at least attract greater attention, than regular brochure formats.

The standard shape of brochures is rectangular, but variations do stand out in display racks and catch the eye. Caution is required on this point, because it was observed that most brochures were in a standard format. If a majority were designed with unusual formats, sizes or covers, the novelty value would diminish greatly. Highlighting a particularly interesting or aesthetic attribute of the destination or attraction might also work to attract attention, and can be combined with format variations.

It is useful to compare these observations with conclusions from the qualitative brochure evaluations conducted for the Scottish Tourist Board (Hoffman Research Co. 1984, 1986). Those studies, albeit focusing on different types of brochure, found that potential consumers wanted to see pictures of the products (e.g., actual photos of hotels). Air and space around photos and information was desired, even if it resulted in bulky publications. Least-liked brochures were found to be associated with a lack of color and photos (i.e., no eye-catching elements) and poor layout or lack of information. Most-liked brochures were visually attractive, full of desired information, and laid out for maximum clarity. Thus, utility and attractiveness were closely inter-related: "Initial reactions to a brochure are determined by how attractively it portrays the area it is presenting, and by how clearly it communicates its information" (Hoffman Research Co. 1984: 7).

Results of consumer research conducted by Gilbert and Houghton (1991: 23) are also pertinent. They looked specifically at how and why tour company brochures were selected by potential consumers and concluded that "what is communicated by the initial visual component of the brochure is extremely important." Design features, language, and images displayed on the covers led the test subjects to make conclusions about the target markets and quality of products being offered in the holiday brochures. Glossy paper and thin brochures were associated with expensive products, while line drawings were associated with cheapness. Colors and imagery were important in shaping perceptions about the orientation of the brochure towards a relaxing or active holiday, or towards a family or youthful emphasis.

Hypotheses Regarding the Utility of Brochures for Trip Planning

H6: Utility will be perceived to stem from both clear descriptions of what the area or site has to offer, and adequate information on how to realize desired benefits.

Participants, and especially the students, did not want to waste time with a brochure that was vague or misleading on what the area or attraction offered. Things to do in the general area of a site were also valued, at least by the students, showing the advantages of joint promotions. Pictures might sometimes be substituted for descriptions if they clearly indicate the benefits offered customers. A risk, however, is that excessive reliance on illustrations will overwhelm the printed messages.

Other obvious factors, such as price and hours, were considered to be important. Discussions revealed that the omission of these facts was considered to be a serious problem with the utility of some of the reviewed brochures. Directories of attractions were felt to be a good feature on destination lure brochures.

H7: An easy to use map and/or directions will be essential.

This hypothesis is related to H6, but seems important enough to stand on its own. Comments elicited during open discussions suggest that many people find maps hard to interpret, so that extra care must be taken in their design and presentation. Those older adults most familiar with the subject area were least concerned with the map, but still found fault with maps in the subject brochures. Maps plus written directions, including access modes and routes, appear to be important for many potential consumers.

Hypotheses Regarding Trip Motivation

From a marketing perspective the effectiveness of a brochure can be defined as its impact on motivating actual travel or on shaping a favorable destination or attraction image. Brochures might be perceived to be both attractive and useful, but have no impact on travel. Participants in the focus groups were therefore also asked, regarding the clients' lure brochure: "Does it encourage you personally to visit any of the sites?" And regarding the visitor's guide which gave details on ten sites, participants were asked: "Would you keep and use this brochure? How? Give reasons." Results are displayed in Tables 3 and 4, and several hypotheses arise from these verbal responses.

H8: Attractive and useful brochures will not in themselves motivate travel, but can easily be an inhibitor.

The clients' lure brochure was not well received by the student group, and none of them felt motivated by it to visit any of the illustrated sites. They found the theme to be negative, the cover bland, and the photographs nice but not alluring. Young adults were more positive, saying that the illustrated activities sparked interest in visiting some of the sites, while indicating that some confusing and sterile pictures acted to discourage trips. Some older adults mentioned an appealing theme and illustrations as sufficient reasons to visit sites, whereas in contrast some said they were not motivated because the cover and theme were unappealing and the illustrations lacked sufficient information.

Students were a little more receptive to the visitor's guide which featured each site on a separate page. Its format and contents were mentioned as reasons for keeping it. On the other hand, inability to use the map would discourage some from keeping or using the brochure, and the photos and text were not appealing to others. Overall, the students showed little interest in visiting museums, so their negative predisposition to some of the attractions must be taken as a partial reason for their negative assessment of the brochures.

Young adults and older adults were entirely positive about the visitor's guide, finding it very useful as a permanent source of information about places nearby to visit. Using it to give visiting friends and relatives a choice of things to do was mentioned several times. The directory provided sufficient information to efficiently plan a trip. The map, judged earlier to be inadequate, was not a factor—presumably because the sites were local and participants assumed they could find them.

Accordingly, the effectiveness of the two subject brochures in motivating a trip and affecting the perceived image of the region and its attractions was judged to be fairly low, although there were definite indications that some of the participants would keep and use the material. It was apparent that a more effective use of the client's brochures would be to direct them

TABLE 3. Does It (the lure brochure) Encourage You Personally to Visit Any of the Sites?

NO

Reasons given by students:

* Would just look at the pictures, not read the map (2 mentions).
* Front cover is nondescript (2 mentions).
* Colors on cover do not attract attention.

Reasons given by young adults:

* Some pictures are confusing and sterile.

Reasons given by older adults:

* The title is not appealing.
* The pictures provide no information on what or where they are.
* Would not even pick up this brochure (poor cover).

YES

Reasons given by students: no positive response.

Reasons given by young adults:

* Would like to participate in, or learn about the illustrated activities (2 mentions).
* I live in this area so should visit these sites.
* The photos are appealing because of people in them.
* The (ethnic) theme looks interesting.

Reasons given by older adults:

* The caption is appealing.
* Pictures are appealing.

---

at local segments with demonstrated interest in the benefits offered (e.g., members of cultural and heritage societies), and to tourists nearing and entering the area, rather than taking a shotgun approach to circulation. It was also recommended to the client that the lure brochure and visitor's guide be combined in the future, as elements of both brochures were considered to be necessary for an attractive and useful advertising tool.

TABLE 4. Would You Keep and Use This (visitor's guide) Brochure? How? Give Reasons.

NO

Reasons given by students:

* Map is poor; cannot use it (2 mentions).
* It's a boring brochure; would not look at it again.
* Descriptions of sites are OK, but that does not make me want to keep it.
* Too much writing; a traveller would throw it out.

Reasons given by young adults: no negative response.

Reasons given by older adults: no negative response.

YES

Reasons given by students:

* If I lived here; it says what is available.
* Everything is readable.
* Would keep it for future reference.
* It has note space and pockets; makes it useful.

Reasons given by young adults:

* Would use it when I had company; give them a choice.
* Can't do everything, so would save it as a reference and reminder.

Reasons given by older adults: no negative response.

* Directory is helpful in planning a trip (2 mentions).
* Would use it to give guests a choice of things to do (2 mentions).
* Would use it to research places before planning a trip.

H9: Utility will partially be a function of perceived ways in which to use a brochure.

Several respondents mentioned that the visitor's guide would be useful in planning a trip with visiting friends and relatives. This suggests that brochure design and contents should be oriented towards specific types of trips and visits. A vacation trip to a far-away destination requires a different brochure than a short visit with a visiting relative or a day-trip for a family, so trip type should be added to target segment characteristics when planning and designing advertising communications. This is corroborated by the Wicks and Schuett (1991) study of people who requested brochures in Illinois, which found that brochures were particularly important sources of information for weekend and day travellers.

CONCLUSIONS

Design and Use of Brochures

The lists of attractiveness and utility attributes derived from the three focus groups certainly provide general support for conventional wisdom on brochure design and use of the AIDA principle. Specifically corroborated were the importance of an attractive, stimulating cover, the use of color and photographs, and the inclusion of benefit-specific information. Brochure designers, and those commissioning them, can use these lists as guidelines on what consumers want in brochures, and what omissions might act as inhibitors to travel.

However, the research findings, as well as some previously reported research, suggest that brochures must be targeted, rather than all-purpose in nature. Gitelson and Crompton (1983) reported on the use of commercial, destination-specific material (including brochures) by automobile travellers in Texas. Better educated and longer-distance travellers made significantly greater use of these types of advertising, and those seeking excitement used more sources of information than those seeking relaxation. Broadcast media were found to be most used by those taking short trips.

Like all other forms of advertising, brochures should be designed and distributed for clear target segments. These can be distinguished by at least several important characteristics:

- location (e.g. local residents, travellers who search for information along their route, residents of distant target areas)
- age (older people might have different reading needs and design preferences)
- length of residence (newcomers might need more incentive to visit a site)
- special interests (those with an interest in the theme are more likely to select a related brochure)
- trip types (day and weekend trips are quite different from long vacations)
- education and income levels
- communication objectives (promoting an area is different from promoting a specific attraction)

Brochures and Destination Choice

The focus groups suggest that an aesthetically pleasing design and interest-generating qualities are needed to get people to pick up and read a destination-specific brochure. Information on benefits appears to be required to stimulate interest in taking trips, but various market segments will look for different benefits. Utility seems to be a function of information, readability (especially of maps) and perceived ways in which to use the brochures to realize desired benefits. If people cannot envisage a specific opportunity for use of the brochure, it might be ignored or wasted. Furthermore, there is no guarantee that a brochure perceived to be both attractive and useful will actually motivate a trip. These observations and hypotheses shed light on the role of brochures in the process by which people form destination images and choose from alternative trip destinations.

Um and Crompton (1990) presented a model on destination choice which highlights the importance of both internal inputs (e.g., attitudes) and external inputs (significative, symbolic and social stimuli, of which brochures are considered to be symbolic). These influence two cognitive constructs, namely the "awareness set" (what destinations or sites are known and preferred), and the "evoked set" of preferred destinations given that a concrete choice must be made, complete with constraints. Considerable research (cited in Um and Crompton 1990) has shown that social stimuli, mostly the impressions and recommendations of friends and relatives, dominate as information sources. For example, Gitelson and Crompton (1983) found that commercial brochures were used by only 25% of a sample of Texas highway travellers, ranking second behind commercial guidebooks in the category of destination-specific literature; friends and relatives were the number one source, being mentioned by 71% of the sample.

Furthermore, Gitelson and Crompton (1983) stated that destination-specific literature serves to inform, not motivate, while social contacts are used to evaluate destination alternatives and to legitimize choices. The brochure can be one factor in influencing the evolution of an "evoked set" from an "awareness set," but is probably not going to be the most important factor (Um and Crompton 1990).

More specifically, Um and Crompton (1990: 446) concluded that "Potential travellers may interpret a complex array of perceptions of destination attributes by simplifying them into facilitators and inhibitors in formulating their destination choice decision." In this light, the brochure can serve as a source of clear, attractive trip facilitators (i.e., information and images on benefits appealing to target segments) and to pre-empt inhibitors through reassurance of the destination or site's accessibility, affordability, friendliness, etc. Negative aspects of brochures, such as the absence of important information, might also become inhibitions.

In conclusion, brochures might have a minor role to play in motivating travel or in leading to specific trip choices. The large amounts of money and effort put into so-called "lure" brochures might very well be wasted unless they are designed, tested, and distributed for specific target market segments and trip types.

Towards a Model of Brochure Design and Utility

Gilbert and Houghton (1991: 20) graphically illustrated a model which they said can be used to maximize consumer selection and use of brochures. Three interacting sets of variables must be considered: how the brochures are physically displayed; travel consultant services (i.e., how brochures are used when advising consumers and selling packages); and consumer filters (i.e., clarity of information, brand name recognition, validity of images to personal needs, graphic design format, colors, people or activities portrayed, physical quality of the brochure).

Results of the current research can contribute to a better understanding of "consumer filters." More work is needed to understand how brochures are actually used (see Wicks and Schuett 1991). And little has been published on the subject of semiotics in brochure design. Buck (1977) examined the messages communicated by tourist brochures in Amish Country–Lancaster County, Pennsylvania. Uzzell (1984) concluded that three levels of meanings must be explored: the superficial but strong projection of sun, sea, sand and sex; the attributes of place which serve to enhance the consumer's self-image; and selling the image of consumers in both reality and fantasy worlds.

Specific Research Issues

The results of focus group research should be considered as a set of hypotheses to be tested, but that is not easy to accomplish. Random sampling of a large population would have cost implications, and must overcome the problem of finding suitable segments and providing them with brochures to evaluate. Consequently, a follow-up test using similarly constructed, but different focus group panels, might be an option. Such a test would attempt to achieve results similar to the lists of attributes derived from the three focus groups reported herein. Modifications could be introduced to have respondents rank the importance of attributes. More segments could be tested and results compared.

Only area residents were used in this research project, so an obvious improvement must be to conduct research in outlying target market areas. Non-residents would ideally be sub-divided by distance and other factors such as fore-knowledge of the destination. Travellers intercepted "en route" would be another prime target group. The difficulty in all cases is finding suitable respondents and convincing them to spend time with interviewers.

There are also a number of issues to be addressed when utilizing focus groups in evaluation of advertising. Gender balance should be maintained, as this was a source of potential bias in one of the sessions described herein. Group discussion can generate many ideas, but it was also found to result in a clustering of responses. Some of the variation among the three groups is likely attributable to the tendency of participants to repeat a good idea. Isolated comments, on the other hand, might very well reflect the views of many others, but the flow of conversation can result in only single mentions. Accordingly, researchers must not presume that only the frequently mentioned factors are important.

Given the findings of these three focus groups, it can be suggested that the group interview (particularly where both individual responses and group discussion are recorded) is a useful method in evaluating advertising media and messages. Ideally, several methods (triangulation) should be employed, and hypotheses generated through group discussions should be tested in follow-up focus groups and/or random-sample surveys.

REFERENCES

Byers, P. and J. Wilcox (1991). "Focus Groups: A Qualitative Opportunity for Researchers." *The Journal of Business Communication*, 28(1): 63-78.

Buck, R. 1977. "The Ubiquitous Tourist Brochure: Explorations in Its Intended and Unintended Use." *Annals of Tourism Research*, 4(4): 195-207.

Calder, B. (1977). "Focus Groups and the Nature of Qualitative Marketing Research." *Journal of Marketing Research*, 14: 353-364.

Checkman, D. (1989), "Focus Group Research as Theatre: How It Affects the Players and Their Audiences." *Marketing Research*, 1(4): 33-40.

Coltman, M. (1989). *Tourism Marketing*. New York: Van Nostrand Reinhold.

Conroy, B. (1987). "Approaches To Teaching Brochure Design." *Tourism Management*, September: 256.

Economic Planning Group of Canada (n.d.). *Tourism Is Your Business: Marketing Management*. Ottawa: Tourism Canada.

Etzel, M. and R. Wahlers (1985). "The Use of Requested Promotional Material by Pleasure Travelers." *Journal of Travel Research*, 23(4): 2-6.

Fern, E. (1982). "The Use of Focus Groups for Idea Generation: The Effects of

Group Size, Acquaintanceship, and Moderator on Response Quantity and Quality." *Journal of Marketing Research*, 19 (Feb.): 1-13.

Gilbert, D. and P. Houghton (1991). "An Exploratory Investigation of Format, Design, and Use of U.K. Tour Operators' Brochures." *Journal of Travel Research*, 30(2): 20-25.

Gitelson, R. and J. Crompton (1983). "The Planning Horizons and Sources of Information Used by Pleasure Vacationers." *Journal of Travel Research*, 21(3): 2-7.

Hodgson, P. (1990). "Designing Better Tour Brochures: The Role of Qualitative Research." In proceedings of the Market Research Seminar, Institute of Travel and Tourism, London.

Hoffman Research Co. (1984). Research on Brochure Design for ATBs in Scotland, for the Scottish Tourist Board, Edinburgh.

Hoffman Research Co. (1986). Research on Accommodation Brochures, for the Scottish Tourist Board, Edinburgh.

Kinnear, T. and J. Taylor (1991). *Marketing Research: An Applied Approach.* New York: McGraw Hill Inc.

Martin, M. (1983). "Marketing With Brochures." *Meetings and Incentive Travel*, June: 4-5.

Morgan, D. and M. Spanish (1984). "Focus Groups: A New Tool for Qualitative Research." *Qualitative Sociology*, 7(3): 253-269.

Nolan, S. (1976). "Tourists' Use and Evaluation of Travel Information Sources: Summary and Conclusions." *Journal of Travel Research*, 14(3): 6-8.

Nykiel, R. (1989). *Marketing in the Hospitality Industry* (second ed.). New York: Van Nostrand Reinhold.

Peterson, K. (1987). "Qualitative Research Methods for the Travel and Tourism Industry." In *Travel, Tourism and Hospitality Research: A Handbook For Managers and Researchers*, B. Ritchie and C. Goeldner (eds.). New York: Wiley.

Reid, R. (1989). *Hospitality Marketing Management* (second ed.). New York: Van Nostrand Reinhold.

Um, S. and J. Crompton (1990). "Attitude Determinants in Tourism Destination Choice." *Annals of Tourism Research*, 17(3): 432-448.

Uzzell, D. (1984). "An Alternative Structuralist Approach to the Psychology of Tourism Marketing." *Annals of Tourism Research*, 11(1): 79-99.

Wicks, B. and M. Schuett (1991). "Examining the Role of Tourism Promotion Through the Use of Brochures." *Tourism Management*, 12(4): 301-312.

Yale, D. (1986). "Stamp Out Banal Brochures." *Business Marketing*, 71(12): 74, 76.

Functional and Aesthetic Information Needs Underlying the Pleasure Travel Experience

Christine A. Vogt
Daniel R. Fesenmaier
Kelly MacKay

SUMMARY. Consumer information acquisition has largely focused on decision making or functional needs. Recently, a set of complementary information needs (i.e., hedonic, aesthetic, and social) have been introduced in the consumer behavior literature. This study examines functional and aesthetic information needs in a tourism consumption context, specifically pre-trip information acquisition for short Midwest trips. Destination selection information needs are shown to be at the core of information acquisition with product knowledge, aesthetic imagery and planning efficiency needs at the "periphery." Suggestions for destination marketing communication strategies and future research are presented.

INTRODUCTION

Traditionally, research on consumer information search has focused attention on the strategies used by individuals to obtain information for

Dr. Christine A. Vogt is affiliated with the Department of Recreation and Park Administration, Indiana University, Bloomington, IN. Dr. Daniel R. Fesenmaier is affiliated with the Department of Leisure Studies, University of Illinois, Champaign, IL. Kelly MacKay is affiliated with the Department of Leisure Studies, University of Illinois, Champaign, IL.

[Haworth co-indexing entry note]: "Functional and Aesthetic Information Needs Underlying the Pleasure Travel Experience." Vogt, Christine A., Daniel R. Fesenmaier, and Kelly MacKay. Co-published simultaneously in *Journal of Travel & Tourism Marketing* (The Haworth Press, Inc.) Vol. 2, No. 2/3, 1993, pp. 133-146; and: *Communication and Channel Systems in Tourism Marketing* (ed: Muzaffer Uysal, and Daniel R. Fesenmaier) The Haworth Press, Inc., 1993, pp. 133-146. Multiple copies of this article/chapter may be purchased from The Haworth Document Delivery Center [1-800-3-HAWORTH; 9:00 a.m. - 5:00 p.m. (EST)].

product-related decisions. In large part, this research has been based on the assumption that motivations for information search are risk related (Bettman, 1979); that is, individuals actively seek information in order to make "more informed" judgments regarding the possible payoff (benefits) of a product purchase given perceived risks (Cox, 1967; Murray, 1991). Consumer behavior research suggests information search may not be oriented solely towards addressing certain functional decision making needs (Olshavsky & Granbois, 1979). Rather, information search may serve other "nonfunctional" elements of consumption behaviors which emphasize the aesthetic, affective, hedonic, and entertainment aspects of product and information acquisition (Hirschman & Holbrook, 1982; Holbrook and Hirschman, 1982; Woods, 1981). This paper presents the results of an exploratory study investigating functional and nonfunctional aspects of information acquisition.

BACKGROUND LITERATURE

The marketing literature on information search is extensive (for reviews cf., Assael, 1984; Bettman, 1979; Engel, Blackwell & Miniard, 1986; Murray, 1991; Sternthal & Craig, 1982). Generally, information search and consumption models suggest information acquisition occurs following either a need arousal (for some product) or that attention is given to some information stimuli. That is, an individual might recognize a need or a desire for some product and subsequently look for information regarding the product (Assael, 1984). In addition, information acquisition occurs when information is introduced to an individual (e.g., sees an advertisement, hears other consumers talking about a product) which then leads him/her to pay attention to the information source and message (Bettman, 1979).

Both information search activation methods, product need arousal and attention to an information stimuli, suggest that an individual enters into a process that requires one to consider whether internal-based knowledge (i.e., memory, past experience) is sufficient to satisfy subsequent decisions, or whether additional knowledge about the product is needed. If the latter case is true, an individual is then motivated to notice and process external-based information. Thus, external-based information is added to existing or internal-based information and requires a series of cognitive steps such as categorization, evaluation, organization and retention following acquisition (Assael, 1984; Bettman, 1979).

In general, the information search and acquisition process embraces a functional perspective of information needs. That is, information is needed to assist in making the variety of decisions required for a pleasure trip (Bettman, 1979; Holbrook and Hirschman, 1982). Yet, much of a travel experience is pleasure-based and consumed through images, such as photographs and the stories of other travellers (Boorstin, 1961; Urry, 1990). Boorstin describes the image-laden tourist experience as:

> Everywhere, picturesque natives fashion papier-mâché images of themselves. Yet all this earnest picturesqueness too often produces only a pallid imitation of the technicolor motion picture which the tourist goes to verify (p. 107). The tourist's appetite for strangeness thus seems best satisfied when the pictures in his own mind are verified in some far country. (p. 109)

Urry (1990) views "tourism to be prefiguratively postmodern because of its particular combination of the visual, the aesthetic, and the popular (p. 87).

In tourism, marketing researchers have maintained a general approach to information consumption and have focused on understanding the assortment of information sources individuals seek (or use) in relation to travel occasions (Capella and Greco, 1987; Etzel and Wahlers, 1985; Fesenmaier & Vogt, 1992; Gitelson & Crompton, 1983; Nolan, 1976; Raitz & Dakhil, 1989; Rao, Thomas & Javalgi, 1992; Schul & Crompton, 1987; Snepenger, 1987; Snepenger, Meged, Snelling & Worrall, 1990). These studies have shown personal experience (i.e., past vacation experience) and information from family members and friends to be the most popular information sources used in vacation decision making. Advertisements and newspaper and magazine articles are generally rated as being less important in the vacation decision making process.

Research by Holbrook, Chestnut, Oliva, and Greenleaf (1984), Hirschman and Holbrook (1982), and Holbrook and Hirschman (1982), however, suggests the basis for information search is also pleasure-seeking. That is, the process of seeking and acquiring travel information may provide travelers a great sense of satisfaction in addition to making vacation decisions. Based on a review of this literature, it appears that travellers may derive pleasure from at least three different elements of information search. First, travel information may be sought simply to improve oneself by enhancing one's knowledge about a certain place. Second, individuals may seek travel information for aesthetic reasons; that is, to obtain information (i.e., primarily through pictures) that conveys the physical attractiveness of a place. Lastly, information search (i.e., reading, watching films, collecting articles and books) may evoke fantasy-like episodes which, in turn, enables an individual to "experience" being at that place.

The goal of this study was to further explain the functional or decision making role of travel information acquisition, and then to explore the supplemental information need of image experiencing or aesthetics. Beyond identifying information needs and reporting the relative strength of these needs, this study was intended to examine the structural relationships represented in the data. More specifically, multidimensional scaling and cluster analysis were used to identify and describe the similarities and differences of the functional and nonfunctional information needs.

To accomplish these goals, the study was limited to information acquisition pertaining to short (2-3 day) overnight vacations in the Midwest region of the United States. This context, which focuses on pre-consumption behaviors, was selected for the following reasons. First, much of the destination marketing efforts by state tourism departments is focused on the "weekend getaway." States, particularly Midwest ones, attempt to influence residents of nearby states, in addition to their own residents, to experience city and rural environments. Midwest states often feature "weekend getaway" trips in travel brochures and advertising campaigns. Thus, destination marketers view short Midwest vacations as a popular product. Additionally, there appears to be an identifiable market of individuals who are interested in acquiring information about short vacations to Midwest destinations. Second, a current U.S. vacation trend is short leisure trips. Thus, a greater understanding of the reasons why individuals request information about trips to close-to-home destinations is critical for destination marketers to successfully create media campaigns. Third, marketing evaluation studies, also called conversion studies, have reported that not everyone who requests travel information is likely to take a trip to the sponsoring destination. In order to understand the reasons why individuals acquire travel information, inquiries that extend beyond decision making reasons (i.e., to select a vacation place, to reserve overnight accommodations) are needed. Overall, it appears that individuals acquire travel information to plan and execute short-length vacations, in addition to satisfying other needs that appear to be less trip related (i.e., to see the beauty of a place, to know about places one may never be able to visit). Destination marketers will be able to provide a higher quality of information (i.e., more useful) to potential tourists by understanding the variety of needs and the relationships between these needs that underlie information acquisition.

DATA COLLECTION

This study was based upon a list of 23,591 individuals who requested tourism information from Brown County, Indiana from March through

June, 1991. It was from this list that 400 individuals were randomly selected as participants in this study. A twelve-page survey instrument was designed to address several advertising objectives, including identifying the needs individuals are attempting to fulfill with travel information. Specifically, individuals were asked to indicate which reasons, from a set of twelve items, describe why they collect information before taking a pleasure trip in the Midwest. For those individuals who do not collect information before taking short trips to Midwest destinations, the following response option was offered "I don't actively seek out travel information before a trip." Seven individuals selected this responses and were omitted from further analyses.

The survey process followed a modified Dillman method (1978) and included an initial mailing of the survey packet (i.e., cover letter, questionnaire, return envelope), a postcard, and then a follow-up mailing to those individuals who had not responded. These mailings occurred during the fall, 1991. An incentive was offered, which was a chance to win one weekend vacation package for two in the Brown County area.

The response rate of the survey effort is summarized in Table 1. As shown, 400 questionnaires were mailed; nine (2%) questionnaires were either returned "undeliverable" or returned by the respondent incomplete. In total, two hundred thirty-four (234) useable questionnaires were returned, resulting in an effective response rate of 59 percent. Demographic data from the study were compared to a previous tourist sample that had achieved a 77 percent response rate and were found to be very similar. It appears, therefore, that non-response bias does not pose a threat to the validity of the data.

DATA ANALYSES AND RESULTS

As previously indicated, the goal of the study was to examine needs travellers attempt to fulfill by collecting information prior to taking short Midwest vacations. The results of the study indicate that individuals seek

TABLE 1. Survey Response				
Overall Sample	Undeliverable	Effective Sample	Number Returned	Effective % Returned
400	9(2%)	391	234	59%

travel information to fulfill a variety of needs. Of the twelve possible needs included in the survey, 52 percent of the respondents checked six or more of the statements with very few (6.7% of the respondents) who checked ten or more statements. As can be seen in Table 2, the primary need respondents sought to fulfill with travel information was to select specific destinations in a region or state (78.6%) and/or to plan specific itineraries of what to see and do (73.4%). Other popular information needs or reasons were to learn about prices of hotels and attractions (71.4%) and to identify places to visit on the way or on the return trip (67.4%). These four responses, with the exception of learning about prices, appear to describe basic decision making needs, such as the selection of products and brands.

Beyond the information needs of destination selection, trip itineraries,

TABLE 2. Information Needs for Pre-Trip Information Search	
Information Needs:	Percent of Times Cited
Select specific destinations in region or state.	78.6
Plan specific itineraries of what to see and do.	73.4
Learn about prices of hotels and attractions.	71.4
Identify places to visit on the way or on the return trip.	67.4
Learn about unique events such as festivals, concerts, or sports events that will occur during my visit.	63.4
Be able to use my vacation time more effectively.	56.3
Find bargains or coupons	48.7
Find out about the beauty of a place before my visit.	47.3
See places that I may never visit.	44.2
Become familiar with a place through recognition of landmarks.	42.9
Locate information which is difficult to find at the destination.	39.7
Be prepared for all aspects of my trip.	32.6

and cost-related information, respondents appeared to rate similarly, in the range of 35 to 55 percent, a group of information needs which are somewhat less decision-related. For instance, 47 percent of the respondents indicated that they search for information before a trip to learn about the beauty of a place; 44 percent of the respondents selected the response "to see places that I may never visit"; and, 40 percent indicated that they search for information before leaving home in order to locate information which is difficult to find at the destination. Based on these descriptive statistics, information acquisition meets a variety of needs including aesthetic and efficiency-based needs.

A second stage in the analysis focused attention on identifying the underlying dimensionality of the set of reasons for travel information search. A matrix of conditional probability values (called coefficient of Jaccard) was created by first, tabulating the number of respondents who checked both reasons (of the two in the matrix) and then dividing this number by the total number of times either reason or both was cited (see Sneath and Sokal, 1973 for excellent discussion of measures of similarity). This coefficient, then, describes how often (in percent terms) pairs of reasons for information search were cited by the respondent.

The results of this analysis are presented in Table 3. The Jaccard coefficients range from .25 to .64, indicating a number of strong relationships among the various reasons for travel information search. Some of the noteworthy relationships include the high correspondence between those destination-related items cited most frequently and trip planning activities (i.e., "selecting specific destinations" and "planning an itinerary"; "selecting a specific destination" and "identifying places to visit en route"). The results presented also show a strong convergence between the items tied closely with the need to efficiently use vacation time.

The results of this analysis suggest that several underlying dimensions exist among the reasons for information search. The conditional probability/similarity (Jaccard) coefficients were subsequently analyzed using Kruskal's nonmetric multidimensional scaling algorithm (Wilkinson, 1990). Solutions were developed for one to five dimensions. Based on goodness-of-fit and interpretation criteria it appears that a two dimensional solution provided the simplest and best fit solution ($R^2 = 0.92$).

An examination of the dimensional mapping (see Figure 1) shows a strong polarity on the dimension shown on the horizontal axis between efficiency needs (to be prepared for all aspects of a trip) and aesthetic needs (to see places that I may never visit). The dimension located on the vertical axis appears to capture the intensity of collecting information. The poles on this dimension suggest that information is used to "find" or

TABLE 3. Perceived Similarities Among Pre-Trip Information Search Needs

Item:	A	B	C	D	E	F	G	H	I	J	K	L
						Items						
A. Select specific dest.	–											
B. Become familiar w/landmarks	0.40	–										
C. Learn about prices	0.59ª	0.38	–									
D. Plan specific itineraries	0.64	0.37	0.54	–								
E. Be able to use vacation time more effectively	0.51	0.36	0.54	0.53	–							
F. Learn about unique events	0.58	0.39	0.55	0.58	0.42	–						
G. Be prepared for all aspects	0.36	0.30	0.32	0.35	0.37	0.26	–					
H. Identify places to visit en route	0.64	0.44	0.53	0.61	0.51	0.50	0.33	–				
I. Find out about beauty	0.47	0.40	0.42	0.46	0.39	0.39	0.35	0.46	–			
J. Find bargains or coupons	0.47	0.30	0.50	0.43	0.40	0.45	0.34	0.45	0.40	–		
K. See places I may never visit	0.43	0.35	0.35	0.43	0.38	0.41	0.25	0.41	0.44	0.33	–	
L. Locate difficult to find information	0.40	0.33	0.38	0.39	0.41	0.37	0.33	0.41	0.35	0.31	0.35	–

ª Coefficients underlined are greater than 0.50.

FIGURE 1. Two dimensional space of pre-trip information search need

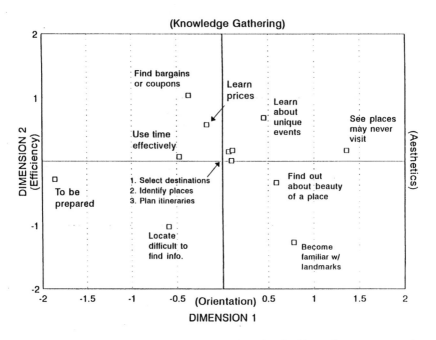

acquire concrete knowledge about a product (to find bargains or coupons), in contrast to "becoming oriented" (to become familiar with a place through recognition of landmarks). Located at the center of the two dimensions are three items, all of which represent decision making needs (i.e., to select specific destinations, to identify places to visit en route, to plan specific itineraries). These multidimensional scaling results suggest that information needs pertaining to decision-making are at the *core* of information acquisition, and efficiency and aesthetic needs are to be considered *periphery* needs.

A final analysis was conducted to further investigate the underlying structure of travel information search. Hierarchical cluster analysis (using Ward's minimum variance method) was conducted using the dimensional scores derived for each item in the MDS analysis (Wilkinson, 1990). This method of cluster analysis begins with each item defining its own cluster and then successively joining with other clusters until only one cluster exists. Figure 2 presents the results of the analysis which seems to indicate that four distinct clusters or groups of information needs exist. Two of the clusters (labelled clusters B and C) appear to be related to destination

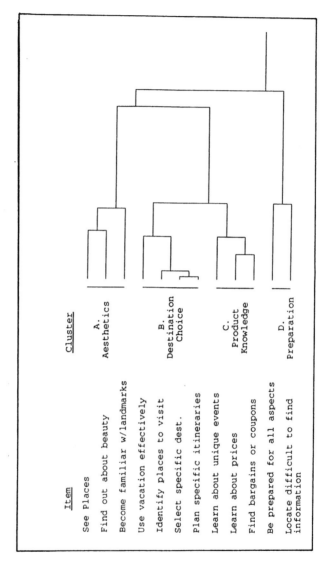

FIGURE 2. Cluster tree of two dimensional MDS Solution

Item

See Places
Find out about beauty
Become familiar w/landmarks

Use vacation effectively
Identify places to visit
Select specific dest.
Plan specific itineraries
Learn about unique events

Learn about prices
Find bargains or coupons

Be prepared for all aspects
Locate difficult to find
information

Cluster

A.
Aesthetics

B.
Destination
Choice

C.
Product
Knowledge

D.
Preparation

142

choice (i.e., selecting a destination, planning itineraries, identifying en-route destinations, using time effectively) and product knowledge (i.e., learning about prices, finding bargains or coupons, learning about unique events during one's visit). These two clusters represent functional information roles which are closely aligned to decision-making (Bettman, 1979).

A third cluster (Cluster A) describes aesthetic or visual aspects of information search (i.e., seeing places never to be visited, finding out about the beauty of a place, becoming familiar with landmarks). A fourth cluster (Cluster D) appears to reflect the needs of travellers to be prepared for what might be encountered during a trip (i.e., preparing for all aspects of a trip, locating difficult to find information). The concept of planning might be unique to or accentuated in the consumption of travel products, however, planning by definition appears to be closely aligned to functional usages of information. Finally, the elements of two clusters (i.e., B and C) are shown to merge earlier then the other two clusters (i.e., A and D) further supporting the *core* (i.e., similar in nature and occurring more frequent) and *periphery* (i.e., less similar and occurring less frequently) concept represented in the multidimensional scaling results.

CONCLUSIONS

The results of the frequency analysis indicate that all of the information needs tested were applicable to short overnight Midwest trips. Moreover, some of the needs were more prominent than others (i.e., those pertaining to decision making and choice), thus it appears that the primary travel information need in the context of getaway trips is to identify places that might be visited. Related to this need to select destinations, as shown in the cluster analysis, is the need to use one's own vacation time more effectively or to select a place that actually achieves what the traveller had intended. Three additional groups of information needs further define the spectrum of reasons for individuals to request or collect travel information before taking a trip. Specifically, these needs are labelled product knowledge, aesthetic, and preparation needs.

The implications of the study's findings are that destination marketer's strategies appear to be correctly oriented toward assisting in the vacation decision making process. First, and foremost, destination's marketing communications need to "sell" or make attractive a visit to the featured destination. While this study does not reveal insight into what influences an individual to select a specific destination, the results do show that destination choice is the top reason for collecting information. Any marketing elements (e.g., toll-free reservation numbers, information on availability of hotel rooms or attraction tickets) that can facilitate selecting a destination would appear to be effective. Next, travellers search for details about their trip. For example, what hotel to stay in, discounts available, and events taking place during one's stay. Marketing communications such as coupon books, calendar of events, and lodging guides appear to serve these types of information needs.

Visual elements of destination communications seem to be somewhat less critical or needed by potential travellers (less than 50 percent indicated those needs). These results suggest that destination image pieces or picture books may not be highly used, if they do not also attempt to satisfy choice and product knowledge needs. It is important to recognize that the results of this study showed that 44 percent of the respondents collect information on places that they may never visit suggesting that a segment of information collectors exist who do not appear to be easily converted to travel to a destination.

Preparing individuals for a trip seems to be less prominent of a need, in comparison to destination choice, product knowledge, and aesthetic needs. However, 40 percent of the respondents indicated that information can be hard to find during a trip and instead requesting information before leaving can be easier. Thus, destination marketers will need to continue to provide information at all steps of decision making and the actual trip in order to serve the varying levels of "preparedness" needs.

The findings of the study suggest several areas for future research. Visual or aesthetic information needs were demonstrated to be a strong, although not central, factor in information acquisition for short vacation trips in the Midwest. Marketing studies (e.g., Hirschman & Solomon, 1984; Holbrook & Moore, 1981; Houston, Childers, & Heckler, 1987) have examined the visual and verbal components of advertisements to determine whether the same meaning is conveyed by the different information forms. Following this research, future tourism marketing studies could test advertisements or brochures with verbal, visual, or mixed orientations to determine whether response would differ depending upon the nature of the trip being considered, level of product knowledge, aesthetic appeal, or planning capabilities. This type of study would allow advertisers to match presentation formats to information needs.

Another area for future research is to determine whether certain types of individuals are more likely to have destination selection needs or any other needs, in comparison to other consumer segments. Also, as noted earlier in the background literature section of this paper, the types of information sources used in travel-related activities vary from one's own personal experiences to the advice of others to advertisements and brochures. A future study could investigate the relationship of information needs and the various types of information sources.

In conclusion, this study has attempted to extend traditional information search theory, which primarily explains functional information needs or search within the context of decision making. A contemporary information theory advocated by Hirschman and Holbrook, among others, suggests that other needs such as aesthetic, hedonic, and social, complement functional needs. This exploratory study has shown that aesthetic information needs supplement functional needs. Additionally, the results suggest that functional needs can be segmented into three elements–product selection, product knowledge, and planning. Future studies can improve on the data properties (e.g., employing Likert-scales) in order to employ more robust and sophisticated statistical modeling techniques. Also in the future, additional information need categories could be developed and tested (e.g., hedonic and social) to further the understanding of information acquisition so that destination marketers can be more effective in delivering information to potential tourists.

REFERENCES

Assael, H. (1984). *Consumer behavior and marketing action.* Boston, MA: Kent Publishing Co.

Bettman, J. R. (1979). *An information processing theory of consumer choice.* Reading, MA: Addison-Wesley Publishing Company.

Boorstin, D. J. (1961). The image: A guide to pseudo-events in America. New York: Atheneum.

Capella, L. M., & Greco, A. J. (1987). Information sources of elderly for vacation decisions. *Annals of Tourism Research, 14,* 148-51.

Cox, D. R. (1967). *Risk-taking and information handling in consumer behavior.* Boston: Harvard University.

Dillman, D. (1978). *Mail and telephone surveys: The total design method.* New York: John Wiley & Sons.

Engel, J. F., Blackwell, R. D., & Miniard, P. W. (1986). *Consumer behavior.* New York: Dryden Press.

Etzel, M. J., & Wahlers, R. (1985). The use of requested promotional material by pleasure travelers. *Journal of Travel Research, 23*(Spring), 2-6.

Fesenmaier, D. R., & Vogt, C. A. (1992). Evaluating the utility of touristic information sources for planning Midwest vacation travel. *Journal of Travel & Tourism Marketing, 1*(2), 1-18.

Gitelson, R. J., & Crompton, J. (1983). The planning horizons and sources of information used by pleasure vacationers. *Journal of Travel Research, 21*(Winter), 2-7.

Hirschman, E. C., & Holbrook, M. B. (1982). Hedonic consumption: Emerging concepts, methods and propositions. *Journal of Marketing, 46*(Summer), 92-101.

Hirschman, E. C., & Solomon, M. R. (1984). Utilitarian, aesthetic, and familiarity responses to verbal versus visual advertisements. *Advances in Consumer Research, 11,* 426-431.

Holbrook, M. B., Chestnut, R. W., Oliva, T. A., & Greenleaf, E. A. (1984). Play as a consumption experience: The roles of emotions, performance, and personality in the enjoyment of games. *Journal of Consumer Research, 11,* 728-739.

Holbrook, M. B., & E. C. Hirschman (1982). The experiential aspects of consumption: Consumer fantasies, feelings, and fun. *Journal of Consumer Research, 9*(Sept), 132-140.

Holbrook, M. B., & Moore, W. L. (1981). Feature interactions in consumer judgments of verbal versus pictorial presentations. *Journal of Consumer Research, 8*(June), 103-113.

Houston, M. J., Childers, T. L., & Heckler, S. E. (1987). Picture-word consistency and the elaborative processing of advertisements. *Journal of Marketing Research, 29*(November), 359-369.

Murray K. B. (1991). A test of services marketing theory: Consumer information acquisition activities. *Journal of Marketing, 55,* 10-25.

Nolan, S. D. (1976). Tourists' use and evaluation of travel information sources: Summary and conclusions. *Journal of Travel Research, 14*(2), 6-8.

Olshavsky, R. W. & Granbois, D. H. (1979). Consumer decision-making–fact or fiction? *Journal of Consumer Research, 6*(Sept.), 93-100.

Raitz, K., & Dakhil, M. (1989). A note on information sources for preferred recreational environments. *Journal of Travel Research, 27*(4), 45-48.

Rao, S. R., Thomas, E. G., & Javalgi, R. G. (1992). Activity preferences and trip-planning behavior of the U.S. outbound pleasure travel market. *Journal of Travel Research, 30*(3), 3-12.

Schul, P., & Crompton, J. (1983). Search behavior of international vacationers: Travel-specific lifestyle and sociodemographic variables. *Journal of Travel Research, 22*(2), 25-30.

Snepenger, D. J. (1987). Segmenting the vacation market by novelty-seeking role. *Journal of Travel Research, 26*(Fall), 8-14.

Snepenger, D.J., Meged, K., Snelling, M., & Worrall, K. (1990). Strategies by destination-naive tourists. *Journal of Travel Research, 29*(Spring), 22-33.

Sneath, P. A., & Sokal, R. R. (1973). *Numerical taxonomy.* San Francisco: W. H. Freeman and Company.

Sternthal, B., & Craig, C. S. (1982). *Consumer behavior: An information processing perspective.* New York: Prentice Hall.

Urry, J. (1990). *The tourist gaze.* London, Sage Publications.

Wilkinson, L. (1990). *SYSTAT: The system for statistics.* Evanston, IL: SYSTAT, Inc.

Woods, W. A. (1981). *Consumer behavior.* New York: North-Holland.

Effects of User and Trip Characteristics on Responses to Communication Messages

Francis P. Noe
Muzaffer Uysal
Claudia Jurowski

SUMMARY. The study examines the effectiveness of environmental messages in relation to demographic, trip characteristics and possible management actions. Three environmental messages were designed to encourage positive behavior and reduce environmentally destructive behavior in a natural recreation area. The study included a survey of actual resource users to determine which symbols in the presentations of the content of the message would evoke a positive response. Research revealed that communication effectiveness can be enhanced by manipulating various symbols in messages and depends upon demographic and trip characteristics as well as environmental orientations of users.

INTRODUCTION

Education and information dissemination techniques have been successfully introduced by natural resource managers to influence and change

Dr. Francis P. Noe is Research Sociologist, National Park Service, Southeast Region, 75 Spring Street, S.W., Atlanta, GA 30303. Dr. Muzaffer Uysal is Associate Professor, and Ms. Claudia Jurowski is a PhD candidate, both at the Department of Hotel, Restaurant and Institutional Management, 351 Wallace Hall, Virginia Polytechnic and State University, Blacksburg, VA 240611-0429.

Address correspondence to Dr. Muzaffer Uysal at the address listed above.

[Haworth co-indexing entry note]: "Effects of User and Trip Characteristics on Responses to Communication Messages." Noe, Francis P., Muzaffer Uysal, and Claudia Jurowski. Co-published simultaneously in *Journal of Travel & Tourism Marketing* (The Haworth Press, Inc.) Vol. 2, No. 2/3, 1993, pp. 147-169; and: *Communication and Channel Systems in Tourism Marketing* (ed: Muzaffer Uysal, and Daniel R. Fesenmaier) The Haworth Press, Inc., 1993, pp. 147-169. Multiple copies of this article/chapter may be purchased from The Haworth Document Delivery Center [1-800-3-HAWORTH; 9:00 a.m. - 5:00 p.m. (EST)].

147

user behavior (Cook and Berrenberg 1981, Roggenbuck et al. 1982). The balance in tipping a decision to action in an open-society is frequently contingent on how credible the communication process is perceived. Information concerning the receptiveness of specific messages is necessary if park managers seek to persuade users to be more safety conscious and more caring about how they treat a natural recreation area. A communication campaign, if properly presented, might help increase the public's level of awareness and aid in the control of adverse behaviors thereby encouraging positive conduct.

Exploitation of the mass media and clever advertising campaigns have been successful in influencing public decision-making (Rogers 1987). There is little difference between the techniques used to induce an action toward purchasing a specific brand of toothpaste, safeguarding sexual activities, or protecting of the environment. Several public campaigns such as the one against drunk driving, have been very effective in increasing public awareness which has led to heightened sensitivity to an issue and a change in public behavior.

However, creating a sense of awareness in the reception of a message is certainly more difficult for some products or ideas than others. Interest often focuses on the superficial and surface issues with regard to the environment. A pleasant view or unobstructed "vision" of nature may be more acceptable to the public than removing an obscure harmful carcinogen that is undetected by the naked eye. The problem is further compounded when the public is totally unaware of the destructive nature of their actions. In such situations, they are unable to judge responsibly. Unfortunately for the environment, this is a common occurrence in which Marion (1990: 247) has found that "most high-impact behavior is a product of carelessness or ignorance."

Countless polls attest to the concern the American public espouses about the environment but this attitude does not necessarily translate into positive action. As indicated in a recent Roper poll (1992), there are limits to "trade-offs," and although consumers are willing to make financial sacrifices "they will not make any and all." Despite championing the protection of the environment, the public believes that they are not responsible for reparations. Additional rationalizations for not participating in environmental preservation or improvement have ranged from (a) they have no spare time, (b) their family would not accept the changes in the household routine, or (c) it's corporate America's fault (Phillips 1990). This paradox represents a monumental problem to resource decision makers who are charged with the conflicting duties of protecting the environment and providing recreational opportunities. The dilemma of responsibility requires park managers to determine the most effective methods for changing environmentally abusive behavior but also providing opportunities for recreational enjoyment. Researchers (Burton 1981; Jackson and Dhanani, 1984) have proposed that the resolution will require a clear understanding of public values and preferences and the incorporation of these into decision making.

Several studies (Dillman and Christensen, 1972; Buttel and Flinn 1974; Dunlap 1975; Geisler et al., 1977; Arcury 1990; Uysal et al. 1992) have found a relationship between demographics and environmental attitudes. These findings suggest that age and education are consistently the single most influential demographic predictor of environmental problem awareness. Arcury (1990) in his study found that the level of environmental knowledge is consistently and positively related to environmental attitudes. Individuals who express the most environmental concern also tend to be relatively well educated (Dillman and Christensen 1972, Buttel and Flinn 1974, 1976, 1978). Those living in urban areas are also more favorably inclined toward preservation or to be pro-environmentalists than those living in rural or adjacent natural park areas (Tremblay and Dunlap 1978, Buttel and Flinn 1978, Mohai and Twight 1986, Saremba and Gill 1991). Most of these studies indicate that a positive association exists between the degree of urbanization and the degree of concern about environmental issues.

Ideological shifts in predicting environmental concern have also been explored by Dunlap and Van Liere (1984). They found that an emerging "dominant social paradigm" could explain more variation in levels of environmental concern than could sociodemographic variables. This research probes both demographic variables and environmental attitudes in an effort to determine the potential effectiveness of specific messages designed to reduce environmentally destructive behavior in a natural recreation area. Environmental messages were structured to encourage positive behavior and management actions were tested to determine what ones would be supported. More specifically, this research examined the effectiveness of proposed messages in relation to demographic, trip characteristics and possible management actions.

The study included a survey of actual resource users to determine which symbols in the presentations of the content of the message would evoke a positive response. By manipulating symbolic expression and metaphors, messages were crafted to address each of the resource issues that the respondents perceived as being problematic. The premise guiding this inquiry is simply that meaning has a referential aspect (Littlejohn 1983). By focusing on the evaluation of how symbols are responded to, communication effectiveness may be enhanced by manipulating different symbols in messages.

METHODS

Site

The study took place at Biscayne National Park located near Miami, Florida. Most of the park is comprised of reef and water, with many keys or islands forming a north-south chain bounded by Biscayne Bay on the west and the Atlantic Ocean on the east. This area is part of a larger more diverse recreational system that includes public parks, beaches, and marinas that cater to boating, diving, sightseeing, and other marine-related recreational activities. The survival of this natural resource will depend upon effective management which is contingent upon public input and cooperation. The direction of this study was motivated by the results of public perceptions in a previous study that found environmental degradation to be caused by inappropriate human behavior[1] (Snow 1989). Public recognition of social problems implies a need to address the situation. As Sykes (1971) explains, "the study of social problems is a political act because when we arrive at some idea of what is a preferable form of society . . . our choice almost always entails an attempt at persuasion, and this is the first step in the restructuring of social reality." Communication of the problems needing attention is also fundamental to persuasion.

The Snow (1989) study revealed that the respondents perceived environment problems to be caused by nature and humankind. The highest-ranked perceived problem was that there were too many insects (76.7%). This illustrates the conflict between preservation and usage because the insect larvae are the natural fish food. The same fishermen who complain about the insect bites also wants good fishing. Inappropriate user behavior ranked second in importance. Respondents noted reckless boat operators (75.9%) and crowding at the docks or in the harbor (67.8%). Pollution on the Bay (63.1%) and litter on the Bay (61.9%) were the other most significant issues that the respondents viewed as having a potential impact on the quality of their recreational experience.[2]

In addition to the issues of boating safety, litter, and insect annoyance raised by the survey respondents, managers of the park raised concerns about damage caused by boats that anchor on or close to the coral reefs. This practice, while not allowed under current regulations, has resulted in serious damage to sections of the coral community.

The results of that study precipitated the need for information that might guide park managers in changing the manner in which the Bay was being treated by its users. Changing human behavior by appealing to new standards of behavior has confronted even the most optimistic of leaders, philosophers, or professionals with difficult decisions and often mixed success. The decision-making process involves evaluating, not always rationally, alternative lines of conduct.

Survey

A mail-back questionnaire was designed to evaluate users' perceptions of proposed environmental and management changes. Specific actions were proposed as possible ways in which the environment could be improved. Respondents were asked to evaluate messages on the basis of their effectiveness. The sample intercept period, July 26-30, 1989, coincided with the opening of the lobster season. It was our intention to contact park users who were active consumers and not just passive sightseers who traditionally form the largest core of park visitors (Noe and Hammitt 1988). We focused our sample on the more consumer oriented park user who potentially would have a greater and more direct impact on the resource.

Respondents

The visitors were approached by trained interviewers at boat ramps at Matheson Hammock, Convoy Point-Bayfront Park, and Black Point. Five-hundred and ten visitors willingly agreed to receive a mail-back questionnaire of which 485 provided valid addresses. Two-hundred and ninety-five questionnaires were filled out and returned from the sample amounting to an effective return rate of 60% (an acceptable average for a field study of this kind). A modified Dillman (1978) procedure was used to help insure an adequate return rate.

The respondents in the survey were predominantly male (90%), married (75%), and an average age of 38 (median age of 36) making them a relatively youthful sample. Eighty-five percent had completed at least 16 years of education. The level of education is reflected in their occupations and incomes: 69% were employed in technical, business or professional jobs, and earned an approximate, median, annual income of $40,000 to $50,000. The majority (96.6%) were Floridian residents and 92% resided in city or suburban areas. Ninety-three percent of the visitors used the park during the day with an average stay of about 5-8 hours. The sample of respondents were repeat visitors and used the park frequently averaging about 22 visits a year.

Analysis

The analysis section of this study consisted of three stages. First the nine NEP statements were factor analyzed which resulted in two factor groupings reflecting ecocentric (attitude 1) and anthropocentric (attitude 2) beliefs. Second, three messages were compared across the selected visitor and trip characteristics using analysis of variance (ANOVA). Age, gender, marital status, education, and occupation were included as the visitor characteristics; and destination type, travel group, residence, and number of visits in the past year as the trip characteristics. In addition, multiple classification analysis (MCA) was employed to investigate the combined effect of selected independent variables on the messages. The final stage of the analysis attempted to examine the association between the messages and environmental attitudes (1 and 2) and management actions (1 to 5). The degree of association between these was explored by using Pearson correlation coefficients.

Variables

Independent variables: Attitudes toward the environment were measured by the New Environmental Paradigm (NEP) that was developed by Dunlap and Van Liere (1978) and was designed to be tested in diverse social and cultural situations. The scale was constructed to capture an ecologically integrative view of man and nature. The concept behind the scale was represented as a kind of world view, built on the idea of "spaceship earth," where mankind lives in harmony with nature. This perspective differs from the view that some will argue is still a more dominant attitude in modern technological society in which the proper role of nature is to be controlled in the service of mankind (Samova, Porter, and Nemic 1981). The content of the NEP scale includes items structured to test these opposing views of how the public perceives the natural environment. The studies surveying park users found a pattern among the scale items indicating two dimensions of meaning, one emphasizing an ecologically dominated interest, while a second was anthropocentrically oriented (Noe and Snow 1990). In an earlier study emphasizing ethnic differences between users, a similar pattern was found for Hispanic and non-Hispanic users (Noe and Snow 1989). The NEP scale seems to isolate two distinct scale dimensions among National Park users. Although the NEP may not be a single neatly formed scale, it has successfully measured beliefs about dominating or living in harmony with the environment. Clearly, there is no single homogeneous set of beliefs toward the environment, and the public's viewpoint in all probability is already being modified toward a more global orientation regarding the balance between nature and technology. Previous testing of the scale in five other parks indicated that a nine-item scale resulting in two dimensions would most likely be sufficient to measure environmental attitudes among park users (Noe and Snow 1990).[3]

Socio-demographic characteristics were measured by age, sex, and marital status of the individual. Status or social class characteristics were measured by the more traditional indicators of occupation, education, and income.

Trip or travel destination characteristics were also measured because they indicated to what extent an individual or group sought out such an experience. Such variables like place of residence, composition of the travel group, number of previous visits, and whether the park was a major or pass through destination characterize the type of trip variable.

Five proposed management actions (see Exhibit A) were also included to determine the degree of support or opposition in relation to respondents' evaluations of messages based on effectiveness. Proposed actions were Likert measured from strongly favor (1) to strongly oppose (5).

Information diffusion about Biscayne Bay was measured by determining what channels of communication were being used by the visitor to learn about the park and what importance they played in gathering information.

Dependent variable: A set of three message variables was tested. Messages were designed as short paragraph-length statements exhorting the visitor to care for the environment. Respondents were asked to rate and evaluate the effectiveness of the three messages in motivating people to be more responsible when visiting the park. Messages were rated on a five-point Likert-type scale (5 = excellent; 4 = good; 3 = neutral; 2 = not so good; 1 = not good at all).

Message One:

> Storms and cold weather, particularly during the winter months, can severely damage the coral reefs in Biscayne Bay. There is little we can do to protect these living underwater treasures from the whims of Nature. Man also damages the corals through careless and thoughtless actions. Throwing an anchor over board without looking, diving, and standing on corals, and running a boat aground can be controlled. We should take charge and direct how we will keep and preserve the Bay, now and in the future.

EXHIBIT A. Management Actions

Action 1: Restrict use of motorized boats in seagrass areas.
Develop exclusive zones for snorkeling and scuba diving.
Separate scuba diving and spearfishing from snorkeling areas for safety.
Limit spearfishing to designated areas.
Require reduced boat speeds over patch reefs.

Action 2: Inform bay users about protecting the environment.
Develop a campaign on safe boat operation.
Require mandatory public instruction on resource protection, if a bay user is found damaging the bay.

Action 3: Allow boats to anchor using buoyed tie-up on patch reefs.
Permit anchoring of boats in rubble areas of sand and debris within a patch reef.
Permit use of mushroom-type anchors for mooring near patch reefs.

Action 4: Promote an information campaign for a litter-free bay.
Inform bay users about protecting the environment.

Action 5: Prohibit use of chemical spraying on bay area.
Ban boat anchoring on patch reefs.
Continue current regulations on boat anchoring off patch reefs.

Note: Respondents were asked to rate the degree to which they favor oppose management actions being considered for the park, (1 = strongly favor; 2 = somewhat favor; 3 = neutral; 4 = somewhat oppose; and 5 = strongly oppose).

Comment–this appeal offers a two-sided approach, nature vs. man in the destruction of coral. The approach was positive and avoided negative connotations. It characterized coral as a living treasure. It also employed symbols that connote man in "charge," controlling, and directing his actions since a more anthropocentric view of nature is characterized by that perception. Since this sample of Bay users was consumers of the resource, namely lobstering, this approach might have appeal.

Message Two:

Biscayne Bay offers an oasis of escape for family and friends. Bordered by a modern technological city, the Bay plays host to millions of micro-organisms busily building underwater cities of coral very much like those of man. Like human engineers, these micro-organisms are fussy about where they build their homes. The water must be clear and clean, but fairly shallow so light energy can penetrate and produce food to nourish the many different species of fish and plant life. And like our city, the coral city can be threatened by pollution, waste, and litter. Together we can stop these harmful practices and save the Bay's coral cities.

Comment–This appeal offers a one-sided appeal personalizing the Bay as an environment for family and friends. Since there is a strong association with family or friendship groups, and Bay use, we thought such a symbolic reference might increase interest in protecting the coral. A metaphor characterizing coral as a living city needing clear, clean water attempted to make the association with the city and suburbs of Dade county that face similar needs where the majority of visitors reside. The tone was positive although "stopping" harmful practices was stressed.

Message Three:

The Caribbean-like habitat of Biscayne Bay offers many challenges for man to overcome. It is sometimes difficult to live in harmony with nature, and the balance of nature can be upset easily. The Bay's recreational riches are far greater than all the gold that was transported by the Spanish galleons to the Old World. Today, the riches of boating, relaxing, sailing, diving, swimming, and snorkeling bring wealth to the Bay's inhabitants. But there is a price to pay . . . not in gold, but in care and understanding. We have a responsibility to know and learn how to use the Bay without hurting it.

Comment–A one-sided message focusing on the challenge of dealing and living in harmony with nature. Symbols of riches and Spanish galleons were used to point out the recreational riches the Bay has to offer. Visitors were urged to learn and understand how to live responsively with the Bay. This approach attempted to capitalize on the rich cultural history of the area rooted in a Latin past and contemporary presence.

The three messages represented collectively different levels of involvement with the environment. In the first appeal, there was a call for self control over one's action. The second appeal called for a collective effort in organizing action. The third appeal made learning not action, whether individual or collective, the focus of concern. We would expect there to be greater backing of the appeal scaling for less personal responsibility such as in appeals 2 and 3.

RESULTS

Respondents were asked whether they considered three different appeals effective in motivating people to be more responsible when visiting the park. They were asked to judge whether the appeal was excellent (5), good (4), neutral (3), not so good (2) or not good at all (1).

Appeal One which characterized coral as a living treasure was directed at resource consumers. The message encouraged the audience to take charge of the preservation of the Bay. The mean score of 4.09 on this variable indicates that the majority of the respondents found this to be a good message. Table 1 presents the results of ANOVA with MCA options with respect to demographic variables. Those between the age of 31 and 50, married persons, and those without a masters degree or doctorate were somewhat less enthusiastic about the message, although not at a statistically significant level. Females expressed a significantly more favorable view toward this message than did males. Those employed in white-collar technical and managerial/professional occupations seemed to approve more strongly of ideas expressed in this appeal. Table 2 shows the results of ANOVA and MCA with respect to trip variables. The strongest support at a statistically significant level came from those who chose the Biscayne National Park as their major destination and visited the park less than 7 times in the past 12 months. Couples and families with school age children as well as those traveling with two or more families or relatives also seemed to rate appeal one more agreeable. Those who did not live in a city tended to rate the appeal lower than those who lived in cities.

The second appeal that used a metaphor characterizing coral as a living city encouraged halting harmful practices. It was directed toward family and friendship groups, especially those living within the local city and suburbs. The mean score of 4.00 indicates that the message was generally perceived as good (Table 3). The most significant deviations seem to be attributable to age. As with appeal one, the age group 31-50 approved of this appeal somewhat less than the other groups. Also, although not at a statistically significant level, females, singles, those without a college degree and those in unskilled, sales/clerk or managerial/professional occupations showed more endorsement of this type of suggestion than did the other groups.

TABLE 1. MCA Summary Statistics for the Combined Effects of Demographic Characteristics on Message 1

Grand Mean: 4.09

Independent Variables	N	Unadj. Dev.	Adj. Dev.	Eta	Beta	F-test Sig.
Age				0.10	0.10	0.472
30 and under	43	0.17	0.13			
31 to 50 years old	143	−0.05	−0.06			
51 and over	32	0.01	0.11			
Gender				0.16	0.17	0.021
Male	195	−0.05	−0.05			
Female	23	0.44	0.47			
Marital Status				0.02	0.02	0.946
Married	169	−0.01	−0.01			
Widowed/Divorced	20	0.07	0.07			
Never Married	33	0.01	0.00			
Education				0.08	0.10	0.733
Some College or less	91	−0.05	−0.06			
College Graduate	54	0.03	0.01			
Graduate Work	18	−0.03	−0.01			
Masters Degree	40	−0.01	0.04			
Doctorate	15	0.25	0.32			
Occupation				0.10	0.13	0.507
Unskilled	29	−0.05	−0.20			
Sales/Clerk	31	−0.08	−0.06			
Skilled	15	−0.08	−0.02			
Technical	16	0.29	0.36			
Managerial/Professional	127	0.00	0.02			

Multiple R^2 = .055   Multiple R = .234
Note: Unadj. Dev.: Unadjusted deviation from the grand mean; Adj. Dev.: Adjusted deviation from the grand mean.

TABLE 2. MCA Summary Statistics for the Combined Effects of Demographic Characteristics on Message 2

Grand Mean: 4.00

Independent Variables	N	Unadj. Dev.	Adj. Dev.	Eta	Beta	F-test Sig.
Age				0.21	0.21	0.063
30 and under	44	0.43	0.43			
31 to 50 years old	144	-0.11	-0.09			
51 and over	32	0.11	0.17			
Gender				0.09	0.03	0.660
Male	197	-0.03	-0.01			
Female	23	0.28	0.10			
Marital Status				0.12	0.09	0.488
Married	167	-0.07	-0.01			
Widowed/Divorced	20	0.16	0.26			
Never Married	33	0.26	-0.12			
Education				0.08	0.10	0.733
Some College or less	9	0.10	0.11			
College Graduate	55	-0.16	-0.13			
Graduate Work	18	-0.22	-0.23			
Masters Degree	40	-0.22	-0.19			
Doctorate	15	-0.36	-0.37			
Occupation				0.08	0.11	0.640
Unskilled	29	0.07	0.11			
Sales/Clerk	31	0.01	-0.04			
Skilled	15	-0.09	-0.14			
Technical	17	-0.24	-0.35			
Managerial/Professional	128	0.02	0.05			

Multiple R^2 = .081   Multiple R = .285

TABLE 3. MCA Summary Statistics for the Combined Effects of Demographic Characteristics on Message 3

Grand Mean: 3.96

Independent Variables	N	Unadj. Dev.	Adj. Dev.	Eta	Beta	F-test Sig.
Age				0.06	0.08	0.524
30 and under	44	0.06	0.05			
31 to 50 years old	142	0.02	0.04			
51 and over	32	−0.16	−0.23			
Gender				0.08	0.10	0.160
Male	195	−0.03	−0.04			
Female	23	0.28	0.33			
Marital Status				0.05	0.03	0.938
Married	166	−0.03	−0.01			
Widowed/Divorced	20	0.11	0.04			
Never Married	33	0.09	−0.08			
Education				0.30	0.33	0.000
Some College or less	91	0.38	0.41			
College Graduate	53	−0.19	−0.24			
Graduate Work	18	−0.50	−0.51			
Masters Degree	40	−0.17	−0.15			
Doctorate	16	−0.57	−0.59			
Occupation				0.07	0.08	0.877
Unskilled	29	−0.18	−0.21			
Sales/Clerk	30	0.06	−0.02			
Skilled	15	−0.01	−0.04			
Technical	16	0.06	−0.04			
Managerial/Professional	128	0.02	0.05			

Multiple R^2 = .116   Multiple R = .340

While those who chose the park as their major destination gave the most favorable marks to appeal one, this same group demonstrated significantly less approval for appeal two (Table 4). In like manner, another variable demonstrates the contrast between the two appeals. While those who visited the park least frequently rated one more favorably than the mean, the same group rated appeal two less effective. A second variable identified a similarity between appeals one and two, though not at a significant level. Respondents who lived in cities rated both appeals higher than those who did not. Almost the same travel groups that favored appeal one more strongly, also favored the second appeal. The only difference between the attitude toward the two variables in light of travel groups appears to be in a change of attitude of the two special interest groups who seem to favor the second appeal more than the first.

The third appeal focuses on the challenge of living in harmony with nature and extols the value of the Bay to users and inhabitants. It urges visitors to learn and understand how to use the Bay without harming her. The mean of score 3.96 on this variable indicates that it is somewhat less popular than the other two. At the same time, it seems to meet the requirements of a broader group.

This was the only appeal which did not record significant differences between age groups. The only age group to deviate from the mean was that of the 51 and over group (Table 5).

Appeals two and three both received higher scores from females but not at the statistically significant levels as did appeal one. Married respondents when compared to singles tended to measure this appeal in the same manner–somewhat less favorably.

The only significant difference in demographic characteristics on appeal three can be found in the level of education. Those who did not continue education beyond high school were considerably more attracted to the rhetoric of the third appeal than those who had continued their education (Table 5).

No significant differences were found for the combined effects of trip variables (Table 6). However, once again there seems to be a difference between those who use the park as a major destination and those who use it as part of a trip that includes a few other destinations. Those who include Biscayne Bay as part of a few but not many other destinations favor much more strongly the third appeal than those who just visit the Bay.

Respondents who traveled in family groups appear to like this appeal more than other groups, especially more than the two special interest groups. In addition, population density seemed to affect respondents' atti-

TABLE 4. MCA Summary Statistics for the Combined Effects of Trip Variables on Message 1

Grand Mean: 4.09

Independent Variables	N	Unadj. Dev.	Adj. Dev.	Eta	Beta	F-test Sig.
Destination				0.19	0.23	0.004
Major destination	150	0.11	0.13			
One of few destinations	32	−0.25	−0.26			
One of many destinations	33	−0.24	−0.26			
Travel Group				0.17	0.15	0.168
Alone	6	−0.76	−0.87			
Couple	30	0.31	0.39			
Family w/ preschool children	7	−0.24	−0.22			
Family w/ schoolage children	32	0.06	0.07			
Family with both	15	0.31	0.31			
Group of friends	81	−0.13	−0.31			
Two or more families or relatives together	42	0.03	0.01			
Special interest groups	2	−0.09	−0.09			
Residence				0.23	0.21	0.029
Small town or city	21	−0.09	−0.01			
City (population 25,001-100,000)	23	0.08	0.02			
Suburb within 25 miles of a large city	82	−0.17	−0.17			
Large city (population over 100,000)	89	0.15	0.17			
Number of visits in the last 12 months				0.17	0.21	0.029
1-6 times	66	0.16	0.15			
7-15 times	52	−0.11	−0.11			
16-30 times	53	−0.19	−0.19			
31 or more	44	0.11	−0.09			

Multiple R^2 = .157   Multiple R = .397

TABLE 5. MCA Summary Statistics for the Combined Effects of Trip Variables on Message 2

Grand Mean: 4.00

Independent Variables	N	Unadj. Dev.	Adj. Dev.	Eta	Beta	F-test Sig.
Destination				0.18	0.16	0.076
Major destination	152	−0.11	−0.10			
One of few destinations	32	0.22	0.24			
One of many destinations	33	0.31	0.25			
Travel Group				0.13	0.13	0.403
Alone	6	−0.33	−0.41			
Couple	30	0.10	0.05			
Family w/ preschool children	7	−0.28	−0.27			
Family w/ schoolage children	33	−0.09	−0.04			
Family with both	16	0.19	0.15			
Group of friends	81	−0.07	−0.04			
Two or more families or relatives together	42	0.15	0.12			
Special interest groups	2	0.00	0.17			
Residence				0.13	0.11	0.469
Small town or city	21	−0.09	−0.05			
City (population 25,001-100,000)	23	0.31	0.31			
Suburb within 25 miles of a large city	82	−0.09	−0.08			
Large city (population over 100,000)	91	0.03	0.00			
Number of visits in the last 12 months				0.12	0.10	0.323
1-6 times	67	−0.03	−0.03			
7-15 times	52	0.18	0.18			
16-30 times	53	0.04	0.03			
31 or more	45	−0.22	−0.20			

Multiple R^2 = .072   Multiple R = .269

TABLE 6. MCA Summary Statistics for the Combined Effects of Trip Variables on Message 3

Grand Mean: 3.96

Independent Variables	N	Unadj. Dev.	Adj. Dev.	Eta	Beta	F-test Sig.
Destination				0.13	0.13	0.193
Major destination	153	−0.03	−0.03			
One of few destinations	31	0.33	0.33			
One of many destinations	32	−0.15	−0.17			
Travel Group				0.13	0.13	0.403
Alone	6	−0.30	−0.34			
Couple	30	−0.10	−0.05			
Family w/ preschool children	7	0.04	0.05			
Family w/ schoolage children	33	0.10	0.11			
Family with both	17	0.15	0.20			
Group of friends	79	−0.11	−0.14			
Two or more families or relatives together	42	0.20	0.18			
Special interest groups	2	−0.40	−0.46			
Residence				0.13	0.14	0.452
Small town or city	21	0.13	0.20			
City (population 25,001-100,000)	23	0.25	0.27			
Suburb within 25 miles of a large city	81	−0.01	0.01			
Large city (population over 100,000)	91	−0.08	−0.10			
Number of visits in the last 12 months				0.13	0.13	0.751
1-6 times	68	−0.01	−0.04			
7-15 times	52	0.09	0.14			
16-30 times	52	−0.10	−0.10			
31 or more	44	0.01	0.02			

Multiple R^2 = .050   Multiple R = .223

tudes toward this appeal with more favor being shown by those who lived in smaller towns and cities.

Tables 7 and 8 present the results of Pearson correlations between environmental attitudes, management actions and the messages. The first appeal correlated positively with attitude one toward the environment and negatively with attitude 2 (Table 7). The highest correlations between this appeal and the actions respondents favored was found between actions 2, 4, and 5 which indicate that those who favor appeal one also favor prohibiting certain activities, punishing violators and providing information (Table 8). A weak positive correlation exists between appeal two and both environmental attitudes (Table 7). The strongest correlation between actions favored and appeal two appears to be in actions 1, 2, and 3 which suggest the need to restrict and limit usage, punish, inform and control anchorage (Table 8).

TABLE 7. Pearson Correlation Between Messages and NEP Subscales			
NEP Subscale	Message 1	Message 2	Message 3
Attitude 1	0.2882**	0.1758**	0.2316**
Attitude 2	− 0.1973**	0.0115*	− 0.1756**
* $P = 0.05$, ** $P = 0.01$			

TABLE 8. Pearson Correlation Between Appeals and Actions			
	Message 1	Message 2	Message 3
Action 1	0.1603*	0.1507*	0.2424**
Action 2	0.2712**	0.1591**	0.1980**
Action 3	0.1306*	0.1523*	0.0715
Action 4	0.2587**	0.1144	0.2128*
Action 5	0.2147**	0.0833	0.0967
* $P = 0.05$ ** $P = 0.01$			

Appeal three correlates positively with environmental attitude one and negatively with the second environmental attitude. The strongest correlations between appeal three and preferred actions are for actions 1 and 4 which propose restrictions, limits and information. Actions 2, 3, and 5 which had lower correlations with appeal 3 all mentioned boats or anchors.

CONCLUSIONS

Knowledge about the potential effectiveness of individuals that utilize national recreation areas is imperative for messages to be effective enough to change human behavior. The information is particularly important for the management of national parks because they are charged with the converse missions of protecting natural resources and utilization (Dunn 1980). The findings of the study indicated that all three messages were judged effective by the respondents. Each message has merit as a tool to encourage positive behavior through information dissemination. Identifiable characteristics of users with different recreation behaviors separate the three messages.

For example, the first message suggests that the reader take control and implies a need for individual actions. The message appeals to a relatively explicit segment of the Bay users who recognize the consequences of their own actions, are internally-directed and responsive to certain managerial policies. This message would be most effective if it were directed to college graduates who believe in the protection and preservation of the environment through public education and information dissemination. Another consideration in focusing the direction of this message is to recognize that the message appealed most forcefully to those whose major destination was Biscayne Bay and to those who use the Bay on a less frequent basis. The results imply that the respondents who favored the message desire quality experiences and appreciate the environment. The content of message one could be included in specialized outdoor recreation magazines, information packets and on tastefully designed outdoor messages with more emphasis on verbal rather than visual means.

The second message which focused on appealing to friendship groups to work together to stop harmful practices seemed to appeal more to the younger group of respondents who did not have a college degree. This message can be directed to both ecocentric and anthropocentric users of blue-collar and sales/clerk occupations who use the park as one of many destinations on a more frequent basis. Communication messages should be designed with emphasis on visual displays, interpretation and oral narratives. Metaphors can be an effective communication tool to reach users who favor this message.

The respondents who favored the third message appeared to have the same ecocentric attitudes as the respondents endorsing the first message. However, there is a significant difference in the educational level of the two groups. Respondents with less than a college degree favored the third message while college and post graduates supported the first message. The major difference between the two messages was in the type of action required. The first message implied that individuals should take charge and direct the preservation of the Bay while the third suggested that responsible action depends upon knowing and learning how to use the Bay without hurting her. The results imply that the respondents who favor message three desire more information concerning responsible use of the Bay.

To reach those who favored the third choice, the message could incorporate symbols that connote cultural heritage of the users such as the reference to the gold transported by the Spanish galleons in message three. Direct marketing of the conservation and preservation efforts could be accomplished through the collection of names and addresses of onsite users who show interest in learning more about how to protect the Bay. Outdoor signs that indicate the availability of such information and how to request it as well as personnel available to answer questions will be effective means of communicating with those who seek more information.

This exploratory study revealed that not any one message was rated more effective than another but that the effectiveness of the message depends upon the certain demographic and trip characteristic and environmental orientations of the users.

The study intended no generalization to other parks. However, the same messages with appropriate place specific changes can be developed in similar surveys to examine the degree of responsiveness to assorted messages. There is evidence from this research that clusters may exist within user groups. An extension of this research would seek to profile visitor segments based on their evaluation of selected messages. Such profile studies may be of help to park managers to develop communication programs to influence recreation behavior.

NOTES

1. The original study by Snow (1989) sampled registered boat owners in the Miami-Dade county area and actual on-site users who were intercepted at access points such as boat ramps, beaches, and marinas about their perception of problems associated with the Bay.

2. The complete list of other site-related issues and lesser perceived problems affecting Biscayne Bay National Park are discussed in more detail in Cofer-Shabica et al. (1990).

3. The items were Likert-scaled and of those abstracted from the original scale are the following: (1) we are approaching the limit on the number of people the earth can support, (2) the balance of nature is very delicate and upset easily, (3) humans have the right to modify the natural environment to suit their needs, (4) mankind was created to rule over the rest of nature, (5) when humans interfere with nature, it often produces disastrous consequences, (6) plants and animals exist primarily to be used by humans, (7) to maintain a healthy economy, we will have to develop a steady-state economy where industrial growth is controlled, (8) humans must live in harmony with nature in order to survive, and (9) mankind is severely abusing the environment. Items 2, 3, and 6 are reverse-scored on the Likert scale. The ecocentric attitude (1) consisted of 1, 2, 5, 7, 8, and 9 subscales 3, 4, and 6 made up the anthropocentric attitude (2).

REFERENCES

Arcury, A.T. (1990). Environmental Attitude and Environmental Knowledge. *Human Organization*. 49(4):300-304.

Audience Research. (1955). *A Survey of the Public Concerning the National Parks*. Princeton, NJ.

Burton, T.L. (1981). You Can't Get There from Here: A Personal Perspective on Recreation Forecasting in Canada. *Recreation Resource Review*. 9:38-43.

Buttel, F.H. and W. L. Flinn. (1974). The Structure of Support for the Environmental Movement, 1968-1970. *Rural Sociology*. 39(1):56-69.

Buttel, F.H. and W. L. Flinn. (1976). Environmental Politics: The Structuring of Partisan and Ideological Cleavages in Mass Environmental Attitudes. *Sociology Quarterly*. 17:477-490.

Buttel, F. H. and W. L. Flinn. (1978). The Politics of Environmental Concern: The Impacts of Party Identification of Political Ideology on Environmental Attitudes. *Environment and Behavior*. 10(1):17-36.

Citibank, Mastercard, and Visa. (1991). *Our National Parks: Preserving a Priceless Heritage*. New York, NY.

Cofer-Shabica, S.V., Snow, R.E., and F.P. Noe. (1990). Formulating Policies Using Visitor Perceptions of Biscayne National Park and Seashore, in Fabbri, P. (ed). *Recreation Uses of Coastal Areas*. Kluwer Academic Publishers: Netherlands.

Cook, S.W. and J.L. Berrenberg. (1981). Approaches to Encouraging Conservation Behavior: A Review and Conceptual Framework. *Journal of Social Issues*. 39(2): 73-107.

Dillman, D. (1978). *Mail and Telephone Surveys: The Total Design Method*. New York: John Wiley & Sons, Inc.

Dillman, D. A. and J.A. Christensen. (1972). The Public Value for Pollution

Control, pp. 237-256. In W. Burch et al., (eds) *Social Behavior, Natural Re-sources and the Environment.* New York: Harper & Row.

Dunn, D. R. (1980). Future Leisure Resources. In T. L. Goodale and P.A. Witt, eds. *Recreation and Leisure: Issues in an Era of Change,* pp. 115-124. State College, PA: Venture Publishing.

Dunlap, R.E. (1975). The Impact of Political Orientation on Environmental Atti-tudes and Actions. *Environment and Behavior.* 7:428-545.

Dunlap, R. E., and K. Van Liere. (1978). The Environmental Paradigm Scale: A Reexamination. *Journal of Environmental Education.* 17:9-12.

Geisler, C. C., Martinson, O.B., and E.A. Wilkening. (1977). Outdoor Recreation and Environmental Concern: A Restudy. *Rural Sociology.* 42(2):242-249.

Geller, J. and P. Lansley. (1985). The New Environmental Paradigm Scale: A Reexamination. *Journal of Environmental Education.* 17(1):9-12.

Jaccard, J. (1981). Toward Theories of Persuasion and Belief Change. *Journal of Personality and Social Psychology.* 40:260-269.

Jackson, L.E. and A.D.B. Dhanani. (1984). Resources and Resource Use Conflict in Alberta. In B.M. Barr and P.J. Smith, (eds)., *Environment and Economy: Essays on the Human Geography of Alberta,* pp. 79-94. Edmonton: University of Alberta Press.

Leiss, W. (1981). The Limits to Satisfaction: An Essay on the Problem of Needs and Commodities. Toronto: University of Toronto Press.

Marion, L.J. (1990). Ecological Impacts of Nature-Dependent Tourism. *The Tour-ism Connection: Linking Research and Marketing.* Twenty-first TTRA Confer-ence Proceedings, pp. 243-249.

Mohai, P., and B.W. Twight. (1986). Rural-Urban Differences in Environmental-ism Revisited. Paper presented at the Annual Meeting of the Rural Sociologi-cal Society, Salt Lake City, UT.

Noe, F.P. and W. Hammitt. (1990). Visual Preferences. Washington, DC.: USDI Science Monograph No. 18.

Noe, F. P. and B. Snow. (1990). The Environmental Paradigm and Further Scale Analysis. *Journal of Environmental Education.* 21:20-26.

Phillips, S. (1990). Americans on Environment: Let Someone Else Clean It Up. *Atlanta Constitution*, August 1, 3A.

Rogers, E.M. (1987). Communication Campaigns. In *Handbook of Communica-tion Science,* Berger, C. R. and S.H. Chaffee. Newbury Park, CA: Sage Publi-cations.

Roggenbuck, J.W., Hall, O.F., and S.S. Oliver. (1982). The Effectiveness of Inter-pretation in Reducing Depreciative Behavior in Campgrounds. *U.S. Army of Corps of Engineers DACM-39-81-M-2264.* Vicksburg, MS.

Roper. (1992). Natural Resource Conservation: Where Environmentalism is Heading in the 1990's. Roper Organization.

Samova, L.R., Porter, R. and R. Nemic, J.C. (1981). Understanding Intercultural Communication. Belmont, CA: Wadsworth Publishing.

Saremba, J. and A. Gill. (1991). Value Conflicts in Mountain Park Settings. *Annals of Tourism Research.* 18(1):455-472.

Snow, R.E. (1989). Recreation Resource Management and Planning Study for the Biscayne National Park. Report: Center for Public and Urban Research, Georgia State University.

Sykes, G. (1971). *Social Problems in America*. Glenview, Il: Scott, Foreman & Co.

Tremblay, Jr., K.R. and R.E. Dunlap. (1978). Rural-Urban Residence and Concern with Environmental Quality: A Replication and Extension. *Rural Sociology*. 43:474-491.

Uysal, M., Noe, F.P. and C. D. McDonal. (1992). Environmental Attitude by Trip and Visitor Characteristics: US Virgin Islands National Park. Unpublished paper.

The Influence
of Tourists' Characteristics on Ratings
of Information Sources for an Attraction

Kathleen L. Andereck
Linda L. Caldwell

SUMMARY. Information sources about a product or service potentially affect a tourist's purchase decision. The characteristics of tourists influence the manner in which they search for, rate, and use information about tourism related products or services. The purpose of this paper is to determine the relationship between the characteristics of visitors to an attraction and information source importance ratings. It concludes that word-of-mouth information is rated most important, followed by past experience and other media sources. Additionally, several demographic and trip characteristics are related to ratings of information sources, as are visitor motives.

INTRODUCTION

Understanding tourists' decisions to purchase specific tourism products or services is becoming increasingly important to tourism marketing managers. The process of consumer behavior encompasses several stages: searching for

Dr. Kathleen Andereck is Assistant Professor, Department of Leisure Studies, University of North Carolina at Greensboro, 420-J HHP Building, Greensboro, NC 27412. Dr. Linda Caldwell is Assistant Professor, Department of Leisure Studies, University of North Carolina at Greensboro.

The authors wish to thank the North Carolina Zoological Park, North Carolina Zoological Society and University of North Carolina at Greensboro Research Council for supporting this study.

[Haworth co-indexing entry note]: "The Influence of Tourists' Characteristics on Ratings of Information Sources for an Attraction." Andereck, Kathleen L., and Linda L. Caldwell. Co-published simultaneously in *Journal of Travel & Tourism Marketing* (The Haworth Press, Inc.) Vol. 2, No. 2/3, 1993, pp. 171-189; and: *Communication and Channel Systems in Tourism Marketing* (ed: Muzaffer Uysal, and Daniel R. Fesenmaier) The Haworth Press, Inc., 1993, pp. 171-189. Multiple copies of this article/chapter may be purchased from The Haworth Document Delivery Center [1-800-3-HAWORTH; 9:00 a.m. - 5:00 p.m. (EST)].

171

information, purchasing, using, evaluating, and disposing of the product or service (Moutinho, 1987). Research in tourism consumer behavior must continue to try to understand the factors related to purchase decisions.

One of the major factors influencing consumer decisions to purchase a product or service is information sources about the product or service. *Information search or information seeking* is the process of consulting various sources before making a purchasing decision. Consumers recognize the need for more knowledge, which activates the decision to search for information about alternatives (Moutinho, 1987). Awareness of a particular product or service and resulting purchase decisions largely depend on the information consumers are able to gather and the credibility of such information (Raitz & Dakhil, 1989). The availability of information in tourism is especially important because often consumers are located far from the product or service of purchase, and/or the product or service is a one time event (Wicks & Schuett, 1991).

The search process may be spontaneous and short lived or occur over a longer period of time and involve intense exploration of the product or service. Information may be sought internally from an individual's memory, usually from a previous trip to the same or a similar destination (Wicks & Schuett, 1991). Searches may also be conducted externally, which involves an active process in that information must be sought out. Additionally, several information sources may be used (Moutinho, 1987; Runyon & Stewart, 1987). External sources can be: (1) interpersonal sources such as friends or family, (2) marketer-dominated sources such as advertisements or promotional materials, or (3) objective sources such as product rating and consumer information services (Berkman & Gilson, 1986).

Several product/service related factors encourage consumers to conduct external information searches. These are higher prices, perceived differences in product alternatives, greater product importance, higher perceived risk, less experience with the product/service, and situational determinants (Capella & Greco, 1987; Newman, 1977). Vacation decisions often are associated with many of these factors suggesting that some external information search probably occurs (Capella & Greco, 1987). Gitelson and Crompton (1983) suggest that external information searches are important in tourism for related reasons:

1. A trip involves using discretionary money and free time, and is a high risk purchase.
2. The intangible nature of services suggests that secondary or tertiary sources must be used as a consumer is not able to actually observe the potential purchase.
3. Vacationers are often interested in visiting new, unfamiliar destinations as a primary travel motive.

A number of studies have indicated that of all the external sources of information available to tourists, the interpersonal sources of family and friends are often relied on most heavily (Rao, Thomas & Javalgi, 1992; Raitz & Dakhil, 1989; Capella & Greco, 1987; Gitelson & Crompton, 1983; Walter & Tong, 1977; Nolan, 1976).

RELATED STUDIES

Past studies have found that consumers differ in their likelihood to seek out product knowledge (Moutinho, 1987; Thorelli & Becker, 1981), ranging from intensive seekers to those that engage in very limited searches. Consumers also differ in the number of sources consulted for product or service information and the importance placed on the sources; frequently consumers seek information from several sources prior to making a purchase decision. Numerous factors may influence a consumer's information seeking behavior. Past information seeking research based on information search theory has found several general relationships between consumer characteristics and search behavior (Snepenger, Meged, Snelling & Worrall, 1990; Raitz & Dakhil, 1989; Capella & Greco, 1987; Runyon & Stewart, 1987; Newman, 1977).

Demographic Characteristics

Individual demographic characteristics may influence information seeking behavior (cf. Hirschman & Wallendorf, 1982). Research in consumer behavior has generally found that people of higher income and education search more for product/service information (Runyon & Stewart, 1987; Robertson, Zielinski & Ward, 1984; Newman, 1977). Age tends to be inversely related to amount of search, while the relationship between search behavior and other demographic characteristics, such as social class and occupation, tends to depend on the product/service being investigated (Newman, 1977).

Certain demographic characteristics of travelers have been linked to information search behavior. Studies have found that college educated individuals were more likely to use destination specific literature (Gitelson & Crompton, 1983), and people of higher socio-economic class frequently used travel agents as information sources (Woodside & Ronkainen, 1980).

Gitelson and Crompton (1983) found that older people were more likely to use a travel agent than younger people. Older people have also been reported to heavily rely on information from friends and family

(Capella & Greco, 1987). Raitz and Dakhil (1989) and Schreyer, Lime and Williams (1984) suggested that younger people value information provided by peers more highly than that provided by family members, and may rely on a narrower set of information sources, respectively. Snepenger et al. (1990), however, found no difference in information search strategy based on average age among visitors to Alaska, although it appeared that men were less likely to use travel agents than women.

Other findings have suggested that family groups are more likely to gain information from the media than other groups (Gitelson & Crompton, 1983). Snepenger et al. (1990), however, found that information search strategy did not vary by group size.

Social-Psychological Factors

Perceived benefits of information search will influence search behavior. Consumers that already have knowledge of the product will usually engage in limited search activity perceiving that the benefits of additional information search are minimal (Robertson et al., 1984). Studies of the relationship between experience and information search have had mixed results, however. Likely the relationship is mitigated by many factors, such as product/service satisfaction (Runyon & Stewart, 1987). Generally, however, it seems that consumers with more knowledge of a product or service engage in different types of information search than those with limited knowledge, and frequently less information seeking behavior will occur (Anderson, Engledow & Becker, 1979). Such individuals will rely more heavily on internal information search. Two tourism studies related to this idea found that: (1) information seeking for travelers to South Carolina was related to previous visitation, with professional sources used more by first-time visitors (Woodside, 1980); and (2) information seeking was greater with unknown destinations (Van Raaij, 1986).

Information search behavior also may partly depend on consumer preferences for information sources, and preferences for sources in particular purchase situations. It seems that the specific product/service being purchased influences preferences for information sources, as does the specific point in time during the purchase process (Runyon & Stewart, 1987).

Finally, motives for visitation can influence information seeking. Motivation is a state of need that "pushes" a person toward actions that may bring satisfaction. In the case of tourists, motivation is related to the need for optimal arousal and is largely effected by social factors (Moutinho, 1987). It has been proposed that by tourist motivation one intends "a meaningful state of mind which adequately disposes an actor or group of actors to travel, and which is subsequently interpretable by others as a valid explanation for such a decision" (Dann, 1981). Although propensity to travel is related to favorable perceptions of a destination which can be influenced by information, actual travel to the destination will not occur without specific motives (Henshall, Roberts & Leighton, 1985). It is consumer needs and motives that activate goal-oriented behavior. Specific motives for travel are related to past vacation experiences, personal experience and knowledge, and information gained from interpersonal, marketer dominated and objective sources (Moutinho, 1987).

A few studies have found that travel motives influence information search behavior. The vacation motive of novelty or variety, and a search for variety in the trip can both lead to more intensive information searches and the use of a greater variety of sources (Crompton, 1979; Engle, Kollat & Blackwell, 1973). Motives for visitation may also affect the types of information sources used. Market segments of visitors to Alaska based on Cohen's (1972) novelty-seeking topology differed in the amount of search behavior and the specific sources most people utilized (Snepenger, 1987).

STUDY PURPOSE AND HYPOTHESES

Marketing managers of attractions must have knowledge of the importance visitors place on various information sources because of its influence on purchase decisions. The effectiveness of information varies with the nature of the product/service and the characteristics of the people interested in consuming the product/service. The purpose of this paper is to explore the relative importance visitors to an attraction placed on various information sources. Additionally, this study will determine the relationship between visitor characteristics and information source importance ratings. It is hypothesized that:

1. Word-of-mouth will be rated as the most important information source influencing visitors' decisions to visit an attraction.
2. Differences in importance ratings of information sources will be related to:

    a. visitor demographic characteristics of education, income, age, and residence;
    b. visitor trip characteristics of vacation versus other trip type, distance traveled, and repeat visitation;
    c. visitor motives for visitation.

METHODS

Procedures and Sample

The North Carolina Zoological Park (NCZP) is located near Asheboro, North Carolina. The zoo is a natural habitat zoo with 10 major exhibits featuring African animals. The NCZP covers 1,448 acres making it one of the world's largest zoos in physical size, and a major part of the state's growing tourism industry.

Data were collected from visitors to the North Carolina Zoological Park (NCZP) in Asheboro, NC from April 13, 1990 through August 7, 1990.[1]

Dates for data collection were randomly selected, though the proportion of week days and weekend days selected were based on visitation figures from previous years. Data were collected on 36 days.

Visitors selected for the study were asked to provide information at three different time points: (1) before entering the zoo via an intercept interview; (2) after the visit was completed via a self-administered questionnaire; and (3) one month after the visit via a self-administered mail questionnaire. Details of this process follow.

On the days of data collection, research assistants stationed themselves outside the entrance to the zoo, near the ticket booth. Assistants approached every n*th* visitor and asked for his or her cooperation in the study. Due to the nature of the study, large and/or organized groups were not selected for inclusion. The sampling interval was pre-determined based on a three year history of visitation rates for that same day. For example, weekends have typically attracted a greater number of visitors to the zoo, thus the sampling interval was larger on weekend days than on weekdays. Assistants were given some discretion to alter that figure if actual visitation rates were not consistent with expected rates.

When the visitor was first approached to participate in the study, he or she was informed of the nature of the project, that there would be three questionnaires including one that would be mailed, and that it was important for the same person to fill out all three questionnaires. As an incentive to participate fully in the study, a free zoo t-shirt was offered. This t-shirt was mailed to the visitor upon receipt of the mail-back questionnaire.

If the visitor agreed to participate in the study, the research assistant asked a set of questions on the pre-visit instrument. The visitor then completed a set of self-administered questions. The "interview" technique was utilized to establish rapport and therefore increase response rate for the entire study.

After the initial questionnaire was completed, which took approximately seven minutes, the visitor was asked to return after his or her visit to complete a post-visit questionnaire. This questionnaire was entirely self-administered, and took approximately 10 minutes. Visitors also completed a separate address card for mailing purposes at this time. A third questionnaire was mailed to the visitor approximately four weeks after his or her visit to the zoo. Visitors who completed all three questionnaires were mailed a free zoo t-shirt upon receipt of the mail-back questionnaire.

Initially, 883 people were approached at the zoo to participate in the study; 795 people agreed to participate. Of those 795 people, 740 (93.1%) returned after their zoo visit to complete the post-visit questionnaire. These individuals were mailed a questionnaire one month later, and 630 returned their questionnaires for an 86.1% response rate. The 630 people who returned their mail-back questionnaires represented 72.1% of the total number of initial contacts made at the onset of the study.

Variables

All variables of interest in this paper were part of the pre-visit interview and were measured in several ways. To determine the importance of various information sources, respondents were asked to respond to the query "How important were the following sources of information?" using a five point scale, where 1 = not important and 5 = extremely important. Nine sources of information were listed: past experience, word of mouth, brochure, TV commercial, TV appearance or program, highway sign or billboard, newspaper ad or article, magazine ad or story, and radio ad or program. These 9 sources of information were later factor analyzed to produce 3 main sources of information which were used as dependent variables in later analyses. The process by which these variables were collapsed is described in the results section.

Measurement of the independent variables is described below.

a. Visitors responded to *education* categories of: (1) less than high school, (2) high school graduate, (3) some college, (4) two-year college graduate, (5) four year college graduate, and (6) advanced graduate degree. Categories were then combined into Low (1 and 2), Medium (3 and 4) and High (5 and 6).

b. *Income* was measured in incremental $10,000 categories up to over $100,000. These were collapsed into categories of $20,000 up to over $80,000.

c. *Age* was categorized in tens from less than 20 to over 70. Again, these were further reduced by increments of 20 years.

    d. The *residence* variable was formed from information about respondents' states of origin, with one category representing North Carolina residents and all others falling in a second category.

    e. On the questionnaire visitors were asked if this trip to the zoo was part of a longer vacation, yes or no. Response to this question constitutes the *vacation* variable.

    f. *Distance traveled* was the actual number of miles traveled to the zoo, categorized as (1) 40 miles or less, (2) 41 to 80 miles, (3) 81 to 120 miles, (4) 121 to 160 miles and (5) 161 miles or more.

    g. Whether or not respondents were *repeat visitors* was measured by asking if they had been to the zoo before: no; yes, one or two times before; or yes, three or more times.

    h. The final independent variables of *motives* for visitation were measured by asking respondents to rate a number of motive items with 1 being not important to 5 being extremely important. These items were then collapsed into scales base on *a priori* theorizing and principle components factor analysis with orthogonal rotation. Final scales consisted of four general motives for visiting the zoo: (1) recreation/novelty, (2) education/recreation, (3) education for others in my group, and (4) photography of animals and plants. (See Andereck, Caldwell & Debbage, 1991 for details.) Each of these scales were then collapsed into three categories of low motivation (mean of 1 to 2.49), neutral motivation (mean of 2.5 to 3.49), or high motivation (mean of 2.5 to 5).

Data Analysis

The major type of data analysis employed was multivariate analysis of variance (MANOVA) followed by one-way analysis of variance (ANOVA) with post hoc Bonferroni t-tests to determine which dependent measures were influenced by the independent variables. Pillai's trace (V) was the multivariate test statistic used. The MANOVA technique was originally developed to analyze the effects of experimental treatments on a set of two or more dependent variables, but can also be used in non-experimental studies which employ random selection. MANOVA is analogous to the more commonly used ANOVA in univariate analysis. However, in situations when more than one dependent variable is being investigated, and the dependent variables are conceptualized as measuring aspects of a single underlying variable, the multivariate test is more appropriate. Using univariate statistics to measure multivariate data increases the chance of finding significant results where none exit (Type I error). Additionally, the likelihood of making a Type I error increases as the number of dependent variables increases (Biskin, 1983).

RESULTS

The NCZP attracts a large variety of visitors. A demographic profile of these visitors appears in Table 1. Most visitors were from North Carolina (84%) and had traveled fairly short distances. The highest frequency of visitors were middle aged, with fairly evenly distributed education levels and a median income of $40,000-$50,000. More respondents were women (55.9%), and most visitors to the zoo were traveling in family groups. More than half of the respondents (54.5%) had visited the zoo before.

Findings suggest that two information sources stand out as the major sources that influenced visitors: word-of-mouth (mean = 3.36) and past experience (mean = 3.20) (Table 2). This supports the first hypothesis that word-of-mouth information will be rated as the most important information source influencing visitors' decisions to visit the zoo. No single information source, however, stands out as being extremely important. For all sources, the highest frequency of responses are in the very important to neutral range.

Before testing the second hypothesis, the nine information sources were factor analyzed to identify information sources that tended to group together. Principle components factor analysis with orthogonal rotation resulted in three distinct factors (Table 3). Past experience and word-of-mouth both were factors by themselves, explaining 16.0 percent and 15.7 percent of the variance, respectively. All of the other information sources factored together explaining 68.3 percent of the variance. An index of these seven sources was created to use in additional analysis. The result was three information source dependent variables: *experience, word-of-mouth (WOM), and media.*

Relationships between individual independent variables and the three information sources, tested with MANOVA, appear in Table 4. Results indicate that there are several statistically significant relationships (alpha ≤ .05) between visitor characteristics and the manner in which visitors rated information sources. Of the demographic variables, both education and residence are significant. Also, two trip related variables are significant: whether the respondent was on vacation and if s/he was a repeat visitor. Finally, all four of the visitation motives are related to the importance rating of information sources.

Follow-up ANOVAs indicate how respondents' characteristics influenced ratings of individual dependent measures. Results suggest that

TABLE 1. Profile of North Carolina Zoological Park Visitors.		
Characteristic	**Frequency**	**Percent**
State Origin (n = 795)		
North Carolina	668	80.0
Virginia	29	3.6
South Carolina	17	2.1
Other States	77	9.6
Other Countries	4	0.5
Age (n = 791)		
20 or less	37	4.7
21-30	206	26.0
31-40	301	38.0
41-50	143	18.1
51-60	57	7.2
61-70	43	5.4
over 70	4	0.5
Group Composition (n = 786)		
Couple with children	299	38.0
Couple without children	138	17.6
Multi-generational family	121	15.4
Two or more families	90	11.4
Adult with children	51	6.5
Group of friends	51	6.5
Alone	16	2.0
Other	20	2.5
Repeat Visitation (n = 795)		
First time visitor	361	45.4
1-2 previous visits	275	34.6
3 or more previous visits	159	20.0

Characteristic	Frequency	Percent
Distance Traveled (n = 793)		
0-40 miles	206	25.9
41-80 miles	347	43.7
81-120 miles	167	17.2
121-160 miles	65	8.1
over 160 miles	38	4.8
Education (n = 790)		
Less than high school	40	5.1
High school diploma	175	22.1
Some college	176	22.3
Two years college	87	11
Four years college	176	22.3
Advanced graduate degree	136	17.2
Household income (n = 729)		
less than $20,000	120	16.5
$20,001-40,000	297	40.7
$40,001-60,000	209	28.7
$60,001-80,000	67	9.2
$80,001 and more	36	4.9
Sex (n = 791)		
Female	442	55.9
Male	349	44.1

TABLE 2. Importance of Information Sources in Decision to Visit the Zoo.

Information Source	1 Not Import. (%)	2 Slight. Import. (%)	3 Neutr. (%)	4 Very Import. (%)	5 Extrem. Import. (%)	Mean
Word-of-mouth (n = 726)	91 (12.5)	84 (11.6)	145 (20.0)	283 (39.0)	123 (16.9)	3.36
Past experience (n = 729)	150 (20.6)	55 (7.5)	149 (20.4)	251 (34.4)	124 (17.0)	3.20
Brochure (n = 695)	189 (27.2)	63 (9.1)	178 (25.6)	200 (28.8)	65 (9.4)	2.84
TV commercial (n = 696)	217 (31.2)	67 (9.6)	175 (25.1)	177 (25.4)	60 (8.6)	2.71
TV appearance or program (n = 685)	230 (33.6)	69 (10.1)	196 (28.6)	136 (19.9)	54 (7.9)	2.58
Highway sign or billboard (n = 703)	240 (34.1)	86 (12.2)	181 (25.7)	131 (18.6)	65 (9.2)	2.57
Magazine ad or story (n = 693)	219 (31.6)	73 (10.5)	215 (31.0)	144 (20.8)	42 (6.1)	2.59
Newspaper ad or article (n = 695)	231 (33.2)	84 (12.1)	200 (28.8)	145 (20.9)	35 (5.0)	2.52
Radio ad or program (n = 684)	247 (36.1)	78 (11.4)	189 (27.6)	136 (19.9)	34 (5.0)	2.46

people with lower educational levels rated media as more important than people with higher educational levels, although education did not influence importance ratings of experience or WOM (Table 5).

The information source of past experience was rated differently by individuals depending on their state of residence, if they were on vacation, or if the visit to the zoo was a repeat visit. North Carolinians rated experience higher than residents of other state, as did people not on vacation and, as would be expected, visitors that had previously visited the zoo (Table 5).

TABLE 3. Factor Analysis of Information Sources.

Source	Factor Scores		
Past experience/familiarity	**.9680**	.0757	.0933
Word-of-mouth	.0845	**.9723**	.1809
Highway sign/billboard	− .0277	.2078	**.7126**
Newspaper ad/article	− .0388	.1562	**.8441**
Radio ad/program	.1798	.1316	**.8580**
T.V. commercial	.2492	.0806	**.8362**
T.V. appearance/program	.2364	.0992	**.8577**
Magazine ad/story	.0356	.1458	**.8291**
Brochure	− .0116	.0096	**.7472**

People that had never visited the zoo before rated WOM information higher than did repeat visitors (Table 5).

Finally, motivation to visit the zoo influenced ratings of all information sources except experience for the photography motive (Table 6). Generally, however, as the level of motivation to visit the zoo increased, so did the importance rating of all information sources.

DISCUSSION AND CONCLUSIONS

Results reveal that visitors to the NCZP use a number of sources of information, with word-of-mouth rating as the most important source, followed by past experience. This finding is consistent with other studies that have also reported the importance consumers place on word-of-mouth information. Gunn (1988) suggests that part of the reason for this is the perceived credibility of information passed on by friends and family. Regardless of potential biases in the information, it is usually unquestionably believed because the informant is viewed as credible. This finding points

TABLE 4. MANOVA Between Independent Variables and Information Sources.

Variables	V[1] Value	Approx. F	D.F.	p
Demographic				
Education	.0463	5.408	6, 1368	0.0001
Income	.0265	1.520	12, 2049	0.1096
Age	.0044	0.503	6, 1366	0.8067
Residence	.0386	9.144	3, 684	0.0001
Trip Factors				
Vacation	.0159	3.679	3, 683	0.0120
Distance traveled	.0324	1.490	12, 1635	0.1208
Repeat visit	.2853	37.943	6, 1368	0.0001
Motives				
Recreation/Novelty	.0384	4.471	6, 1368	0.0002
Education/ Recreation	.0568	6.668	6, 1368	0.0001
Education Relational	.1038	12.478	6, 1368	0.0001
Photography	.0618	7.274	6, 1368	0.0001

[1]Pillai's trace

to the necessity of maintaining high levels of satisfaction among visitors to the zoo.

Education, although effecting ratings of information sources, does not appear to influence information seeking behavior in the manner found in other studies. In this case, respondents with a low education level rate media as more important than respondents in other education groups. It is not clear why these findings are not consistent with previous studies.

It is not surprising that state of residence is related to information sources, with experience being more important to North Carolinians than to residents of other states. North Carolinians have visited the zoo more frequently that out-of-state visitors.[2] This rational is similar for vacationers versus nonvacationers. Most vacationers who are on an extended trip have not visited the zoo at an earlier time.[3]

TABLE 5. Univariate Analyses for Significant MANOVA Demographic and Trip Characteristic Variables.

Variables	Variable Means[1]			Univariate F	D.F.	p value
Education	**Lo**	**Med.**	**High**			
Experience	3.12[a]	3.23[a]	3.22[a]	0.40	2	.6705
WOM	3.31[a]	3.42[a]	3.35[a]	0.42	2	.6580
Media	2.99[a]	2.69[b]	2.47[b]	12.98	2	.0001
Residence	**NC**	**Other**				
Experience	3.31[a]	2.55[b]		30.25	1	.0001
WOM	3.35[a]	3.43[a]		0.36	1	.5500
Media	2.69[a]	2.62[a]		0.40	1	.5292
Vacation	**Yes**	**No**				
Experience	2.85[a]	3.29[b]		12.22	1	.0005
WOM	3.39[a]	3.35[a]		0.09	1	.7688
Media	2.70[a]	2.67[a]		0.07	1	.7949
Repeat visit	**No**	**1-2**	**3+**			
Experience	2.42[a]	3.63[b]	4.03[c]	122.18	2	.0001
WOM	3.50[a]	3.19[b]	3.36[ab]	4.33	2	.0136
Media	2.73[a]	2.58[a]	2.72[a]	0.76	2	.4688

[1]Means with different letters indicate statistically significant differences at the .05 level.

The final trip variable of repeat visitation is very strongly related to the information source of experience, as would be expected. Visitors that have made previous trips to the zoo rely increasingly heavily on an internal search for information. Visitors that have not previously visited the zoo, however, place a higher level of importance on word-of-mouth information than repeat visitors.

The interesting thing about this set of analyses is that importance of media is not what was expected. Media is more important to those who had lower levels of education than more highly educated individuals, and

TABLE 6. Univariate Analyses for Significant MANOVA Motive Variables.

Variables	Variable Means[1]			Univariate F	D.F.	p value
Recreation/ novelty motive	**Low**	**Neut.**	**High**			
Experience	2.58ª	3.06ªᵇ	3.27ᵇ	5.02	2	.0068
WOM	2.94ª	3.18ªᵇ	3.43ᵇ	4.08	2	.0173
Media	2.63ªᵇ	2.29ª	2.77ᵇ	9.51	2	.0001
Education/ recreation motive	**Low**	**Neut.**	**High**			
Experience	2.60ª	2.98ªᵇ	3.31ᵇ	8.71	2	.0002
WOM	2.89ª	3.12ªᵇ	3.47ᵇ	8.38	2	.0003
Media	2.15ª	2.53ᵇ	2.76ᵇ	8.59	2	.0002
Education motive	**Low**	**Neut.**	**High**			
Experience	2.59ª	3.09ᵇ	3.45ᶜ	19.14	2	.0001
WOM	3.02ª	3.26ªᵇ	3.53ᵇ	8.68	2	.0002
Media	2.22ª	2.52ᵇ	2.90ᶜ	20.25	2	.0001
Photography motive	**Low**	**Neut.**	**High**			
Experience	3.19ª	3.07ª	3.30ª	1.83	2	.1605
WOM	3.11ª	3.25ª	3.61ᵇ	11.17	2	.0001
Media	2.34ª	2.67ᵇ	2.89ᵇ	14.46	2	.0001

[1]Means with different letters indicate statistically significant differences at the .05 level.

is more important to in-state residents and vacationers. This finding could be an artifact of the operationalization of the variable media. The variable media includes seven types of media sources, including brochures, TV commercials and programs, and various print media sources (see Table 2). All of these media sources except brochures, and to some extent magazine ads, tend to be locally oriented (that is, within the state of North Carolina).

Vacationers and out-of-staters may not have even had the opportunity to be influenced by these media sources. It is possible, however, that they may have made use of brochures since these are available at welcome centers and other places across North Carolina, as well as included in North Carolina travel information packages and sent in response to inquiries for zoo information.

Additionally, while others have suggested that people of higher social class search more for product and service information (Runyon & Stewart, 1987; Robertson et al., 1984; Newman, 1977), Runyon and Stewart also suggest that individuals of lower social classes watch more TV than their higher social class counterparts. As well, individuals of lower social classes are more receptive to advertising, especially advertisements which have strong visual characteristics. Print ads and billboards for the NCZP are well known for their striking visual images. These findings may help to explain why those of a lower educational level rely more heavily on media than people in other educational categories. It should be pointed out, however, that the overall importance of media for all groups ranged from being not important to neutral. Still, approximately 25 percent of respondents rated each specific media information source as very or extremely important which justifies continued promotional efforts.

Findings of this study indicate that motives play a significant role in the utilization of product information. In particular, the findings suggest that people who are strongly motivated, regardless of their motivation, rate all information sources higher. This is consistent with Crompton (1979) and Engle et al. (1973) who found that the vacation motive of novelty and variety led to more intensive information searches. It appears that the more highly motivated or purposeful the individual, the more important it is to gather information about the trip. It may be that a strong perception of a need will activate information search behavior.

It should be noted, however, that the causal nature of this relationship is unclear. It is possible that information sources have contributed to the development of motivation to visit the zoo. For example, someone who has been influenced to visit the zoo through recommendation of a close friend may *become* highly motivated to visit the zoo. Future research may wish to address this issue of causality further.

Overall, results of this study agree with prior consumer behavior research in that search behavior differs among individuals. Additionally, the high level of importance placed on interpersonal sources of information is consistent with past research. Differences between the findings of this study and other studies may be due in part to the specific nature of the destination being investigated. While past tourism information search studies have focused on vacations in general, or a vacation to a broad geographic region, this study focussed on one particular attraction. It is possible that similar findings may emerge from future information search research for specific attractions.

NOTES

1. These dates represent when the actual intercept study was conducted. Mail back surveys were returned through October, 1990.
2. Relationship confirmed by Chi-squared analysis ($X^2 = 61.92$; D.F. = 2; p = 0.000).
3. Confirmed with Chi-squared analysis ($X^2 = 89.93$; D.F. = 2; p = 0.000).

REFERENCES

Andereck, K.L., Caldwell, L.L. & Debbage, K. (1991). A market segmentation analysis of zoo visitors. In *Tourism: Building Credibility for a Credible Industry* (pp. 359-372). Travel and Tourism Research Association 22nd Annual Conference, Long Beach, CA, (June 9-13).

Anderson, R.D., Engledow, J.L. & Becker, H. (1979). Evaluating the relationships among attitudes toward business, product satisfaction, experience, and search effort. *Journal of Marketing Research, 16*: 394-400.

Berkman, H.W. & Gilson, C. (1986). *Consumer behavior: Concepts and strategies,* third edition. Boston: Kent Publishing Company.

Biskin, B.H. (1983). Multivariate analysis in experimental leisure research. *Journal of Leisure Research, 15*: 344-358.

Capella, L.M. & Greco, A.J. (1987). Information sources of elderly for vacation decisions. *Annals of Tourism Research, 14*: 104-117.

Cohen, E. (1972). Toward a sociology of international tourism. *Social Research, 39*: 164-182.

Crompton, J.L. (1979). Motivations for pleasure vacations. *Annals of Tourism Research, 6*: 408-424.

Dann, G.M.S. (1981). Tourist motivation: An appraisal. *Annals of Tourism Research, 8*: 187-219.

Engle, J., Kollat, D. & Blackwell, R. (1973). *Consumer behavior.* Hinsdale, IL: Dryden Press.

Gitelson, R.J. & Crompton, J.L. (1983). The planning horizons and sources of information used by pleasure vacationers. *Journal of Travel Research, 22*: 2-7.

Gunn, C.A. (1988). *Tourism planning.* New York: Taylor and Francis.

Henshall, B.D., Roberts, R. & Leighton, A. (1985). Fly-drive tourists: Motivation and destination choice factors. *Journal of Travel Research, 23*: 23-27.

Hirschman, E.C. & Wallendorf, M. (1982). Motives underlying marketing information acquisition and knowledge transfer. *Journal of Advertising, 11*: 25-31.

Moutinho, L. (1987). Consumer behavior in marketing. *European Journal of Marketing, 21*: 5-44.

Newman, J.W. (1977). Consumer external search: Amount and determinants. In Arch G. Woodside, Jagdish N. Sheth & Peter D. Bennett (Eds.), *Consumer and industrial buying behavior* (pp. 79-94). New York: North-Holland.

Nolan, S.D. (1976). Tourists' use and evaluation of travel information sources: Summary and conclusions. *Journal of Travel Research, 14*: 6-8.

Raitz, K. & Dakhil, M. (1989). A note about information sources for preferred recreational environments. *Journal of Travel Research, 27*: 45-49.

Rao, S.R., Thomas, E.G. & Javalgi, R.G. (1992). Activity preferences and trip-planning behavior of the U.S. outbound pleasure travel market. *Journal of Travel Research, 30*: 3-12.

Robertson, T.S., Zielinski, J. & Ward, S. (1984). *Consumer behavior.* Glenview, IL: Scott, Foresman and Company.

Runyon, K.E. & Stewart, D.W. (1987). *Consumer behavior and the practice of marketing,* third edition. Columbus, OH: Merrill Publishing Company.

Schreyer, R., Lime, D.W. & Williams, D.W. (1984). Characterizing the influence of past experience on recreation behavior. *Journal of Leisure Research, 16*: 34-50.

Snepenger, D. (1987). Segmenting the vacation market by novelty-seeking role. *Journal of Travel Research, 26*: 8-14.

Snepenger, D., Meged, K., Snelling, M. & Worrall, K. (1990). Information search strategies by destination-naive tourists. *Journal of Travel Research, 29*: 13-16.

Thorelli, H. & Becker, H. (1981). Information seekers and information systems. *Journal of Marketing, 44*: 9-24.

Walter, A.G. & Tong, H. (1977). A local study of consumer vacation decisions. *Journal of Travel Research, 15*: 30-34.

Wicks, Bruce E. and Schuett, Michael A. (1991). Examining the role of tourism promotion through the use of brochures. *Tourism Management, 11*: 301-312.

Woodside, A.G. (1980). First time versus repeat visitors: Analyzing multiple travel market segments. Paper presented at the 11th annual Travel and Tourism Research Association Conference, Savanna, Georgia.

Woodside, A.G. & Ronkainen. (1980). Vacation travel planning segments. *Annals of Tourism Research 3*: 385-394.

Van Raaij, W.F. (1986). Consumer research on tourism: Mental and behavioral constructs. *Annals of Tourism Research 13*, 1-9.

Image Formation Process

William C. Gartner

SUMMARY. The image formation process has been an area of inquiry for more than 20 years. The process of image formation is intricately entwined with the destination selection process. Understanding the different techniques utilized to form destination images is necessary to developing an image consistent with what a destination has to offer. This paper presents a typology of the different image formation agents, describes the process of touristic image formation and provides recommendations for selecting the appropriate image formation mix. It is an attempt to develop a theoretical basis for the touristic image formation process.

INTRODUCTION

The tourist destination selection decision process has been an area of substantial investigation. Numerous models (Mathieson and Wall, 1982; Schmoll, 1977; Mouthino, 1987) have been proposed in an attempt to capture the different factors affecting destination selection. Included in each model is the recognition of "push" and "pull" factors (Dann, 1977). Motivations for travel comprise "push" factors and desirable features or attributes of destination attractions exert "pull" forces. A person may become motivated to travel whenever he/she, or the decision making body, realizes life at home is not fulfilling certain needs.

Kotler (1982) identifies three stages of what he terms "need arousal."

Dr. William C. Gartner is Director of Tourism Center and Associate Professor of Agricultural Economics at the University of Minnesota.

[Haworth co-indexing entry note]: "Image Formation Process." Gartner, William C. Co-published simultaneously in *Journal of Travel & Tourism Marketing* (The Haworth Press, Inc.) Vol. 2, No. 2/3, 1993, pp. 191-215; and: *Communication and Channel Systems in Tourism Marketing* (ed: Muzaffer Uysal, and Daniel R. Fesenmaier) The Haworth Press, Inc., 1993, pp. 191-215. Multiple copies of this article/chapter may be purchased from The Haworth Document Delivery Center [1-800-3-HAWORTH; 9:00 a.m. - 5:00 p.m. (EST)].

The first stage involves some internal or external stimuli which triggers a predisposition toward product class. The second stage is consideration of the needs that can be met through the purchase of a particular product and the third stage is the wants that become activated by the recognized needs.

Internal stimuli relate to the recognition of needs not being met at home (push) and external stimuli may result from advertisements or destination information (pull). Research on internal stimuli leading to motivations for travel has been an understandably difficult process. The basic underlying motive for travel is generally recognized to be physical escape which brings with it psychological escape (Grinstein, 1955; Crompton, 1979a).

Even when research focuses on one specific type of activity many motives for activity selection have been found (Stankey and Schreyer, 1985). While researchers may have difficulty identifying specific motives for activity choice, most destination selection models recognize that motives spring from unmet needs in the home environment and destinations selected are expected to fulfill those needs.

DESTINATION SELECTION

Goodall (1991) has developed a destination selection process (Figure 1) building on the work of Goodall et al. (1988), Mouthino (1987), Woodside and Sherrell (1977), and Um and Crompton (1987). The universe of possible destinations form the initial opportunity set. However certain destinations are not even considered because they are unknown to the decision making body or are unattainable in terms of money, time or some other constraint. What remains form the realizable opportunity set. Most likely the realizable opportunity set is large and requires further reduction to a consideration set. If the realizable opportunity set remains large, additional evaluation with respect to operational constraints is undertaken reducing the number of destinations to a choice set. Destinations are now evaluated against expected returns. Attributes provided by each destination are evaluated separately. It is at this point that place images acquired become secondary to attitudes held with respect to the product class. Without digressing much into attitude theory the difference between the two is defined by Mazanec and Schweiger (1981) as: " 'Images' as opposed to 'attitudes' must not contain judgments relating to objective, denotative evaluation criteria. The image construct implies some overriding impression or stereotype." Prior experience with the product class, activity preference, knowledge of performance characteristics are a few of the factors that determine attitudinal position. Experience through prior travel to an area is not necessary for attitudes to be formed toward the type of image projected or acquired about a destination.

After destination attribute evaluation has taken place the pool of possible destinations is reduced further to a decision or evoked set (Howard and Sheth, 1969). The size of the decision set is small, generally containing no more than three destinations (Thompson and Cooper, 1979; Woodside and Sherrel, 1977) although as propensity to travel increases the decision set may enlarge (Woodside and Sherrell, 1977). A final evaluation is made of all the destinations remaining in the decision set resulting in final destination selection.

If Goodall's model is operational then destination image becomes an important component of destination selection as soon as an individual decides to travel. Only destinations which the decision making body is aware of will be included in the perceived opportunity set. Awareness implies that an image of the destination exists in the mind(s) of the decision makers. As more and more destinations are eliminated through the evaluation process only those destinations with a strong image for the types of activities deemed important to the decision making group or individual remain viable for selection. Touristic destination images can be viewed as "pull" factors. Therefore, understanding how images are formed is critical to developing the "pull" potential of a destination.

IMAGE COMPONENTS

Destination images are formed by three distinctly different but hierarchically interrelated components: cognitive, affective and conative. The interrelationships between these components will determine product predisposition.

The cognitive image component is defined by Scott (1965) as an evaluation of the known attributes of the product or the understanding of the product in an intellectual way. Boulding (1956) in his seminal work on image describes the cognitive component as images derived from fact. The cognitive component may be viewed as the sum of beliefs and attitudes of an object leading to some internally accepted picture of its attributes. The amount of external stimuli received about an object is instrumental in forming a cognitive image.

For example, Zagreb, the capital of Croatia, has a cognitive image based on its location within what used to be the country of Yugoslavia. Some peoples' cognitive image of Zagreb may have been formed by previous travel to the city whereas other people may not even know Zagreb is in Croatia. If they have heard of it they may think it is in another

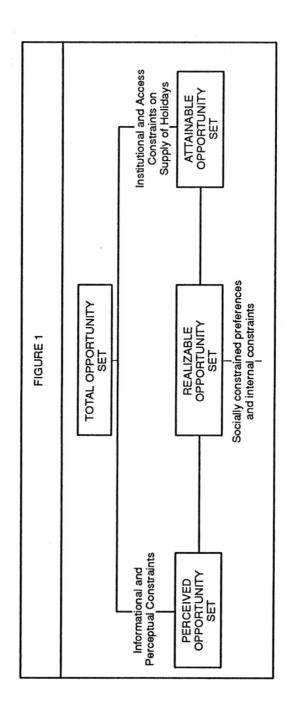

FIGURE 1

194

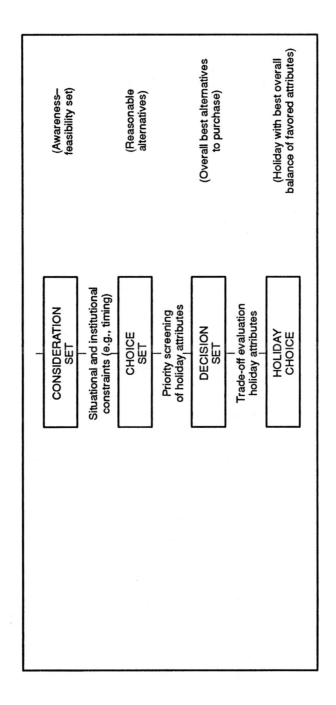

CONSIDERATION SET (Awareness—feasibility set)

Situational and institutional constraints (e.g., timing)

CHOICE SET (Reasonable alternatives)

Priority screening of holiday attributes

DECISION SET (Overall best alternatives to purchase)

Trade-off evaluation holiday attributes

HOLIDAY CHOICE (Holiday with best overall balance of favored attributes) country. The cognitive image one has of Zagreb, in this case, is subject to the cognitive image one has of the country in which they believe it is located.

Due to the inability to pretest the tourism product, touristic images will often be based more on perceptions than reality. The process of forming cognitive images will determine which destinations move into the perceived, realistic and attainable opportunity sets.

The affective component of image is related to the motives one has for destination selection. Motives determine what we wish to obtain from the object being considered thus affecting object valuation (Boulding, 1956). If we consider Zagreb an exotic city with a culture different than our own, and our travel motives are predisposed to learning more about different cultures, then travel to Zagreb has more value to us than travel to a city with which we are familiar. If on the other hand the news media has made us aware of civil unrest in Zagreb, and we place high value on safety and security, Zagreb is valued less as a destination option. The affective component of image becomes operational when the evaluation stage of destination selection begins. Using Goodall's model, this takes place when the choice set of destinations is considered.

The conative image component is analogous to behavior because it is the action component. After all internal and external information is processed a decision is reached. One destination from the decision set is selected. The conative component's relationship to the other two components is direct. It depends on the images developed during the cognitive stage and evaluated during the affective stage.

Gunn (1972) was one of the first to identify the different ways in which cognitive images are formed. He argued images are formed through induced and organic agents. Induced images emanate from the destination area and are a function of the marketing efforts of destination promoters. Organic images are formed from sources not directly associated with a destination area. News stories, documentaries, movies and other ostensibly unbiased sources of information form organic images. The key difference between organic and induced image formation agents is the control the destination area has over what is presented.

Phelps (1986) argues that destination images are either of a primary or secondary nature. Secondary images are formed from information received from some external source and primary images are formed through visitation. In a sense Phelps has combined Gunn's two types of image formation into one and created a separate category for her other type.

One could argue what difference does it make how images are formed? After all it is the final outcome which is most important. Assuming that the destination selection process outlined above adequately simulates reality, how images are formed and the component parts of that formation process are important areas of inquiry. If it can be shown that different image formation agents affect the formation of destination images differently than the final outcome can be directed through the selection of an appropriate image formation mix.

IMAGE FORMATION AGENTS

The selection of the terminology, image formation agents, is derived from the definition of agent as a force producing a specific result. The selection of one type of image formation agent over another is intended to influence the recipient of the message in a particular way, hence a specific result. To be included as a separate category in the typology that follows a different result must be obtained. The image formation process can be viewed as a continuum of separate agents that act independently or in some combination to form a destination image unique to the individual. The first agent on the continuum is labeled Overt Induced I.

Overt Induced I

Overt Induced I agents consist of traditional forms of advertising. The use of television, radio, brochures, billboards, and print media advertising by destination area promoters are direct attempts to form particular images in the minds of prospective visitors. The person receiving the message is not confused over who is sending it. It is clearly a blatant attempt, by the promoters of the destination area, to construct an image of the salient attributes of the destination in the minds of the targeted audience. Depending on the type of media chosen the cost of reaching an individual with the message may be very low although total cost can be very expensive. Television advertising carries the highest price with total cost based on program viewership numbers. Television's primary advantages are the emotional appeal and visual images it is able to convey combined with extensive market exposure. Byerly (1985) reports that the average American child will spend 27,000 hours watching television before graduation from high school. This compares to only 18,000 hours in a classroom during the same period of time. This exposure to television is a prime source of image formation.

Radio advertising can also be used to develop destination images but due to the lack of visual imagery its primary use is to disseminate information, rather than constructing an elaborate mental picture, resulting in increased awareness. Due to radio's lack of range it is generally used to develop local area images or support special promotional programs.

Brochures, a staple of almost every tourism dependent business and destination area, are necessary to increase awareness and reinforce existing images. Brochures, which also includes guide books and information booklets, are usually sent in response to some request for additional information indicating that an image has already been formed of the area and further elaboration of that image is needed. Often the request originates from some destination advertisement predisposing a decision maker to request more information from the destination. Etzel and Wahlers (1985) refer to the information produced and sent to inquirers as Destination Specific Travel Literature (DSTL).

Brochures which are sent to travel agencies for distribution may be more important than DSTL in developing images. However, the exposure brochures receive is extremely limited. Gilbert and Houghton (1991) found that travel agents' clients spent, on the average, only 54 seconds scanning racks for a suitable brochure.

Print media, such as special interest magazines, are often used for targeting specific markets. The interests of the magazines' subscribers are known and destination attributes can be presented which match readers' interests.

Mandese (1991), reporting the results of a study in which 500 ad executives were surveyed, claims that cable television and special interest magazines provide the best overall effectiveness combined with value for traditional advertising vehicles. Broadcast television and radio were close behind. Broadcast television is rated the best in terms of reach or market penetration and radio works well when used for marketing and promotional support.

People living in a country with a market based economy have been subjected to advertising since they were old enough to comprehend the world around them. They are bombarded with hundreds of messages a day and disregard most of them (Assael, 1984). It does not require much experience with advertising before people learn that what they are told about a product's attributes does not always conform to reality. This skepticism results in low credibility for Overt Induced I types of image formation. Countering the low credibility is high market penetration. Traditional forms of advertising are intended to reach large amounts of people. Advertising rates reflect the number of people expected to be contacted. Depending on the media chosen the cost of reaching an individual may be very low. However it is not possible to pay per individual as indivisibility constraints require all or nothing.

Overt Induced II

Overt Induced II image formation agents consist of information received or requested from tour operators, wholesalers, and organizations which have a vested interest in the travel decision process but which are not directly associated with a particular destination area. Tour operators are gatekeepers of information (McLellan and Noe, 1983; Bitner and Booms, 1982) and the type of information distributed by them contributes to the images people hold about certain areas (Murphy, 1983). A major function of tour operators is to create attractive destination images for the areas to which they arrange tours (Lapage and Cormier, 1977). In most cases country images influence the images tour operators project to their clients (McLellan and Foushee, 1983) however, because tour operators are interested in increasing their business only selected images will be passed on to their clients. This may lead to unrealistic portrayals of place and result in destination images not supported or desired by the destination's host society. Doobie (1976) contends that tour operators and wholesalers are the interpreters and coordinators of demand, ultimately influencing destination selection (Jenkins and Henry, 1982). Britton (1979) and a report by IUOTO (1976) contend that foreign companies influence the image of a destination through their advertising which often leads to unjustified expectations.

Destination area promoters do have some control over the images projected through tour operators. Most foreign tour operators have to be registered in the country in which they are doing business and are subject to pressure, subtle or direct, to project specific destination images. However realistic images may not always be presented and because of the high credibility tour operators have with their clients this source of image formation may surpass the importance of all the Overt Induced I forms of image formation especially in countries where foreign travel is heavily dependent on package tours. Countering the high credibility is lower market penetration. Independent tour operators or wholesalers generally do not have the resources to fully utilize Overt Induced I types of image formation agents with most concentrating on specialty markets.

Covert Induced I

The use of a recognizable spokesperson is an attempt to overcome the credibility problem inherent in Overt Induced I image formation. Traditional forms of advertising are still utilized for developing destination images but the images are supported and recommended by a known, at least to the intended audience, celebrity. In a sense, destination promoters are not relying on the credibility projected through their advertisement to convince prospective visitors of the destination's touristic attributes but instead rely on the credibility of the celebrity spokesperson to do this for them. For example, shortly after the movie *Crocodile Dundee* became a recognized box office hit the movie's male star, Paul Hogan, was seen in tourism advertising for Australia.

A recognizable spokesperson will attract attention to the endorsed product using their attractive and likeable qualities to differentiate their advertisement from the clutter of other advertising messages (Atkin and Block, 1983). Credibility is enhanced whenever the product advertised has a high psychological or social risk (Friedman and Friedman, 1979) which may be the case with long haul international travel. Increasing credibility can be accomplished by using two sided messages which acknowledges an attribute weakness and counters it with a strength (Kamins et al., 1989). For example, "Indonesia may not be the most frequently visited Pacific Rim destination but it is the most exotic."

Use of a celebrity spokesperson increases message recall especially when the celebrity is identified and the brand name is mentioned early in the advertisement (Lukeman, 1991). Market penetration remains the same as identical forms of advertising used in Overt Induced I are used in Covert Induced I. Balancing the increase in credibility is a higher cost for advertising if the second party spokesperson is compensated for the endorsement.

If adequate funds are not available to hire a celebrity, an endorsement from a satisfied customer is another method commonly used to increase credibility (Farrant, 1989). Satisfied customer endorsements appear to work well for high financial risk purchases (Atkin and Block, 1983).

Covert Induced II

The fourth component of image formation is termed Covert Induced II. A person influenced by this agent is not aware that destination promoters are involved in the development of the projected image. Articles, reports, or stories about a particular place, from an ostensibly unbiased source with no vested interest in increased travel to the destination, constitute Covert Induced II image formation agents. Familiarization tours for travel writers or special interest media groups are the vehicle used by many destination area promoters to project a particular image through the writings of the people who are hosted. Travel writers facing publication deadlines upon return home often write about their most recent travel experience. Credibility is increased as the image is now presented by a person who does not appear to have any connection with the destination except through prior visitation. The reader of the article is rarely informed that the author's travel expenses were covered by his/her hosts in the destination area.

Costs for Covert Induced II image development are considerably less than for Overt Induced I or Covert Induced I types of image formation agents as they relate only to the expenses associated with hosting a familiarization tour. Publication and production costs are borne by the publication purchasing the writer's work. The increase in credibility and decline in cost is somewhat offset by a reduction in market penetration. If the image formation is to be effective, the published article, report, etc. must be read by the intended audience. This requires the intended reader to be predisposed to the area or specific activity featured in the article. There is also no direct control over what is written as those who hosted the familiarization tour do not exercise veto power over the travel writer's work. Covert Induced II types of image formation are especially useful for small resorts or destination areas with a limited advertising budget.

Autonomous

Autonomous image formation agents consist of independently produced reports, documentaries, movies, and news articles. There are two sub-components in the Autonomous category: News and Popular Culture.

One of the most common Autonomous image formation agents is news reporting. Generally destination area promoters have no control over what appears in a news story and the projected image is based on someone else's interpretation of what is happening in the area. News reporting, because of its supposedly unbiased presentation, is assumed to have significant impacts on tourism image development. If the event reported is of major importance the opportunity for image change, in a relatively short period of time, is present.

Gartner and Shen (1992) studied tourism image change for the People's Republic of China (PRC) resulting from media coverage of the Tiananmen Square conflict. Not all aspects of the PRC's touristic image changed as a result of the conflict, but some significant changes were noted. Although images of the PRC's attraction base remained relatively stable, images of some services (e.g., safety and security) and the hospitality of the local people declined significantly. A related study by Roehl (1990) examined U.S. travel agents' attitudinal shifts after the conflict and found support for the imposition of trade restrictions on the PRC as a result of Tiananmen Square.

Other examples of image formation or change resulting from news reporting can be found in a study conducted by the U.S. Travel Service (1977), and reports by Britton (1979) and Kent and Chesnutt (1991). The U.S. Travel Service (1977) concluded from a study investigating foreigners' perceptions of the United States that many images were based on news reports depicting violence within the country. Britton (1979) contends that the North American Press convinced American tourists that travel to Jamaica was unsafe in the mid 1970's even though violence in the country was confined to a small area around Kingston. Kent and Chesnutt (1991) blame media reports of crime in downtown Atlanta, in part, for the decline in patronage of the Underground Atlanta attraction complex.

High credibility and market penetration combine to make news reporting a powerful source of image formation. Unfortunately as events are unfolding destination promoters can do very little to control the images portrayed through news reports. Even when authoritative governments censor news this only serves to lend credibility to what has already been presented.

Damage control for destination images which are impacted by major news events however can still be initiated and directed. Milo and Yoder (1991) have examined the process of news coverage during a major event and have identified opportunities for destination promoters to control the impact of the event on touristic image. At the start of a major news event broadcast media request little local support for news coverage except through affiliate stations. After the event, however, follow up stories are sought by independent reporters and local officials are often asked to provide assistance. It is during this phase of news coverage that image damage control is possible. Ahmed (1991) argues that negative events can be turned around and become positive image forces by organizing festivals and events to commemorate the event. He cites the example of Johnstown, Pennsylvania's 1890 year-long celebration of a devastating flood which occurred in 1989. This form of image reversal should be reserved for natural disasters as celebrating human disasters (e.g., Tianamen Square) would not have the same effect.

It is possible that the effect of negative autonomous change agents, although significant in the short term, may not be an important factor in long term image change. Thurstone (1967) contends that in the absence of any reinforcing information, images may revert back to those held before the exogenous shock. Ritchie and Smith (1991) studied awareness retention levels from a positive autonomous change agent, the 1988 Winter Olympic Games in Calgary, which received substantial media exposure in North America and Europe. They found awareness decay for Calgary to be substantial, occurring only a short period of time after the autonomous image formation agent was no longer present.

Popular culture also portrays images of people and places. Feature length movies are one example. Increased travel to Australia occurred shortly after the release and subsequent box office success of *Crocodile Dundee*. As previously mentioned, the film's male star became a tourism spokesperson for the country. Popular culture in the form of non-news television programming (e.g. documentaries, sitcoms) often plays an important image formation role. For example, the Pacific Travel News (1984) reported that Americans' image of Korea was primarily based on the popular television program "M.A.S.H." depicting a Korea of over 30 years ago.

News and Popular culture forms of Autonomous image formation, because of their high credibility and market penetration, may be the only image formation agents capable of changing an area's image dramatically in a short period of time. One of the reasons for this may be the massive amounts of information people are exposed to in a relatively brief period. News does not age well and significant events receive major exposure as they are happening. For example, people may have acquired some cognitive image of the People's Republic of China through years of exposure to induced, organic and autonomous agents but when news reports of the Tiananmen Square conflict were carried daily on American television stations the amount of information received in such a short time could easily have overwhelmed old images.

Unsolicited Organic

Unrequested information received from individuals who have been to an area, or believe they know what exists there, constitute the Unsolicited Organic image formation agents. Information about various destinations is received by almost everyone on a regular basis. Dinner with friends, discussions during business meetings, or anywhere the topic of conversation focuses on a specific place results in Unsolicited Organic image formation. If the person receiving the information has not requested it, information retention is low. Credibility levels depend on the source providing the information but generally they will be higher than for the Overt Induced I forms of image formation. Countering higher credibility is low market penetration as individual communication is less pervasive than mass media.

If the person receiving the information has not developed a destination image based on previous exposure to Induced or Autonomous image formation agents, Unsolicited Organic information may become an important image formation source. Costs to the destination area of Unsolicited Organic image formation are indirect. If the person providing the information has been to the area and their report is unfavorable then it may have an impact on the travel plans of the person receiving the information. Lost sales in the destination as a result of an unfavorable image being projected through others constitutes an indirect cost.

Solicited Organic

When a destination is part of the consideration set an active information search may include requests, from knowledgeable sources, about what exists at the destination. What sets Solicited Organic apart from Overt Induced II sources is that the individual or group providing the information has no vested interest in the outcome of the decision. Friends or relatives usually constitute the Solicited Organic Image information agents. This stage of image information is also termed "word-of-mouth" advertising. Studies by Harris and McLaughin (1988), Paradice (1985) and Jenkins (1978) support the importance of "word-of-mouth" information as one of the most relied upon sources of information for destination selection. Sources selected to provide specific destination information have high credibility making Solicited Organic image formation agents an extremely important part of the destination selection process.

The number of people requested to provide specific destination information is very low as eventually additional sources provide no new information. A point is reached where any additional information only serves to reinforce information already acquired. Stutman and Newell (1984) refer to this as acquiring salient beliefs. When the point of substantial reinforcement of previously stated beliefs is reached, the information seeker will stop the search process and assess acquired beliefs against their own beliefs and motivations. Although there is no direct cost to destination area promoters for Solicited Organic image formation the experience provided through destination visitation is of critical importance in forming positive salient beliefs about travel to the area. The types of people who are requested to provide Solicited Organic image information are those who share common social class or family life cycle characteristics with the requestor (Engel, Kollat, and Blackwell, 1973; Thoreli, 1971) reinforcing the need to adequately identify a target market for the types of touristic products offered at the destination.

Organic

The final end of the image formation continuum is termed Organic and consists of information acquired about a destination based on previous travel to the area. Examples of image changes resulting from visitation are found in studies conducted by Gyte (1988), Khan (1991), and Phelps (1986). The Organic image formation has the highest credibility as it is based on personal experience. People holding organic images from prior travel to an area feed back into the image formation cycle as providers of Unsolicited Organic or Solicited Organic information.

CHARACTERISTICS OF DESTINATION IMAGE

1. The larger the entity the more slowly images change. The speed of change is inversely related to the complexity of the system. A tourism image is made up of many different parts including the natural resource base on which activities often take place, the socio-cultural system that governs the provision and type of touristic services and the built environment that serves the needs of tourists and may also provide some of the attractions.

Boulding (1956) suggests that information affecting held images can cause three effects. In the first instance information is received that does not conform to held beliefs which results in a state of cognitive dissonance. The individual will attempt to avoid incoming information thereby reducing the dissonance. If enough information is avoided the image remains essentially the same. In the second instance the information keeps coming and can not be avoided thus resulting in a gradual image change. In the third instance enough new information is received which results in a general reassessment of the image previously held and leads to an entirely new image. The key element then in image change is the amount and extent of new information which contrasts with the image currently held. Autonomous image change agents, if constant and prolonged, will eventually be unavoidable causing a shift in image. However, as Gartner and Shen (1992) have shown, not all aspects of touristic image will be affected similarly. Induced image change agents can also overwhelm people with new formation but due to their low credibility and relatively easy avoidance image change will be slower.

Gartner and Hunt (1983) studied the change in Utah's image occurring over a twelve year period. There was evidence linking increased visitation to an improved state image although the image of the region in which Utah was located had also improved leading to the conclusion that an improvement in a larger entity, the region, had benefitted all states in the region. Further evidence of the relatively long time factor involved in changing touristic images can be found in Crompton (1979b), and Cumings (1983).

2. Induced image formation attempts must be focused and long term. As a result of the time it takes to change touristic image any induced image formation programs must be focused on specific destination images and budgeted for long term exposure. If destination promoters have scarce financial resources, or resources fluctuate on an annual basis, they would be better off concentrating their efforts on improving their product (e.g., ensuring quality services) and utilizing organic formation agents to promote their product. Images tend to have stability (Crompton and Lamb, 1986) and as discussed above, in the absence of any major autonomous impacts will take years to shift. Therefore consistency is a requirement for long term image change using induced formation agents.

According to Uzzell (1984: 81) "Advertising is . . . informing people of the existence of a consumer product or service, favorably disposing them toward it and changing their opinions, attitudes and behavior so that they will want to consume that product or service." Because people resist accepting information that differs from that previously held, any induced image change must be based on a long term strategy intended to overload the individual or decision making body with information that overturns any previously held images and consequently refocus attitude evaluation on a perceptually different product.

Consistency should not be confused with repetition of the same message. Exposure to the same advertisement can result in a diminishing marginal rate of effectiveness (Schumann et al., 1990; Cacioppo and Petty, 1979; and Appel, 1971). Six exposures to the same commercial may be the point at which diminishing returns occur (Grass and Wallace, 1969). Maintaining consistency requires the selection of an appropriate image mix using different image formation agents.

3. The smaller the entity in relation to the whole the less of a chance to develop an independent image. This conclusion has its exceptions and generally they relate to distance from market and strength of brand image. Hunt (1971) found that distance from one's permanent residence to a destination was a factor in the image held of that destination. Crompton's (1979b) study on images of Mexico supports Hunt's conclusions. Khan (1991) studied the image of Wisconsin's tourism regions and compared those images to the prevailing state image. His findings lend support to the argument that brand image, in this case the image of the state of Wisconsin, can overpower images of smaller entities within the state.

A brand as defined by Okoroafo (1989) is a name, design, symbol, or a combination of these used to identify a service or product. Slogans such as "I Love New York," "Discover Iowa Treasures," or "Say Yes to Michigan" all create a point of reference and develop a perception based on the images evoked from these brand identification statements. Brand Identification does not rule out the creation of a strong independent image at the community level but that image will be stronger in localized areas and less distinct the more one is removed from the destination community. Communities in a region can use this tendency to their advantage however as they can "piggy back" on a strong state image in their advertising and promotion programs.

As mentioned, there are exceptions. It is possible for a smaller entity to have such a strong image that it overpowers the larger entity's brand image. For example if the results of the U.S. Travel Service (1977) study on foreigners' perceptions of the United States were extended it would not be unlikely to find that images of certain states were related more to the images held of large cities. In this case cities receiving media exposure would form the brand image against which the state's image is compared.

4. Effective image change depends on an assessment of presently held tourism images. Changing an area's image requires knowledge of its current projected image(s) and initiating efforts to move that image(s) in a new direction. Image change efforts are essentially wasted if baseline data establishing the present image position is not known. Understanding images held by target markets is necessary to avoid establishing a new image which moves the destination into a position currently held by an able and strong competitor. Numerous techniques have been used for establishing baseline images including correspondence analysis (Calantone, R. et al., 1989), free elicitation of descriptive adjectives (Reilly, 1990), factor analysis (Fakeye and Crompton, 1991) multidimensional scaling (Gartner, 1989; Goodrich, 1978) and repertory grid mapping (Gyte, 1988).

IMAGE MIX

The selection of the right image formation agents to build a desired touristic image depends on many factors. The first, obviously, is the amount of money budgeted for image development. Many small communities are unable to use expensive Induced formation agents. Focusing on quality service, unique attraction packages, and using lower cost image formation agents may be the wisest choice for cash poor rural communities.

A second concern is the characteristics of the target market. If the decision making body is comprised of a family unit, induced image formation agents may be a top priority. Gitelson and Crompton (1983) found family groups were most likely to use media sources for information acquisition. They also found that college educated individuals were more likely to use specific destination literature (DSTL).

Third, demographic characteristics should be considered. Capella and Greco (1987) found that people over 60 years of age were more inclined to rely on Solicited Organic image information agents as this group's destination selection was greatly influenced by families and friends. Some print media (i.e., magazines and newspapers) were also important information sources for this group. Within the Organic end of the spectrum, college students relied more on information received from peers than from family members (Raitz and Dakhil, 1989). Age has also found to be a factor in determining credibility ratings of various companies (Weaver and McCleary, 1984) and further investigation may show a relationship between age and different types of image formation agents.

Fourth, timing is critical. Van Raaij and Francken, (1984) found Overt Induced I sources of image formation (i.e., advertising) to be important information sources early in the decision process. Overt Induced II (e.g., tour operators) sources enter into the information search process at a later stage. Throughout the information acquisition period Solicited Organic sources were used at the same rate. However, the longer the planning horizon the more likely a multitude of sources will be used (Nolan, 1976).

Fifth, the type of image(s) projected needs to be addressed. If a strong brand image already exists, less money and effort will be required to develop a local area image which is consistent with the dominant brand image. On the other hand, if a strong unique image, independent or counter to prevailing brand image is to be projected all image formation agents should be considered as important contributors. The amount of money required for a small entity to establish an image different from the prevailing brand image requires large numbers of tourists be hosted to justify the expense and time involved in forming an unique image. Consequently mass tourism markets will have to be developed. Small scale tourism developments, using alternative forms of tourism, should avoid widespread use of induced formation agents and rely primarily on the organic types to develop their touristic image. In this way, the type of images formed will be consistent with the type of experience offered.

Finally, the product itself determines the type of image formation agents that are most useful. Country, state or regional image formation benefits more from the induced agents than for specific products (e.g., resorts) which need the more organically based agents to succeed. Nolan (1976) found resort patrons were more likely to consult friends or relatives when making a vacation selection than those traveling simply to a state who relied more heavily on state produced promotional literature.

A brief summary of the different types of image formation agents discussed in this paper compared against credibility, market penetration and cost is displayed in Figure 2. Comparisons reflect the author's interpretations based on literature reviewed in this paper and other sources not cited herein.

CONCLUSION

The image formation process is intricately entwined with the destination selection process. At all stages in the selection process, touristic images help determine which destinations remain for further evaluation and which are eliminated from further consideration. Understanding how touristic images are formed can assist destination promoters in developing appropriate destination images for selected target markets. The various image formation agents all have their advantages and disadvantages which can be summarized into the categories of cost, market penetration and credibility. Given certain constraints (e.g., time, money) destination promoters can select the right mix of image formation agents to maximize their scarce resources. As competition increases and more destinations promote their touristic attributes, touristic image, as a selection factor, will become increasingly important. Destination promoters without an image formation strategy will find it increasingly difficult to maintain, increase, or develop their unique share of the tourism market.

As with any other type of research more investigation is needed to develop guidelines for assessing image change and selecting an appropriate image formation mix for a particular destination. Most tourism image research has been piecemeal without a theoretical basis for support. Although most tourism marketing experts accept the importance of touristic image in the destination selection process, little effort has been undertaken to develop a holistic understanding of the entire image formation process. This paper is an intermediate attempt to accomplish that objective, but much work still needs to be completed before all aspects of tourism image formation are understood and appropriately applied.

FIGURE 2. Image Formation			
Image Change Agent	Credibility	Market Penetration	Destination Cost
Overt Included I			
Traditional forms of Advertising (e.g., Brochures, T.V., Radio, Print, Billboards, etc.)	Low	High	High
Overt Included II			
Information received from tour operators, wholesalers	Medium	Medium	Indirect
Covert Included I			
Second party endorsement of products via traditional forms of advertising	Low/Medium	High	High
Covert Included II			
Second Party Endorsement through apparently unbiased reports (e.g., Newspaper, Travel Section articles)	Medium	Medium	Medium
Autonomous			
News and Popular culture: documentaries, reports news stories, movies, television programs	High	Medium/High	Indirect
Unsolicited Organic			
Unsolicited information received from friends and relatives	Medium	Low	Indirect
Solicited Organic			
Solicited information received from friends and relatives	High	Low	Indirect
Organic			
Actual Visitation	High	- - -	Indirect

REFERENCES

Ahmed, Z. (1991). "Marketing Your Community: Connecting a Negative Image." *Cornell H.R.A. Quarterly*, February:24-27.

Appel, V. (1971). "On Advertising Wearout." *Journal of Advertising Research* 11(February):11-13.

Assael, H. (1984). Consumer Behavior and Marketing Action. Boston, MA: Kent Publishing.

Atkin, C., and Block, M. (1983). "Effectiveness of Celebrity Endorsers." *Journal of Advertising Research* 23(Feb/March):57-61.

Bitner, J., and Booms, H. (1982). "Trends in Travel and Tourism Marketing: The Changing Structure of Distribution Channels." *Journal of Travel Research* 20(4):39-44.

Boulding, K. (1956). *The Image-Knowledge in Life and Society*. The University of Michigan Press, Ann Arbor: Michigan.

Britton, R. (1979). "The Image of the Third World in Tourism Marketing." *Annals of Tourism Research* 6(3):331-358.

Britton, S. (1982). "Political Economy of Third World Tourism." *Annals of Tourism Research* 9(3):331-358.

Byerly, C. (1985). "Media and Sexism: An Instruction Manual for Secondary School Teachers." Washington Office of the State Superintendent of Public Instruction, Olympia, Washington.

Cacioppo, J., and Petty, R. (1979). "The Effects of Message Repetition and Position on Cognitive Response, Recall and Persuasion." *Journal of Personality and Social Psychology* 37(1): 97-109.

Calantone, R., Di Benedetto, C., Hakam, A., and Bojanic, D. (1989). "Multiple Multinational Tourism Positioning Using Correspondence Analysis." *Journal of Travel Research* 28(2):25-32.

Capella. L., and Greco, G. (1987). "Information Sources of Elderly for Vacation Decisions." *Annals of Tourism Research* 14(1):148-151.

Crompton, J. (1979a). "Motivations for Pleasure Vacation." *Annals of Tourism Research* 6(4):408-424.

Crompton, J. (1979b). "An Assessment of the Image of Mexico as a Vacation Destination and the Influence of Geographical Location upon That Image." *Journal of Travel Research* 17(4):18-24.

Crompton, J., and Lamb, C. (1986). *Marketing Government and Social Services*. New York: John Wiley & Sons.

Cumings, B. (1983). "Korean American Relations: A Century of Contact and Thirty-five Years of Intimacy." In W.J. Cohen (ed) *New Frontiers in American East Asian Relations*. New York:Columbia University Press.

Dann, G. (1977). "Anomie, Ego-enhancement and Tourism." *Annals of Tourism Research* 4(4):184-194.

Doobie, L. (1976). Interpreters and Co-ordinators of Tourism Demand." I.T.A. Bulletin No.3 from C. Jenkins (1982).

Engel, J., Kollat, D., and Blackwell, R. (1973). *Consumer Behavior*. New York: Holt, Rinehart and Winston.

Etzel, M., and Wahlers, R. (1985). "The Use of Requested Promotional Material by Pleasure Travelers." *Journal of Travel Research* 23(4):2-6.

Fakeye, P., and Crompton, J. (1991). "Image Differences Between Prospective First-Time, and Repeat Visitors to the Lower Rio Grande Valley." *Journal of Travel Research* 30(2):10-16.

Farrant, A. (1989). "Local Testimonials Increase Advertising Effectiveness." *Air Conditioning, Heating and Refrigeration News* 176(January):12.

Friedman, H., and Friedman L. (1979). "Endorser Effectiveness by Product Type." *Journal of Advertising Research* 19(Oct/Nov):63-71.

Gartner, W., and Shen, J. (1992). "The Impact of Tiananmen Square on China's Tourism Image." *Journal of Travel Research* 30(4):47-52.

Gartner, W., and Hunt, J. (1983). "An Analysis of State Image Change Over a Twelve Year Period (1971-1983)." *Journal of Travel Research* 26(2):15-19.

Gartner, W. (1989). "Tourism Image: Attribute Measurement of State Tourism Products Using Multidimensional Scaling Techniques." *Journal of Travel Research* 28(2):16-20.

Gilbert, D., and Houghton, P. (1991). "An Exploratory Investigation of Format, Design, and Use of U.K. Tour Operators' Brochures." *Journal of Travel Research* 30(2):20-25.

Gitelson, R., and Crompton, J. (1983). "The Planning Horizons and Sources of Information Used by Pleasure Vacationers." *Journal of Travel Research* 21(3):2-7.

Goodall, B. (1991). "Understanding Holiday Choice." In *Progress in Tourism, Recreation and Hospitality Management* edited by C. Cooper. Belhaven Press: London, pp 58-77.

Goodall, B., Radburn, M., and Stabler, M. (1988). "Market Opportunity Sets for Tourism." Geographical Paper No. 100, Department of Geography, Reading, from Goodall 1991.

Goodrich, J. (1978). "A New Approach to Image Analysis Through Multi-Dimensional Scaling." *Journal of Travel Research* 16: 10-13.

Grinstein, A. (1955). "Vacations: A Psycho-Analytic Study." *International Journal of Psycho-Analysis* 36(3):177-185.

Gunn, C. (1972). *Vacationscape: Designing Tourist Regions.* Austin: Bureau of Business Research, University of Texas.

Grass, R., and Wallace, W. (1969). "Satiation Effects of Television Commercials." *Journal of Advertising Research* 9(September):3-8.

Gyte, D. (1988). "Tourist Cognition of Destination: An Exploration of Techniques of Measurement and Representation of Images of Tunisia." Department of Geography, Trent Polytechnic: Nottingham.

Harris, C., and Mclaughlin, W. (1988). "The 1987 Idaho Leisure Travel and Recreation Survey." *Tourism Research: Expanding Boundaries* in Proceedings of the 19th Annual Travel and Tourism Research Association Conference, Montreal, Canada, June 19-23, pp 131-138.

Howard, J., and Sheth, J. (1969). *Theory of Buyer Behavior.* John Wiley & Sons: New York.

Hunt, J. (1971). *Image–A factor in Tourism*. Doctoral Dissertation, Colorado State University, Fort Collins: Colorado.

IUOTO, International Union of Official Travel Organizations. (1976). *The Impact of International Tourism on the Economic Development of the Developing Countries*. World Tourism Organization: Geneva (from S. Britton, 1982).

Jenkins, R. (1978). "Family Decision Making." *Journal of Travel Research* 16(4):2-7.

Jenkins, C. (1982). "The Effects of Scale in Tourism Projects." *Annals of Tourism Research* 9(2):229-249.

Jenkins, C. and Henry, B. (1982). "Government Involvement in Tourism in Developing Countries." *Annals of Tourism Research* 15(4):21-25.

Kamins, M., Brand, M., Hoeke, S., and Moe, J. (1989). "Two-Sided Versus One-Sided Celebrity Endorsements: The Impact of Advertising Effectiveness and Credibility." *Journal of Advertising* 18(2):4-10.

Kent, W., and Chesnutt, J. (1991). "Underground Atlanta: Resurrected and Revisited." *Journal of Travel Research* 29(4): 36-39.

Khan, S. (1991). *Nonresidents Perceptions of Wisconsin's Tourism Regions*. Unpublished M.S. Thesis, University of Wisconsin-Stout, Menomonie, Wisconsin, 1991.

Kotler, P. (1982). *Marketing for Nonprofit Organizations*. Prentice Hall: Englewood Cliffs, New Jersey.

Lapage, W., and Cormier, P. (1977). "Images of Camping: Barriers to Participation?" *Journal of Travel Research* 15(4):21-25.

Lukeman, G. (1991). "Analysis Shows New Way to Think About TV Recall Scores." *Marketing News* 25(April):24.

Mandese, J. (1991). "Exec Views on Media Clash with Plans." *Advertising Age* 62(August):13.

Mathieson, A., and Wall, G. (1982). *Tourism: Economic, Physical and Social Impacts*. Longman Scientific and Technical: New York.

Mazanec, J. and Schweiger, G. (1981). "Improved Marketing Efficiency Through Multi-Product Brand Names. An Empirical Investigation of Image Transfer." *European Research* 9(1):32-44.

McLellan, R., and Noe, F. (1983). "Source of Information and Types of Messages Useful to International Tour Operators." *Journal of Travel Research* 8(3):27-30.

McLellan, R., and Foushee, K. (1983). "Negative Images of the United States as Expressed by Tour Operators from Other Countries." *Journal of Travel Research* 2(2):2-5.

Milo, K., and Yoder, S. (1991). "Recovery from Natural Disaster: Travel Writers and Tourist Destinations." *Journal of Travel Research* 30(1):36-39.

Moutinho, L. (1987). "Consumer Behavior in Tourism." *European Journal of Marketing* 21(10):3-44.

Murphy, P. (1983). "Perception of Attitudes of Decision Making Groups in Tourist Centers" in *The Image of Destination Regions*. Edited by M. Stabler. Croom Helm, Inc.: New York, pp. 133-160.

Nolan, S. (1976). "Tourists' Use and Evaluation of Travel Information Sources: Summary and Conclusions." *Journal of Travel Research* 14:6-8.

Okorofa, S. (1989). "Branding in Tourism." In *Tourism Marketing and Management Handbook.* Edited by S. Witt. Prentice Hall: New York, pp. 23-26.

Pacific Travel News (1984). "Evaluating Korea." February:38-40.

Paradice, W. (1985). "Recreation Information Dissemination and the Visitor Choice Process in Australian Natural Environments." Tourism Recreation Research 10(2): 19-27.

Phelps, A. (1986). "Holiday Destination Image: The Problem of Assessment: An Example Developed in Menorca." *Tourism Management* 7(3):168-180.

Raitz, K. and Dakhil, M. (1989). "A Note About Information Sources for Preferred Recreational Environments." *Journal of Travel Research* 27(4):45-48.

Reilly, M. (1990). "Free Elicitation of Descriptive Adjectives for Tourism Image Assessment." *Journal of Travel Research* 28(4):21-26.

Ritchie, B., and Smith, B. (1991). "The Impact of a Mega-Event on Host Region Awareness: A Longitudinal Study." *Journal of Travel Research* 30(1):3-10.

Roehl, W. (1990). "Travel Agent Attitudes Toward China After Tiananmen Square." *Journal of Travel Research* 29(2):16-22.

Schmoll, G. (1977). *Tourism Promotion.* Tourism International Press: London.

Schumann, D., Petty, R., and Clemons, S. (1990). "Predicting the Effectiveness of Different Strategies of Advertising Variation: A Test of the Repetition-Variation Hypotheses." *Journal of Consumer Research* 17 (September): 192-202.

Scott, W. (1965). "Psychological and Social Correlates of International Images," in *International Behavior: A Social-Psychological Analysis*, edited by H.C. Kelman. Holt, Rinehart and Winston: New York.

Stankey, G., and Schreyer, R. (1985). "Attitudes Toward Wilderness and Factors Affecting Visitor Behavior: A State-of-Knowledge Review." In *Proceedings of the National Wilderness Research Conference: Issues, State-of-Knowledge, Future Directions*, compiled by R. Lucas. Intermountain Research Station: Ogden, Utah, pp 246-293.

Stutman, R., and Newell, S. (1984). "Beliefs versus Values: Salient Beliefs in Designing Persuasive Messages." *The Western Journal of Speech Communication* 48(Fall):362-372.

Thompson, J.. and Cooper, P. (1979). "Attitudinal Evidence on the Limited Size of Evoked Set of Travel Destinations." *Journal of Travel Research* 17(3):23-25.

Thoreli, H. (1971). "Concentration of Information Power Among Consumers." *Journal of Marketing Research* 8: 427-432.

Thurstone, L. (1967). "The Measurement of Social Attitudes." Chapter 2 in *Readings in Attitude Theory and Measurement* edited by Martin Fishbein, New York: John Wiley & Sons, Inc.

Um, S., and Crompton, J. (1987). "A Cognitive Model of Pleasure Travel Destination Choice." Department of Recreation and Parks, Texas A&M University, Texas.

United States Travel Service (1977). *International Travel Market Reviews of*

Selected Major Tourism Generating Countries. U.S. Department of Commerce, Washington D.C.

Uzzell, D. (1984). "An Alternative Structuralist Approach to the Psychology of Tourism Marketing." *Annals of Tourism Research* 11(1):79-99.

Van Raaij, W., and Francken, D. (1984). "Vacation Decisions, Activities and Satisfactions." *Annals of Tourism Research* 11(1):101-112.

Weaver, P., and McCleary, K. (1984). "A Market Segmentation Study to Determine the Appropriate Ad/Model Format for Travel Advertising." *Journal of Travel Research* 23(1):12-16.

Woodside, A., and Sherrell, D. (1977). "Traveller Evoked, Inept and Inert Sets of Vacation Destinations." *Journal of Travel Research* 6(1):14-18.

Collaborative Alliances: New Interorganizational Forms in Tourism

Steven Selin

SUMMARY. Interest in collaborative alliances as a management strategy and as an object of scientific inquiry is on the rise in the tourism field. Rapid economic, social, and political change is providing powerful incentives for tourism interests to recognize their interdependences and to engage in joint decision-making. Whether the issue is multi-national firms, tourism coalitions, or cooperative marketing strategies–collaboration is the common ground linking these recent trends. This paper provides a framework for understanding this trend toward collaborative action. Constraints to collaboration are identified as well as societal forces prompting collaborative responses from tourism stakeholders. Basic assumptions underlying scientific inquiry in this area are outlined and a theoretical process model of collaboration is presented. Implications for management strategy and research are discussed.

INTRODUCTION

There is a quiet revolution changing the face of the tourism industry. On an international scale and locally, tourism planners and operators are dis-

Dr. Steven Selin is Assistant Professor, Division of Forestry, West Virginia University, Morgantown, WV 26506-6125.

[Haworth co-indexing entry note]: "Collaborative Alliances: New Interorganizational Forms in Tourism." Selin, Steven. Co-published simultaneously in *Journal of Travel & Tourism Marketing* (The Haworth Press, Inc.) Vol. 2, No. 2/3, 1993, pp. 217-227; and: *Communication and Channel Systems in Tourism Marketing* (ed: Muzaffer Uysal, and Daniel R. Fesenmaier) The Haworth Press, Inc., 1993, pp. 217-227. Multiple copies of this article/chapter may be purchased from The Haworth Document Delivery Center [1-800-3-HAWORTH; 9:00 a.m. - 5:00 p.m. (EST)].

covering the power of collaborative action. Whether the issue is multi-national firms, tourism coalitions, or cooperative marketing strategies, collaboration is the common ground linking these new initiatives. This recent trend is underlined by the "tourism partnership" theme selected for the 1992 Travel and Tourism Research Association conference (Travel and Tourism Research Association, 1992). Traditional communication systems are being revised as tourism professionals adjust to the rapid and turbulent change of the 1990s. Economic and political trends are providing powerful incentives for tourism interests to recognize their interdependencies and to engage in joint decision-making.

This paper will provide a framework for understanding this trend toward collaborative action. Structural and situational constraints to collaboration are identified as well as those political and economic forces providing powerful incentives to forge collective responses to tourism industry challenges. Next, recent advances in collaboration theory drawn from the management sciences provide insight into collaborative processes occurring in the tourism field. Theoretical propositions are illustrated with examples from the tourism field. Implications for future research and management action are discussed.

CONSTRAINTS TO COLLABORATION

A number of tourism scholars have developed conceptual models describing the fully-functioning tourism system (Gunn, 1988; Mill and Morrison, 1985; Murphy, 1985). While there are minor differences between them, these models generally describe components of the supply-side of tourism such as: Attractions, services, transportation, and promotional entities as well as the demand-side representing the tourist. These tourism models generally describe an ideal system characterized by close communication between each of the components. As these authors point out, in reality, communication systems have always been underdeveloped in the tourism industry. A number of structural and situational factors constrain effective collaboration between tourism suppliers and planners. Table 1 illustrates some of these constraints.

Tourists purchase a wide array of goods and services during the planning, travel to and from, and destination phases of their trips. This fact makes it difficult for any individual tourism business to capture a controlling share of the market. This has led to geographic and organizational fragmentation within the tourism industry and contributes to a lack of communication between these fragmented tourism sectors. Fragmentation

TABLE 1. Factors Constraining Effective Tourism Communication

---

- Geographic and Organizational Fragmentation
- Long Chain of Distribution Systems
- Jurisdictional Boundaries
- Ideological Differences
- Centralized Government Decision-Making
- Competitive Rhetoric
- Pay for Representation Systems
- Emphasis on One-Way Communications

---

also makes it difficult to communicate travel packages to prospective tourists, requiring complex distribution systems.

Many public agencies have policies and staff functions which either directly or indirectly affect tourism development. Federal, state, and city departments of forestry, parks, highways, wildlife, and planning all have functions which affect tourism development (Gunn, 1988). Often, these agencies view their roles narrowly–building highways, growing trees, or managing healthy game populations–and do not recognize or appreciate how its agency decisions impact tourism. These jurisdictional constraints often hamper integrated tourism planning and collaboration. In addition, ideological differences between these agencies often lead to polarized views and antagonism rather than collaboration.

Many of these same agencies have historically used a comprehensive-rational model of decision-making with its emphasis on centralized planning (Schatz, McAvoy, and Lime, 1991). This approach to planning has constrained communication by limiting public participation to a minor role in agency decisions. Collaboration is also underdeveloped in the tourism field because of competition between tourism interests. Combat analogies are used by federal, state, and city tourism departments to justify increased expenditures on tourism promotion. Nations, states, and cities are at "war" with adjacent entities over a controlling slice of the tourism pie. These competitive pressures often constrain opportunities for regional cooperation in tourism marketing.

Another factor limiting communication is the "pay for representation" system characteristic of tourism marketing at the city and regional level. Typically, tourism businesses purchase memberships in a Chamber of Commerce or regional association entitling them to participate in regional tourism marketing decisions. Rarely do community or regional tourism planning groups benevolently look out for the interests of all tourism operators in their region.

ANTECEDENTS TO COLLABORATION

Anecdotal and case study evidence richly document the emerging trend towards collaborative action in the tourism field. This increased interest in collaborative relationships has not occurred by chance. A host of societal forces are providing powerful incentives for tourism interests to form collective responses to industry challenges. These societal forces and collaborative responses are summarized in Table 2.

It is increasingly difficult for individual tourism organizations to make decisions unilaterally without taking other tourism interests into account. The fast pace of social, economic and technical change has placed intense pressure on tourism businesses to adapt product offerings quickly to meet the needs of sophisticated consumers. Increased competitive pressures

TABLE 2. Emerging Collaborative Systems in Tourism (Adopted from Gray, 1988)

Rapid Economic and Technological Changes

- Cooperative Marketing Strategies (Witt & Moutinho, 1989)
- Industry-University Partnerships (Smith, Hetherington, & Brumbaugh, 1986)

Global Interdependence

- Multi-National Firms (Buckley & Witt, 1990)
- International Trade and Professional Consortia (Smith, 1991)

Blurred Boundaries Between Government and Business

- Public-Private Partnerships (Murphy, 1985)
- Intergovernmental Collaboration (Teye, 1988)
- Tourism Coalitions; Working Groups; Associations (Miller, 1987)

Crisis Situations

- Image Enhancement Initiatives (Milo & Yoder, 1991)
- Infrastructure Redevelopment Projects

---

have prompted collaboration between tourism interests trying to gain access to new technologies or spread the cost of marketing innovation over several parties.

Cooperative marketing has become widespread in the tourism industry. In cooperative marketing relationships, tourism interests share the cost of some marketing task–typically, product development, promotions, research, or pricing. Industry-university partnerships are growing in importance as training programs expand and tourism centers provide research services and technical assistance to the tourism industry.

Tourism has indeed become a global industry. New communication and transportation technologies have effectively reduced the size of the world. Competition for the international travel market has increased markedly over the past decade. The recent expansion of major airlines into overseas markets illustrates this globalization of the tourism industry. New patterns of relationships have emerged between nations as they discover their economic and political interdependence.

The number of multi-national tourism companies has grown dramatically in the past decade. Developing nations are aggressively promoting joint ventures with international hotel chains which match local labor with Western capital and management skill. Hilton International has vigorously expanded their operations in developing and developed nations. International trade and professional consortia have also fostered collaboration between tourism interests. Organizations like the World Tourism Organization (WTO) play an important role in standardizing international tourism statistics and terminology. The recent New Horizons Conference held in Calgary was convened to expressly develop linkages between tourism stakeholders internationally (Smith, 1991).

Collaboration in the tourism industry has also been stimulated by the blurring of boundaries between government and business. Osborne and Gaebler (1992) describe how fiscal constraints and public pressure for accountability have forced government agencies to adopt an entrepreneurial approach to service delivery. Public agencies are increasingly playing a catalyst or empowering role in community, state, and federal affairs. Cost-sharing has become the call of the 1990s. This change in philosophy has resulted in new relationships between public and private sector agencies interested in tourism.

Public-private sector partnerships have been formed by tourism departments seeking to stretch resource allocations. In Arkansas, the Partners in Tourism program has been successful in obtaining corporate support for promotional campaigns and the annual Governor's Conference on Tourism. Intergovernmental collaboration has increased as well. Tourism coalitions have been formed in a number of states to increase recreation opportunities and provide improved informational services to tourists. In Utah, representatives from several federal land management agencies and the Utah Travel Commission have established a scenic byway coordinating committee. The committee has established an extensive scenic byway system and is presently developing interpretive facilities along each byway (Stalder, personal communication, April 21, 1992).

Crisis will continue to act as a catalyst for collaborative action in the tourism field. Natural disasters, political unrest, and recession can profoundly upset the delicate balance in tourist trade. The recent San Francisco earthquake prompted an aggressive inter-agency effort to repair structural damage and allay prospective tourists' fears regarding future catastrophe (Milo and Yoder, 1991).

COLLABORATION THEORY

The previous discussion provides a descriptive account of the rise of collaborative alliances in tourism settings. Concurrently, there is rising scholarly interest in moving beyond pragmatic descriptions of collaboration to a deeper theoretical understanding of issues related to forming and maintaining collaborative alliances. Several recent journal issues and conferences have been devoted to this theme (Gunn, 1990; Reid, 1987).

Collaboration has been the subject of scholarly inquiry for several years in the sociological and management science disciplines. Recent conceptual advances can provide a signpost to tourism scholars interested in examining collaboration. The following discussion outlines several underlying assumptions of this research and presents a conceptual model of collaboration in a tourism context.

Assumptions

Several key assumptions provide a conceptual framework for understanding collaborative processes within the tourism field. First, it is assumed that tourism organizations operate in a "turbulent environment" (Trist, 1977). In other words, there are many external social, economic, and political events to name a few which influence the tourism industry. The Persian Gulf War has illustrated how fears of terrorism can dramatically diminish the public's demand for overseas travel. However, it is also assumed that tourism organizations have the ability to influence their environment through strategic planning.

joins them (Gray, 1985). It is important at this stage that a consensus is reached about who has a legitimate stake in the issue and just what the joint issue is. Schatz, McAvoy, and Lime (1991) provide an example of problem-setting in their description of collaboration between the United States Forest Service and regional outfitters adjacent to the Boundary Waters Canoe Area in northern Minnesota. Conflict over restrictive policies led to a series of workshops where outfitters and Forest Service officials worked to identify issues of mutual concern. Once workshop participants agreed on mutual problems they could proceed to the next stage of collaboration.

Direction-Setting

During the direction-setting phase of collaboration, stakeholders share interpretations about the future of the domain and begin to identify and appreciate a sense of common purpose (McCann, 1983). From the previous example, once Forest Service officials and local outfitters agreed on issues of mutual concern, they proceeded to identify and prioritize future collaborative actions which all participants subscribed to.

Structuring

For collaboration to persist over time, there is a need to manage stakeholder interactions in an increasingly systematic manner (Gray, 1985). Structuring refers here to the process of institutionalizing the shared meanings that emerge as the domain develops. Murphy (1983) described a structuring process that occurred in the city of Victoria, Canada. Over 40 delegates from various tourism sectors were convened by the Chamber of Commerce to initiate community-wide tourism planning. After several workshops to identify common concerns and long-term goals, it was decided to form a single umbrella organization to coordinate the tourism industry in Greater Victoria. Through this institutionalizing process, participants attempt to achieve a "negotiated order" (Day and Day, 1977) so that interactions among organizations can be better managed.

While collaboration may progress through this natural order, there are many internal and external forces that can interrupt or enhance this natural cycle. We are primarily interested in identifying those conditions that either facilitate or constrain the development of collaborative domains within the tourism field.

CONCLUSIONS

Case study and anecdotal evidence suggest societal forces are providing powerful incentives for collaboration between tourism organizations to achieve mutually beneficial goals. The tourism field is experiencing unprecedented institution-building at the interorganizational level. A recent conference held in Canada focused specifically on interorganizational collaboration in achieving sustainable or "green" tourism goals (Tourism Management Colloquium, 1991). Planners observe an integration of tourism development, planning, and marketing activities (Gunn, 1988). While tourism scholars often advocate integrated collaborative planning, this revolution is being driven by the rapid economic, social, and political change of the 1990s. Tourism practitioners are collaborating out of self-interest aside from any altruistic concern for their competition.

Tourism practitioners will need new skills to recognize when to compete and when to collaborate. Many tourism managers are more comfortable making decisions within the hierarchical structure of one organization. Managers must also be able to make lateral decisions to sustain effective collaboration. The previous discussion has focused heavily on collaboration between tourism suppliers. Collaboration is also needed between tourism suppliers and prospective tourists to adjust marketing mixes to changing customer needs. Schrage (1992) describes how industrial designers are building "rapid prototypes" with clients instead of for them. This type of customer collaboration could easily be adapted to design new tourism products.

Basic and applied research is needed to better understand collaborative processes in the tourism field. Collaboration theory and methods can be borrowed from the management sciences (Selin and Beason, 1991). Interpretive case studies and longitudinal research will be needed to capture the complexity of collaborative processes. Tourism managers need information about convening, managing, and sustaining collaborative relationships. By examining successful and unsuccessful partnerships, programs can be developed to assist managers in nurturing all phases of collaboration.

There is a dynamic tension between competitive and collaborative forces in the tourism field. It is noteworthy that at a time when competitive pressures are mounting, many tourism interests are engaging in joint decision-making and resource sharing. However, collaborative systems are still underdeveloped in the tourism field due to many geographic, organizational, and political constraints. Nevertheless, evidence is accumulating that suggests traditional relationships are being transformed.

REFERENCES

Brown, L.D. (1980). Planned change in underorganized systems. In T.G. Cummings (Ed.), *Systems theory for organization development.* New York: Wiley.

Buckley, P.J., & Witt, S.F. (1990). Tourism in the centrally planned economies of Europe. *Annals of Tourism Research,* 17 (1): 7-18.

Day, R. & Day, J.V. (1977). A review of the current state of negotiated order research. *The Sociological Quarterly,* 18: 126-142.

Evan, W.M. (1966). *The organization-set: Toward a theory of interorganizational design.* (Edited by J.D. Thompson.) Pittsburgh: University of Pittsburgh Press.

Gray, B. (1985). Conditions facilitating interorganizational collaboration. *Human Relations,* 38: 911-936.

Gray, B. (1989). *Collaborating: Finding Common Ground for Multiparty Problems.* San Francisco: Jossey-Bass.

Gunn, C.A. (1988). *Tourism Planning.* New York: Taylor & Francis.

Gunn, C.A. (1990). The new recreation-tourism alliance. *Journal of Park and Recreation Administration,* 8 (1): 1-8.

McCann, J.E. (1983). Design guidelines for social problem-solving interventions. *Journal of Applied Behavioral Science,* 19: 177-189.

Mill, R.C., & Morrison, A. (1985). *The Tourism System.* Englewood Cliffs, NJ: Prentice Hall.

Miller, M.L. (1987). Tourism in Washington's coastal zone. *Annals of Tourism Research,* 14 (1): 58-70.

Milo, K.J., & Yoder, S.L. (1991). Recovery from natural disasters: travel writers and tourist destinations. *Journal of Travel Research,* 30 (1): 36-39.

Murphy, P.E. (1983). Tourism as a community industry: An ecological model of tourism development. *Tourism Management,* 4 (3): 181-190.

Murphy, P.E. (1985). *Tourism: A Community Affair.* New York: Metheun.

Osborne, D., & Gaebler, T. (1992). *Reinventing Government.* Reading, MA: Addison-Wesley.

Reid, L. (1987). Recreation and tourism workshops. In *Proceedings of the Symposium on Tourism and Recreation: A Growing Partnership,* (pp. 41-57). Asheville, NC: Sagamore Publishing.

Schatz, C., McAvoy, L.H., & Lime, D.W. (1991). Cooperation in resource management: A model planning process for promoting partnerships between resource managers and private service providers. *Journal of Park and Recreation Administration,* 9(4): 42-58.

Schrage, M. (1990). *Shared Minds: The New Technologies of Collaboration.* New York: Random House.

Selin, S.W., & Beason, K. (1991). Interorganizational relations in tourism. *Annals of Tourism Research,* 18 (4): 639-652.

Smith, B. (1991). New horizons in tourism and hospitality education, training, and research. *Journal of Travel Research,* 30 (2): 51-52.

Smith, V.L., Hetherington, A., & Brumbaugh, M.D. (1986). California's Highway 89: A regional tourism model. *Annals of Tourism Research,* 13 (3): 415-433.

Teye, V.B. (1988). Prospects for regional tourism cooperation in Africa. *Tourism Management,* 9 (3): 221-234.

Tourism Management Colloquium. (1991, July). *Call for Papers.* (Available from [Centre for Continuing Education, McGill University, 3461 McTavish St., Montreal, Quebec H3A 1Y1]).

Travel and Tourism Research Association. (1992, February). *Conference Announcement.* (Available from [TTRA Conference, 3160 College Ave #206, Berkeley, CA 94705-2712]).

Trist, E.L. (1977). A concept of organizational ecology. *Australian Journal of Management,* 2: 162-175.

Witt, S.F., & Moutinho, L. (1989). *Tourism Marketing and Management Handbook.* New York: Prentice Hall.

Competing and Cooperating in the Changing Tourism Channel System

Frank M. Go
A. Paul Williams

SUMMARY. The following paper highlights the channel system in tourism in the light of the impact of recent developments in information technology. The changes in the tourism channel system are discussed in terms of demand and supply and how information technology is affecting the marketing distribution channel for tourism producers. The focus of this analysis relates to the pooling of individual energies through and the promotion of cooperation in supplier marketing efforts with compatible partners, so that supplier output is more available and accessible to target markets. Cooperation through networking in the tourism channel system will be the key to gaining competitive edge in the tourism industry.

INTRODUCTION

Tourism comprises businesses engaged in transportation, accommodation, food, beverages, attractions and events, as well as a marketing and distribution network to deliver tourism services to a disperse and increasingly complex market. Recently, innovations in computer communications

Frank M. Go and A. Paul Williams are affiliated with the Department of Hotel and Tourism Management, Hong Kong Polytechnic, Hong Kong.

The authors would like to acknowledge Lorne Whittles and an anonymous reviewer for their constructive comments on an earlier version of this paper.

[Haworth co-indexing entry note]: "Competing and Cooperating in the Changing Tourism Channel System." Go, Frank M., and A. Paul Williams. Co-published simultaneously in *Journal of Travel & Tourism Marketing* (The Haworth Press, Inc.) Vol. 2, No. 2/3, 1993, pp. 229-248; and: *Communication and Channel Systems in Tourism Marketing* (ed: Muzaffer Uysal, and Daniel R. Fesenmaier) The Haworth Press, Inc., 1993, pp. 227-248. Multiple copies of this article/chapter may be purchased from The Haworth Document Delivery Center [1-800-3-HAWORTH; 9:00 a.m. - 5:00 p.m. (EST)].

technology have found increased application in the tourism sector. The information technology revolution is taking place to varying degrees in most tourism sub-sectors. Some tourism sub-sectors, notably the airlines, through the use of CRS, are at the leading edge of technological developments and their successful application, but some, such as the accommodation industry, may be categorized as "laggards" since they are "slow to react to the creative use of communications and information technology" (McGuffie, 1990:30).

The tourism sector can be described as information-intensive because "the relative importance of time and place utility of tourism services is greater than in the case of goods" (Rathmell, 1975:104). With information technology innovations reshaping the basic structure of society and industry, and consumers' increasing demand for information (Davis and Davidson, 1991; Badaracco, 1991), the rates of technological development and diffusion may be anticipated to accelerate in the tourism sector. To be successful in a competitive market such as tourism, it is no longer sufficient to offer more discerning consumers a good product. Increasingly, success in the tourism market, depends on understanding one's customers' expectations, offering customers a perfect product at a lower cost and faster than the competition, by effectively bridging the gap between suppliers and consumers. Information technology is predicted to bridge this gap through the application of computerised reservation systems (CRS) to the travel and tourism industry. Collier claims that "CRS are providing the route to link the needs of the consumer with the products offered by the travel industry" (Collier, 1989:87).

In the following discussion, the tourism channel system is discussed in respect of some important shifts in tourism demand and changes in the competitive environment which confront suppliers when selecting channel systems. Subsequently, the feasibility of networks and the development of network strategy are analyzed with reference to tourism suppliers. The focus of this analysis relates to the pooling of individual energies and the promotion of cooperation in supplier marketing efforts with compatible partners, so that supplier output is more available and accessible to target markets.

THE TOURISM CHANNEL SYSTEM AND VALUE CHAIN

It is argued that the purpose of a tourism channel of distribution is to get sufficient information to the right people at the right time and in the right place, to allow a purchase decision to be made, and to provide a mechanism whereby the consumer can make and pay for the necessary purchase

(Mill and Morrison, 1985:399). The channel system is the critical link in the marketing mix between demand and supply, consumer and producer.

The channel system in tourism refers to the path by which a firm or consumer executes a reservation to use a facility (Leven, 1982). It covers all activities designed to bring consumers more information and thus closer to the travel product; such activities are generally performed by tourism producers and commercial enterprises. An important feature of the travel product is its complexity–or the variety of services it comprises–and the interdependence which exists between the various services. These features of travel services in combination with the complex nature of travel marketing makes it desirable to use intermediaries or indirect channels when getting the message to the market.

Direct channels still exist between buyers and sellers but are chiefly concerned with the sales function at the individual company level, where sales representatives concentrate on (1) maintaining sales contacts with channel intermediaries; (2) maintaining sales contact with local organizations; and (3) following leads furnished by other sources (Kaven, 1974: 116).

However, indirect channels of distribution have become increasingly important to represent the tourism supplier in multiple markets of origin (Bitner and Booms, 1982). As such, travel agents play an increasingly significant role in distributing travel and tourism products to the consumers. Other intermediaries are the tour packagers and tour wholesalers who generally coordinate and promote the development of package tours. The primary advantage for tourism producers is that these wholesalers tend to purchase services in bulk and, more importantly, in advance, allowing producers to anticipate sales volume. Hotel representatives, such as Utell, comprise another intermediary, acting as sales and reservation agents for a number of non-competing hotels and are frequently used by foreign hotels selling to consumers in the travel generating markets. Other types of intermediaries include association executive, corporate travel offices, and incentive travel firms through which suppliers can attempt to influence when, where and how consumers travel. In other words, they control to some degree how much business an individual airline, cruiseline, or hotel may get (Bitner and Booms, 1982). Using intermediaries, i.e., indirect channels in the tourism channel system, means that the tourism firm has third parties playing key roles in contributing to its value chain. The firm must fully understand its relationships with suppliers and intermediaries, in relation to customers to ensure that benefits are optimized. Where appropriate, the hotel industry will be used to demonstrate these relationships in the tourism sector.

A firm's value chain for competing in the market is embedded in a larger stream of activities known as the "value system" (Porter, 1990:34). The value system of a typical international hotel corporation includes related travel and business services such as telecommunications, credit card, and banking services and indirect supplier value chains, like computer reservation systems, brewers, construction firms, real estate, and education and training institutions. The suppliers of related services and manufactured goods provide inputs to the hotel firm's value chain. Within the value chain, the rendering of service by humans, specifically the client-service provider interaction, is the critical success factor in the hotel industry (Geller, 1985), as opposed to manufacturing where the producer and consumer may never come into contact. The role of the channel system in tourism is clearly a major factor in the contribution to the value chain of an individual tourism supplier. If a firm can make its product more accessible and convenient to potential buyers, it has a perceived higher value and should enjoy competitive advantages over other tourism producers.

Porter's (1985:34) analysis highlights this importance in respect of product differentiation and subsequent competitive advantage. It must be noted at this stage that the value chain is not a collection of independent activities, but a system of interdependent activities or linkages. These linkages can lead to competitive advantage (Porter, 1985:48). For example, the linkages in the tourism value chain may be illustrated by the newly introduced computerized reservation systems that connect the information streams of airlines, hotels, car hire companies and travel agents.

At each step of the production process, the manager of the travel and tourism corporation has to choose the optimal combination of inputs, such as manpower, physical capital, financial resources, and the channels for the marketing and delivery of services that shall yield the maximum contribution to the value chain of the organization.

In the lodging industry, for example, hotel ownership may be approached as a business activity, separately from the hotel operations management activity, which may be approached separately from the marketing and reservations function through a hotel franchise or referral system. The key factors for the success of each segment (e.g., ownership, operations management contracting, and franchising) are not homogenous. The key factors for success in gaining market share and profitability shall be elaborated on later in this paper.

SHIFTING TOURISM DEMAND

On the demand side, the need for reliable travel information is essential. Kaven (1974:114) describes the customer's need for information and its complex nature as follows: "the endless combinations and permutations of alternative routes, transportation modes, time, and lodging accommodations make many travel decisions difficult even for the initiated." Communication through the channel system represents a critical element in the marketing mix, in particular in tourism, since in the complex of service, "time and place utility appear to be the essence of the product itself" (Rathmell, 1974:105). And also due to the growth of the more discerning independent traveller, "there is a need for a broader range of information at the point of sale" (Collier, 1989:87).

The fundamental issue of communicating brandname identity in a "crowded" channel system is further complicated by several 'unique' features of the tourism product. The intangibility of the tourism product, rendering it experiential in nature means that the customer is unable to "touch" and "experience" the product prior to purchase, in complete contrast to manufactured goods. Furthermore, the distribution process is impacted by virtue of the tourism product's fixed geographic location in a destination area. The fixed nature of the tourism product requires consumers to travel to the destination area to experience what they are buying. Finally, perhaps the most significant aspect of the tourism product is that it is produced by various components that comprise the functioning tourism system (Gunn, 1972; Go, 1981; Mill and Morrison, 1985; and Blank, 1989) which include the demand (market) side and the supply side.

The role of supply-side components, including attractions, transportation, services and information/promotion, are critically interwoven. Gunn agrees claiming "all components of the supply side are essential to a properly functioning tourism system. All must function in a delicate but tightly integrated balance" (Gunn, 1988:67). In order to offer consumers satisfying experiences, the various suppliers require on-going and excellent communications, shared values, and a customer-driven vision. Unfortunately, the presence of these factors in adequate measure tends to be the exception rather than the rule, often imposing a constraint on a smoothly functioning tourism system. Increased dependency on communication will be critical in the future as the infrastructure of the economy is shifting.

Historically, an economy has relied heavily on a particular kind of infrastructure (Davis and Davidson, 1991:31). Infrastructure is the elementary network on which all activity and especially communication depends. The shift in the infrastructure of today's economy implies a change in travel demand. In the future, suppliers will be much more dependent on the effective functioning of communication within the tourism system, than ever before. The railways and later the highways through to automobile development represent those infrastructures upon which regional economies were transformed into a single national economy. The introduction of the jet aircraft resulted in the large-scale expansion of multi-domestic travel and trade. Each time the infrastructure shifted, tourism demand changed, forcing suppliers to adapt their products to new customer demands.

At the core of today's economy, new information technology is causing a shift in the infrastructure of today's economy and is significantly changing tourism demand. In particular, it is altering long-standing relationships in the channel system in tourism, and creating new forms of competition–sometimes overnight. Specifically, the application of micro-electronic technology in general, and the computer in particular, are playing a fundamental role in market shifts that are most vividly demonstrated by:

- The decline of the independent travel agent catering to the leisure market, and the growth of agents who have invested in large computerized reservation systems with direct access to flights, accommodation, rental cars, and other services (Hitchins, 1991).
- The emergence of the global customer. Instant worldwide news reporting through, for example, the Cable News Network (CNN) has resulted in consumers around the world having access to the same information at the same time. The increasing homogenization of customer needs worldwide has spawned a global lifestyle and raised consumer expectations for ever faster and better information and service delivery. For example, Kendall and Booms (1989) found that information expectations of consumers were rated as more important than physical needs with respect to travel agent facilities.
- The current use of CRS in travel businesses have revolutionized operations, improving, facilitating and speeding up all activities including the booking of flights, car rentals, tours, hotel rooms and other tourist services (German Federal Republic, 1989).

The bargaining power of buyers has also changed dramatically. Consumers are becoming more experienced and knowledgeable, but at the same time are demanding a better quantity and quality of information about globally dispersed tourism products. Single or independent tourism businesses tend to be especially vulnerable in an extremely sensitive economic environment. In contrast, tourism firms operating within a chain or network tend to have better access to the necessary capital, marketing expertise and technology necessary to survive by being able to satisfy these increasing demands.

In the tourism industry, buyers include tour wholesalers, travel agent retailers and consumers. These buyers impact on the tourism industry by forcing down prices, demanding higher quality and greater variety of services, all at the expense of industry profitability. Buyers, sure that they can always find alternative products, have used this knowledge to play one tourism firm against another for example, when meeting planners of a company or association negotiate to hold their conference at a particular hotel.

Wholesalers, travel agencies and tour brokers account for about one third of the roomnights consumed annually in the United States (Brewton, 1987:12). The needs of travel organizations who resell the hotel rooms they buy tends to be different from the user. Although consumers are expected to continue to play the starring role, Leven (1982) suggests that tourism suppliers have become more removed from their clientele, that client decisions are largely controlled by more than just the individual user, and that the "gap" between supplier and consumer will continue to widen.

Shifts in demand are challenging suppliers to make tourism products available and accessible to increasingly demanding customers in often disperse markets. This issue leads us to reassess the tourism channel configuration in relation to the essential and unavoidable activities that are part of the tourism value chain.

TURBULENT CHANNEL ENVIRONMENT
AND COMPETITIVE ADVANTAGE

On the supply side, there are also significant changes which are causing instability and turbulence in the tourism channel system. The very nature of a competitive environment means that there will be some "turbulence" and as Schumpeter (1965) recognized many decades ago, there is no "equilibrium" in competition. "Competition is a constantly changing landscape in which new products, new ways of marketing, new production processes, and new market segments emerge" (Porter, 1990:20). Today's dynamic competitive environment is characterized by change and innovation. Kaven (1974:119) agrees claiming that "so long as competitive innovations occur and entrepreneurs seek to implement them in search of survival, growth and profit, these channels of distribution are subject to change.

In the tourism industry, businesses constantly strive to be identified in the increasingly complex market. Tourism is comprised of a relatively small number of large suppliers and a relatively large number of small suppliers. However, both small and the large suppliers face a universal challenge, albeit perhaps to a different extent, which Kaven (1974:115) refers to as: "hundreds of thousands of establishments are seeking to gain identity with untold millions of potential customers covering the whole spectrum of incomes, interests, knowledge, sophistication and needs." However, only the largest suppliers may have the network in place and the resources to establish and sustain their brand identity successfully.

Competitiveness can be assessed along two dimensions. First, the global dimension measures competitiveness in terms of number of customers attracted, market share, revenues, and expansion. The second dimension focuses on the activities performed in an industry sub-sector and attempts to explain why one sector is more successful than another, for example the airlines in comparison with the accommodation sub-sector. When a country's tourism industry falls behind its competitors in terms of the provision of information, marketing analysis capabilities, and inter-connection among systems and databases, it can have most critical consequences in terms of industry-customer interfacing and affect perceptions and competitiveness most directly (Government of Canada, 1988). The traditional "competitive strategy" paradigm which focuses on product-market positioning is greatly and increasingly dependent in tourism firms on human resources management which is an integral part of the value-chain (Porter, 1990). Therefore, the notion of competitive advantage which provides the means for developing product based advantages at a given point in time (in terms of cost and differentiation) should be complemented with insights into the processes of knowledge acquisition.

The competitive advantage concept offers another perspective on business strategy that facilitates analysis of the competitive environment. The key factors for success of different industries lie in different production functions "at different points along the 'value chain'" (Porter, 1990). The way in which one activity within the value chain is performed affects the cost or effectiveness of other activities. Activities performed in the competition between travel and tourism firms should be designed to contribute to buyer value, and include the following:

> Ongoing production, marketing, delivering, and servicing of the product (primary activities) and those providing purchased inputs, technology, human resources, or overall infrastructure functions to support the other activities, and firms gain competitive advantage from conceiving of new ways to conduct activities. (Porter, 1990:40)

The introduction of computer reservation systems (CRS) and global travel distribution practices designed to create transnational links throughout the world have put channel systems at centre stage in the battle for competitive advantage. Dunning (1970) has explained the growth, distribution, and form of involvement of multinational enterprises (MNE) within the framework of the eclectic theory of international production.

> According to the theory, an enterprise with headquarters in one country will have some form of involvement with firms outside their national boundaries whenever they have a competitive advantage over other firms (whether domestic or foreign) and can combine their advantage with resources located in foreign countries and which are attractive to the MNE. In the process of producing goods and services, firms carry out many other activities, including marketing, training of labour, design and development of products, all of which are interdependent and linked through intermediate products, which mostly take the form of knowledge and expertise. (Dunning and McQueen, 1982:82-83)

The CRS developments have largely arisen through the initiatives of the airline industry. From centralized booking systems, to information providers, to potentially dominant marketing and distribution systems, the CRS role has been critical to airline survival since deregulation in the USA in 1978. Travel agents have adopted links to airline CRS and gained access to an information and booking system which allows them to book (and confirm) seat reservations at the touch of a few keys. Speed, accuracy and reliability of information are just a few of the advantages to the travel agent and ultimately the buyer. At the same time the airlines have instigated an enormous distribution system where travel agents worldwide have access to the marketing and selling information of the airline products.

American Airlines developed SABRE and United Airlines with its APOLLO system were the early entrants and gained significant competitive advantage over their competitors (Truitt, Teye and Farris, 1991:21). In the USA, the penetration of CRS into travel agencies is virtually complete, and the battle is now on for the global market. Only recently have other tourism sub-sectors realized the distributive power of the CRS and its ability to allow access to many new global markets. Hotels, airlines and car hire companies are now linking up with these CRS and hoping to gain significant competitive advantage. The strategic alliance of Marriott, American Airlines, Hilton hotels and Budget Rent-a-Car for the "Confirm" project is a good example (Wolfe, 1991). Activities vary in their contribution to competitive advantage in different industries, and can vary from segment to segment in a particular industry. The application of communications technology and its level of diffusion in the tourism channel system is, to a large extent, shaped by several dimensions, such as:

- the structure of the organizations in a particular sub-sector, e.g., chain-owned, independent, or scheduled versus charter services;
- the size of the operation, whether small, medium, or large;
- the target markets aimed at, e.g., business, pleasure, or group versus independent business;
- the type of service offered, e.g., limited or full service, specialized versus general services (Government of Canada, 1988:4-5).

Within this context, and to facilitate access to global markets, travel and tourism corporations are reassessing their channel configuration. Any "reassessment of a channel configuration begins with the recognition that a channel exists to perform a number of essential and unavoidable activities," that are part of the firm's value chain in taking a product to market (Day, 1990:220). Increased competition and the rising cost of technology have forced tourism companies, especially multinational enterprises, to seek out alternative channel configurations.

The effective acquisition of knowledge will depend on the ability of tourism executives to improve their capability for the superior execution of activities and processes within and beyond their value system. Specifically, tourism organizations have to learn how they can share the knowledge required to create and deliver products and processes better, faster, of higher quality, and at a lower cost and risk. In their quest for enhanced communications capability, some companies have embraced the network concept to foster information sharing beyond corporate boundaries.

MOVING TOWARDS COOPERATION– THE NETWORK CONCEPT

Network Concept

A network is a type of cooperation that does not take the form of a merger or a joint venture, but is rather a limited involvement of the parties designed to solve knowledge and information-related problems through the assistance and contribution of organizations which for instance know and understand local markets (Van Rietbergen, Bosman, and de Smidt, 1990:214). Thus, each of these service providers in the network contributes specific core competencies to the value chain on a short-term or long-term basis. Following this train of thought, the tourism corporation could be viewed as deriving added value to a lesser extent from traditional functions but to a greater extent from those functions that arrange and maintain transactions in integrated networks (de Jong, 1991:8). As Charan (1991:104) states, "networks imply a set of external relationships–a global web of alliances and joint ventures."

Types of Network

Lambooy (1988:28) distinguishes four traditional network types: (a) the "growth pole" model; (b) the "social network"; (c) the "filiere configuration," and (d) the "complex." The concept of "social network" dovetails with Pred's theory (1977) and is applicable in the internationalisation of services.

a. The "growth pole model" is predicated upon the concentration of growth in regions at urban-industrial poles through "key corporations," i.e., companies that play a significant role in the economy, such as for example, car manufacturers, steel manufacturers, or the producers of computers. Through their transactions with other parties, these manufacturers induce business travel demand. Tourism suppliers could capitalise on such a network existing.

b. The "social network" is a concept which recognizes the significance of social relationships among entrepreneurs, employees, and consumers in the decision making process in addition to the price mechanism. For example, family connections often influence market relationships. In this regard, Lambooy refers to the example of politicians who "assist" their family or friends to obtain commissions, in spite of the lower quality and the higher price that may be expected.

c. The "branche configuration" complements the company's value-chain. It is comprised of a network of relationships that may be likened to the branches of a tree, hence the French term "filieres." Relationships in the branche configuration of the international hotel industry might include, for example, real estate brokers, manufacturers of furniture and electronic equipment, financial institutions, transportation corporations, and travel agents and tour operators.

d. Large, key businesses are central to the industrial complex. The notion of "complex" is relevant to networking in the international hotel industry because mega-attractions, like for example, the Euro Disney project near Paris, form the focus for hotel developments.

The dynamic network may be defined as "an organizational architecture that accommodates constant and accelerating change while at the same time stimulating components of the corporate environment to build deep and lasting relationships" (Hickman and Silva, 1987:210).

Why Network?

Earlier discussion in this paper highlighted the external pressures of demand and supply influencing the need to network in the tourism industry. Other synergistic pressures which can be applied to justify networking concern the organization's internal structure. The channel system in tourism will be controlled increasingly through information and communications technologies which tend to be owned by corporations who operate under one or more brand names (Kaven, 1974:119). Consequently, having and communicating a brand name is of increasing significance to achieving competitive advantage in international tourism. As McArdle (1989: 201) correctly indicates "the opportunity exists for operators/companies in the tourist industry to be more proactive in their approach to 'brand' development and extension." Brand name familiarity can be gained through the proper exploitation of informational and promotional media. The growing importance of "branding" will force independent and smaller second-tier tourism chains to obtain affiliation with referral or franchise systems in order to compete in the global environment.

Networks share several characteristics that are relevant to the tourism corporation:

a. Networks raise the cost of entry to a level that few potential competitors can or will pay.
b. Network oriented services are usually enhanced by expanding the network and its facilities tend to be more widely used if the expansion enhances its value to customers.
c. Early investment in a network may result in long-term competitive advantage over new entries especially in industries where customer loyalty, switching costs or habit patterns are dominant.
d. Once a customer franchise is built through network enhancement, it may be difficult to displace.
e. The greater the need for a multinational network due to the high mobility of consumers, the greater the likelihood that a well established service firm will realize a significant portion of its revenues from foreign activity.
f. The technology of networks is changing so fast that it may transform competition in services such as telecommunications (Heskett, 1986:112 and 144).

In an increasingly complex and changing environment, tourism corporations cannot effectively compete through channel systems that are uni-dimensional and static.

While service companies used to have a supporting role in the facilitation of economic transactions in the past, they increasingly tend to take on a transactions determining role (de Jong, 1991:9), and a strategic significance. For instance, the planning and building of commercial accommodations in a tourist destination determines to a great extent the type of tourist market this destination will attract in the future.

Due to the scarcity of required expertise, the high development and operations costs, and the risk factors in the restructuring of the tourism industry, it is becoming more common for tourism companies to seek long-term relationships with production, research and marketing groups around the world. An integrated network of relations between service providers is emerging based on agreements to cooperate with one another by contributing specific knowledge and information that are complementary.

Role of Information Technology and Networking

Another trend which is likely to reinforce the development of the communications network, is the concentration of complementary services that together make up systems of services. This development is embodied by the CRS which are vast networks that the major airlines use to communicate the most up-to-date flight and airfare information to travel agents. When linked to the CRS, agents can check schedules, compare fares, make hotel and rental car reservations, as well as order tickets for Broadway shows. What makes CRS so vital to the airlines is its ability to arrange a dizzying permutation of planes, routes and available seats in the most profitable configuration possible (McCarrol, 1989:50).

The implications of CRS are vast because they have become part of a global network connecting many tourism suppliers including airlines, hotels, and car rental companies. The CRS has in effect become an autonomous profit making organization since tourism producers have to pay for use of the system each time a CRS is used to make a booking. The announcement that SABRE, the CRS division of American Airlines, is more profitable than the airline division, highlights the power and influence of CRS (Hopper, 1990). The sophisticated application of new communications technology will present tourism suppliers the opportunity to cooperate much more closely than before. At the same time, it may result in a greater internationalization of tourism and fiercer competition among travel and host firms.

The CRS, if effectively utilized, can play a crucial role to contributing to the tourism firm's value chain. As the CRS expands, an increasingly complex hierarchical system of transport and travel networks is evolving which provide important opportunities for gaining competitive advantage by those tourism firms with the necessary competencies and skills to capitalize on the new technology.

Information is becoming the critical strategic resource especially in the travel and tourism sector. The power of information technology is also highlighted by Porter and Millar (1985:149) since information technology not only transforms the nature of the products but changes the nature of the competition itself. This is especially true for products such as travel which contain a very high information content. The impact of information technology on the travel and tourism industry cannot be ignored. The required investment in information technology may be high, but it can be shared. Hence, in the future, strategic alliances between tourism corporations should become the norm to exploit any of the opportunities which arise.

Current Networks and the Cooperation of Tourism Producers

Recent developments in the CRS "industry" highlight a number of strategic alliances, primarily with the airline sector dominant. Some of the major airline CRS have become organizationally more "cooperative." For example, Apollo (USA) has developed close links with Galileo (Europe) and Gemini (Canada); Sabre (USA) and Amadeus (Europe) have announced plans to work together; and Worldspan (USA), which also hopes to incorporate System One (USA) in its operations, plans to merge with Abacus (Asia). The result is a move towards three "mega" systems which in effect forms a powerful "oligopolistic" market situation (Truitt, Teye and Farris, 1991:27).

Other tourism sectors hope to link with these powerful systems to facilitate their global expansion. The Confirm project outlined earlier is a prime example, with Marriott, Hilton, Budget Rent-a-Car and American Airlines pooling energies. However, the concern for these other sectors is that the airlines are still dominating tourism distribution channels and plan to remain in this position. As Chervenak (1991:26) states, "the thrust of all three global networks is to control the highest percentage of the world's airline, car rental and hotel reservations."

DEVELOPING A NETWORK STRATEGY

Exploiting Opportunities

Strategic information systems offer tourism corporations great opportunities for gaining competitive advantage when organizations implement them appropriately and manage: (1) to take ownership of information technology, i.e., systems should be user driven and add value, rather than complexity and frustration; (2) not to overburden the development process by building too many features into the system; and (3) to understand and implement the strategies behind new systems or risk limited benefits (Anon., 1989:14).

Since airline deregulation in 1978, the channel system in tourism started to change in a dramatic way, first in the United States and then gradually throughout the world. In particular, because of airline deregulation, airfares changed with unprecedented rapidity. And subsequently, travellers demanded more information, faster, from a broader range of suppliers. In the new channel environment which resulted, tourism managers are compelled to rethink how they should access their markets and maintain relationships with their customers.

The ability of tourism corporations to build and manage a strategic channel system may separate the winners from the losers in the market place of the 1990s. The future marketplace will be characterized by more demanding customers, aggressive and massive financial accumulation, relatively free-flowing resources, and global brands. In an effort to survive, tourism corporations must respond to a rapidly shifting global market place by aligning their channel system and marketing functions with the organizational characteristics of the transnational network. These global opportunities must be exploited, with close, mutually beneficial cooperation, by all tourism producers.

Overcoming Threats

It appears that the "concept of self-interest, the very foundation of a market economy, could be utilized more effectively throughout all parts of tourism" (Gunn, 1988:206). The concept is based on the motivation to achieve and to reap the rewards from such achievement. In the past, this has been directed only internally–within the tourism firm the thinking of managers was guided by best practice. But as Hopper (1990) has suggested this logic may be actually counter productive and therefore no longer valid.

In tourism many externalities influence success. Therefore, when viewing the tourism industry from an external perspective it will be seen that integration within other parts of the travel industry is not only desirable but virtually mandatory. As the travel industry expands, an increasingly complex hierarchical system of transport, tourism and hotel networks is evolving. Gunn (1988:207) cites a number of barriers that prevent or constrain the exercise of adequate networking in the tourism system that are relevant to our discussion. (1) Entrepreneurs often have a misconception of the tourism product. For example, an important part of the hotel product is the travel purpose such as the attractions that brought the traveller to the tourism product in the first place. (2) Small business and government agencies have difficulty in justifying outreach, in part, because capital and operating expenses are not budgeted for this function. (3) For competitive reasons in particular "turf protection" is a major barrier to integration for all businesses and government. (4) The educational systems tend to foster divisiveness rather than integration. As observed by Gunn (1988:207), hotel schools, for example, teach hotel management but seldom are students taught (in depth) how the hotel industry interrelates to and is dependent upon many other sectors and components of the tourism system. Broader education and training programs would assist in alerting managers and students regarding networking potential between the various parts of the functioning tourism system. The issue is no longer whether or not one should adapt to the new technological environment. The current generation of computer systems shows that computerization and hence networking is essential to remaining competitive in tourism (Government of Canada, 1988:2).

Towards an Integrated Network Strategy in Tourism

It should be evident from our analysis that the information technology revolution is reshaping the basic structure of tourism. Though risky as it may be to interpret what the changes mean and what entrepreneurs, executives and others who have to make decisions should do to prepare for the challenges of the future, there seems to be several emerging patterns that point to the increasing importance and application of integrated network strategy in tourism that are worth sharing:

1. Network transactions for value-added skill and knowledge building purposes will become increasingly critical in the tourism industry to (a) assess marketing opportunities, the cost of sales implication, and the difficulties associated with achieving appropriate operating standards in the culturally and economically diverse sectors of the tourism market; (b) to acquire more detailed knowledge of local markets; and (c) to create an organizational structure that sees its mission, markets, and requirements as both local and global.

2. The idea that the tourism firm is part of a network of economic transactions implies that in order to expand geographically and operate profitably the tourism corporation must perform its role effectively in the functioning tourism network (this requires cooperation between the tourism firm and "travel industry partners," such as CRS, rental car, airline

and travel agency firms). "The network avoids the problems of duplication of effort, inefficiency and resistance to change to ideas developed elsewhere by giving subsidiaries the latitude, the encouragement, and tools to pursue local business development within the framework of the global strategy" (Czinkota, Rivoli, and Ronkainen, 1989:609). The main tool for implementing this approach is to develop international teams of managers who meet regularly to develop strategy.

3. Integrated network strategy should be formulated taking into account the host country's tourism policy and regional development priorities. In this regard, a potential obstacle perhaps to effective tourism marketing is the tendency of tourism executives to see problems and solutions in the narrow context of the tourism industry as opposed to the services sector. The latter issue has become more prevalent as a set of global industries, including financial services, telecommunications, and transportation especially through their CRS subsidiaries, are affecting the operation and control of hotel and tourism firms in destinations throughout the world.

4. The greater importance of information and knowledge transactions in the tourism industry shall require managers to gain greater insight in the use of computer technology to facilitate a change in the management process within organizations and to extend their horizons well beyond the traditional trade channel system. Furthermore, it is essential that executives of tourism corporations learn to bridge the gap between business needs and integrate technology with functional processes to create opportunities and advantages. Put differently, "As we change what computers can do, we must change what we do with computers" (Hopper, 1990: 119).

5. In order to function effectively in the integrated network in the fast-moving, competitive market requires an organizational structure which incorporates a much more flexible management mentality than the one which dominates the traditional channel system in tourism. To take advantage of new opportunities and build competitive advantage, tourism corporations are likely to develop the new transnational model (Bartlett and Ghosahl, 1989:6) which is characterized by: (1) the distribution of specialised resources and capabilities through an integrated network; (2) the coordination of flows of products, resources and communication across interdependent units; and (3) a management mentality which treats worldwide tourism operations as an integrated and interdependent strategic network. The transnational network model is significant in relation to the tourism industry because it enables travel and hotel corporations to balance global reach and local adaptability.

CONCLUSION

The continuing process of change in the tourism market requires managers to reassess their corporations' channel configuration in order to remain competitive. Activities performed in the competition between tourism firms should be designed to contribute to buyer value and competitive advantage. Because a channel system is a method of gaining access to a market, changes brought about by computerized reservation systems require adjustments in the organizational and managerial logic, namely the idea that the tourism corporation is part of a network, as opposed to the traditional distribution channel.

Network effects create important opportunities for gaining competitive advantage in the tourism industry in which the basic service consists of linking buyers, sellers and third parties. Networks are designed to build the central competitive advantage of the 1990s. No channel structure, regardless of how de-cluttered or delayered, can compare with the speed and flexibility of networks to link suppliers, intermediaries, and buyers.

Due to increasing application of information technology the process of change and evolution in the channel system in tourism can be expected to continue, perhaps at an even more rapid rate than before. Only those tourism corporations capable of making adjustments to the dynamic characteristics of the tourism market are likely to survive over the long run.

REFERENCES

Anon. (1989). *Looking Forward: A Management Perspective of Technology in the Lodging Industry.* Washington, D.C.: American Hotel & Motel Association and Anderson Consulting.

Badaracco, Joseph L. (1991). *The Knowledge Link; How Firms Compete Through Strategic Alliances.* Boston: Harvard Business School Press.

Bartlett, Christopher A., & Ghosahl, Sumatra (1989). *Managing Across Borders– The Transnational Solution.* Boston: Harvard Business School Press.

Bitner, Mary J., & Booms, Bernard H. (1982). Trends in Travel and Tourism Marketing: The Changing Structure of Distribution Channels. *Journal of Travel Research,* 20 (4): 39-44.

Blank, Uel (1989). *The Community Tourism Industry Imperative: The Necessity, The Opportunities, Its Potential.* State College, PA: Venture Publishing Inc.

Brewton, Charles (1987). A Model for Analyzing the Lodging Industry. *The Cornell H.R.A. Quarterly,* 28 (2): 10-12.

Charan, Ram (1991). How Networks Reshape Organizations for Results, *Harvard Business Review,* Sept-Oct: 104-115.

Chervenak, Larry (1991) CRS, The Past, The Present, The Future. *Lodging,* June p. 25-31.

Collier, David (1989). Expansion and Development of CRS. *Tourism Management*, June p. 86-88.

Czinkota, Michael R., Rivoli, Pietra, & Ronkainen, Ilkka A. (1989). *International Business*. New York: Dryden.

Davis, Stan, & Davidson, Bill (1991). *2020 Vision; Transform your Business Today to Succeed in Tomorrow's Economy*. New York: Simon & Schuster.

Day, George S. (1990). *Market Driven Strategy*. New York: The Free Press.

Dunning, John H. (1970). Technology, U.S. Investment and European Economic Growth. In Kindleberger, C.P. (Ed.), *The International Corporation*. Cambridge, MA:MIT Press.

Dunning, John H. (1979). Explaining Changing Patterns of International Production: In Defence of the Eclectic Theory. *Oxford Economic Papers*, Volume 41.

Dunning, John H., & McQueen, Matthew (1982). Multinational Corporations in the International Hotel Industry. *Annals of Tourism Research*, 9(1) 69-90.

Geller, A. Neal (1985). Tracking the Critical Success Factors for Hotel Companies. *The Cornell H.R.A. Quarterly*, 25 (4): 76-81.

German Federal Republic, Deutscher Verkehrs Verlag GMBH, Neue Medien. *Ti Geschaftsreise*, 1989, 22(20) 14-16.

Go, Frank M. (1981). Development of New Service Products for the Leisure Travel Market–A Systems View. *Revue de Tourisme*, 2.

Government of Canada (1988). *Applications of Technology in the Tourism Industry*. Ottawa: Tourism Canada.

Gunn, Clare A. (1972). *Vacationscape Designing Tourist Regions*. Austin, Texas: Bureau of Business Research, The University of Texas.

Gunn, Clare A. (1988). *Tourism Planning* (2nd Ed.). New York: Taylor & Francis.

Heskett, James L. (1986). *Managing in the Service Economy*. Boston: Harvard Business Press.

Hickman, Craig R., & Silva, Michael (1987). *The Future 500: Creating Tomorrow's Organizations Today*. New York: Nal Penguin.

Hitchins, Fred (1991). The Influence of technology on U.K. *Travel Agents, Travel & Tourism Analyst*, 3, pp. 88-105.

Hopper, Max D. (1990). Rattling SABRE–New Ways to Compete on Information. *Harvard Business Review*, May/June, pp. 118-125.

Jong, de, M.W. (1990) De Dienstensector transacties in transformatie. Rede uitgesproken bij de aanvaarding van het ambt van bijzonder hoogleraar economie en ruimtelijke organisatie van de dienstensector aan de Universiteit van Amsterdam, Leiden: Stenfert Kroese (8 maart).

Kaven, William K. (1974). Channels of Distribution in the Hotel Industry. In John M. Rathmell (Ed.), *Marketing in the Service Sector* (pp. 114-121). Cambridge, MA: Winthrop Publishers Inc.

Kendall, K.W., & Booms, B.H. (1989). Consumer perceptions of travel agencies: Communications, images, needs, and expectations. *Journal of Travel Research*, 27 (4) 29-37.

Lambooy, J.G. (1988). *Regionale Economische Dynamiek een inleiding in de economische geografie*. Muiderberg: Coutinho.

Leven, Michael A. (1982). The Growing Distance Between the Buyer and the User: Channels of Distribution. In A. Pizam, R.C. Lewis & P. Manning (Eds.), *The Practice of Hospitality Management.* Westport, Connecticut: AVI Publishing Company Inc.

McArdle, Jill (1989). Product Branding–The Way Forward. *Tourism Management,* 10 (3) 201.

McCarrol, Thomas, (1989). Big Eagles and Sitting Ducks. *Time* (May 15).

McGuffie, James (1990). CRS Development and The Hotel Sector. *Travel and Tourism Analyst,* 1, p. 29-41.

Mill, Robert Christie, & Morrison, Alastair (1985). *The Tourism System: An Introductory Text.* Englewood Cliffs, N.J.: Prentice Hall.

Porter, Michael E. (1985). *Competitive Advantage.* New York. Free Press.

Porter, Michael E. (1990). *Competitive Advantage of Nations.* New York: Free Press.

Porter, Michael E., & Millar, Victor E. (1985) How Information Gives You Competitive Advantage. *Harvard Business Review,* July-August. p. 149-160.

Pred, A.R. (1977). *City Systems in Advanced Economies: Past Growth, Present Process and Future Development Options.* New York: John Wiley.

Rathmell, John M. (1974). *Marketing in the Service Sector,* Cambridge, Mass: Winthrop.

Rietbergen, Ton van, Bosman, Jeroen, & de Smidt, Marc (1990). *Internationalising van de dienstensector, Nederlandse ondernemingen in modiaal perspectief.* Muiderberg: Dick Coutinho.

Schumpeter, J.A. (1965). *The Theory of Economic Development: An Inquiry into Profit, Credit, Interest, and the Business Cycle (4th Ed.).* Oxford: Oxford University Press.

Truitt, Lauwrence J., Teye, Victor, B., & Farris, Martin T. (1991). The Role of Computer Reservations Systems–International Implications for the Travel Industry. *Tourism Management.* March. p. 21-36.

Wolfe, Carlo (1991). Talking Tech With Marriott. *Lodging Hospitality.* June. p. 39-42.

Index

Page numbers followed by t indicate tables; numbers in italics indicate figures.

Advertising. *See* Marketing communications
Advertising budget in media selection practices, 23
Aesthetic information needs, 135-144
Affective image component, 196
Age
  of British travelers, 66
  brochure design and, 121,124
  in choice of distribution channel, 52
  the environment and
    attitude toward, 149
    response to messages, 156-160
  induced image formation effectiveness and, 208
  sources of information and, 40,173-174,177,180,184
  travel propensity and, 87
Ahmed, Z., 202
AIDA principle (Attention, Interest, Desire, Action), 113
Airline industry
  deregulation, 243
  information technology, 230,237
  networks in, 242
Airline Reporting Corporation, 42
Alaska, 175
  media selection practices, 21-34
  data and method, 24-25
  differentiation by firms, 22-23
  effectiveness, 33
  market structure analysis, 23-24,32-33

media mix decisions, 28-31,29t,30t,32
media use decisions, 26-28,27t,31-32
Alliances in tourism marketing, 102-103,217-225. *See also* Collaborative alliances in tourism marketing; Network concept
American Airlines, 237,241,242
Amish Country, brochure effectiveness in, 129
Anderson, R.D., 174
Arcury, A.T., 149
Arizona state slogan, 98
Arkansas
  Partners in Tourism program, 221
  state slogan, 97
Assael, H., 198
Assurance in service quality, 10
Atkin, C., 200
Atlanta, 202
Attitudes vs. images, 192
Audits of promotional literature, 16
Australia, 203
Autonomous image formation agents, 201-203,210
Awareness set in destination choice, 128

Bacas, Harry, 102
Bartlett, Christopher A., 245
Bateson, J.E.G., 38
Becker, H., 174

Berkman, H.W., 172
Berry, Leonard L., 25,26,33
Bettman, J.R., 134
Biscayne Bay National Park, 150-166
    site, 150-151
    visitor characteristics and
        environmental messages,
        151-166
Bitner, Mary J., 231
Blackwell, R.D., 12-13
Block, M., 200
Booking time for trip for British
        travelers, 70
Booms, Bernard H., 231,234
Boorstin, D.J., 135
Bosman, Jeroen, 238
Boulding, K., 193,196,205
Boundary Waters Canoe Area, 224
Branche configuration, 239
Brand image, 206-207,208
Brand names, 233
    significance of, 240
Britton, R., 199
Britton, S., 202
Brochures
    British travelers use of, 63-64,64t,
        67-72
    design of site-specific, 111-130
        AIDA principle, 113
        attractiveness and utility, 118-123
        consumer filters, 129
        focus groups in research,
            114-118
        research issues, 129-130
        studies of, 112-113
        in trip motivation,
            123-129,125t,126t
    in destination image formation, 198
    importance of as source of
        information, 182,183
    state tourism bureaus, 100
    targeting, 77-89
        effectiveness, 77-78
        frequent travellers and big
            spenders, 77-89

site specific or general purpose
    brochures, 80t,80-81
study methods, 79
travel expenditures and
    brochure use,
    81-86,82t,83t-84t
travel expenditures and
    information source, 85t
travel propensity and brochure
    use, 86-89,87t,88t
travel agents vs. operators, 40,51
types, 112
Brown, L.D., 223
Brown County, Indiana, 136-143
Buck, R., 129
Budget Rent-a-Car, 237,242
Byerly, C., 197

Cable News Network, 234
Cable television, 198,234
Calder, B., 115
Calgary, 202-203
Canada, 224
Capella, L., 208
Capella, L.M., 172
Celebrity spokesperson in destination
    image formation, 199-200
Centralized planning, 219
Channels of distribution. *See*
    Tourism channel system
Chervenak, Larry, 242
Chesnutt, J., 202
Chestnut, R.W., 135
China, 201, 203
Cognitive image component, 193
Cohen, E., 175
Collaborative alliances in tourism
    marketing, 102-103,
    217-225. *See also* Network
    concept
    antecedents to, 220-222
    constraints to, 218-220,219t
    emerging systems, 220t
    theory of, 222-225
        assumptions, 222-223

direction-setting, 224
problem-setting, 223-224
structuring, 224
Collier, David, 230
Coltman, M., 113
Combat analogies in public agencies, 219
Combination packages and British travelers, 63-64,64t,67-71
Communication in tourism industry, 218-220
Communication messages. *See also* Marketing communications
about the environment
public attitudes, 148-149
visitor characteristics and type of message, 152-166
influence on public, 147-148
Communications technology. *See* Information technology
Competitive advantage, 235-238
Complex, 239
Comprehensive-rational model of decision-making, 219
Computerised reservation systems (CRS), 230,234
in competitiveness, 236-237
in networking, 241-242
Computers
communications, 229-230
in network development, 245
in tourism demand, 234
Conative image component, 196
Confirm project, 237,242
Consumer behavior
distribution channel study, 37-54
age in, 52-53
attitudes toward travel agents, 38-39
communications in, 51-52
domestic vs. foreign travelers, 41,47-51,48t,49t,55t
methods, 41-44,45t
respondent characteristics, 43t
tourism communications, 39-41

tour operators vs. travel agents, 44-47,47t,49-50
the environment and
attitudes toward, 148-149,150
Biscayne Bay National Park study, 150-156
sociodemographics in, 149
symbols in, 149-150
targeting communication messages, 165-166
visitor characteristics and communication messages, 152-165
information acquisition, 134-135,172-173
demographic characteristics and, 173-174
social-psychological factors and, 174-175
interaction with personnel
critical nature of, 9-10
employee feedback and initiatives, 16
management control of, 14-15
service quality, 11
word-of-mouth messages in, 13
repeat visitors, 6-7
shifting tourism demand, 232-235
source of information study
data analysis, 178-179
importance of sources, 179,182t,183,183t
methods, 176-179
purpose and hypothesis, 175
visitor characteristics and, 179-188,180t-181t,184t,185t, 186t
stages, 171-172
Consumer filters in brochure effectiveness, 129
Cooperative marketing, 221
Costs. *See also* Travel expenditures
effects of word-of-mouth messages on, 12,204

of hiring celebrity spokesperson, 200
of induced image formation, 207,208,210
of product quality vs, image formation, 206
of targeting repeat visitors, 5-6
Covert Induced I image formation agents, 199-200,210
Covert Induced II image formation agents, 200-201,210
Credibility of destination image formation agents, 204
articles, 201,202
spokesperson, 200
unsolicited information, 203
word-of-mouth, 204
Crisis as catalyst for collaboration, 220t,222
Crocodile Dundee (movie), 203
Crompton, J., 121,127,128,207
Crompton, J.L., 6,59,72,173
Cross-border alliances in tourism marketing, 102-103
CRS. *See* Computerised reservation systems
Cultural information in Biscayne Bay National Park, 155,166
Customer retention. *See* Repeat visitors
Czinkota, Michael R., 245

Dakhil, M., 172,174
Damage control for destination images, 202
Dann, G., 191
Dann, G.M.S., 175
Databases, establishing using repeat customers, 16
Day, George S., 238
Day, J.V., 224
Day, R., 224
Decision time for trip
for British travelers, 70
marketing implications, 81

travel propensity and, 87
Demand factors in media selection practices, 24,26-31
Demand in tourism industry, 232-235
Demographics. *See* Sociodemographics
de Smidt, Marc, 238
Destination
of British travelers, 65,67t
distribution channel and tour purchasing attributes, 49-50
knowledge of and trip expenditures, 83,84-86
response to environmental messages and, 160-164
Destination attribute evaluation, 192-193
Destination choice
information acquisition in, 136
model, 128
process, 192-193,*194-195*
Destination image, 191-210
agents, 197-205,*210*
Autonomous, 201-203
Covert Induced I, 199-200
Covert Induced II, 200-201
Organic, 204-205
Overt Induced I, 197-199
Overt Induced II, 199
Solicited Organic, 204
Unsolicited Organic, 203-204
brochure design and, 121
components, 193
destination selection process, 192-193,*194-195*
effectiveness of, 205-207
first-time vs. repeat visitors, 6
image mix, 207-209
models, 191-192
negative, damage control for, 202-203
Destination marketers
in image formation, 199-200
information on service quality, 10-11

strategies based on tourist
information needs, 143-144
travel writers, 200-201
Destination promoters. *See*
Destination marketers
Destination specific travel literature
(DSTL). *See* Brochures
Differentiation by firms
market structure analysis,
23-24,32-33
strategic and operational
decisions, 22
Direct distribution channels, 231
Directions in brochures, 123
Direct sales, 37-54
consumers' age and, 52-53
consumers' attitudes toward, 38-39
domestic vs. foreign travelers,
41,47-51
purchase decision parameters,
44-47,46t
respondent characteristics, 43t
study methods, 41-44,45t
tourism communications,
39-41,51-52
Distance traveled and source of
information, 178,181
Distribution, 229-245. *See also*
Direct sales; Tourism
channel system
Domestic travelers, choice of
distribution channel,
41,47-52,48t,49t,50t
Dominant social paradigm, 149
Doobie, L., 199
Dunlap, R.E., 149,152
Dunning, John H., 236-237

Eclectic theory of international
production, 237
Economic Planning Group of
Canada, 112
Education
of British travelers, 66

the environment and
attitude toward, 149
response to messages,
156-160,165-166
in network development, 244
sources of information and,
173,177,179,181,184-187
Empathy in service quality, 10
Employee-customer contact. *See*
Personnel-visitor contact
Engel, J.F., 12-13
England. *See* United Kingdom
Engledow, J.L., 174
Environment
communication messages
symbols in, 149-150
visitor characteristics and
response to, 151-166
in media selection practices, 32-33
public attitudes toward
action and awareness,
148-149,150
dominant social paradigm, 149
park actions and messages,
164-165
sociodemographics in, 149
Environment of tourism industry,
222-223,235-238
Etzel, M., 198
Evan, W.M., 223
Evoked set in destination choice, 128
Experience
in destination image formation,
204-205
in destination selection, 192-193
importance as source of
information, 179,183,185
information searching and, 174
tourism as, 9
in tour purchasing decisions, 52
External communications, 172-173
characteristics, 7
management control of, 14
repeat travelers and, 4,9
strategic use of, 16

External stimuli, 192

Fakeye, Paul, 6
Families. *See also* Travel groups
    induced image formation
        effectiveness, 208
    as information source in
        destination choice, 128
    response to environmental
        messages, 160-164
    as source of information, 173
    age and, 173-174
    for British travelers, 73
    use of Biscayne Bay National
        Park, 155
Farrant, A., 200
Females
    response to environmental
        messages, 156-160
    sources of information, 179,181
Fesenmaier, D.R., 59
Fick, G.R., 10
Financial risk, influence on
        consumer behavior, 50-51
First-time visitors. *See* New
        customers
Focus groups
    in advertising evaluation, 130
    in brochure design research,
        116-118
    characteristics, 115-116
    follow-up tests, 129
Foreign travelers, choice of
        distribution channel,
        41,47-52,48t,49t,50t
Formal external communications
    characteristics, 7
    management control, 13-14
    repeat travelers' use of, 4,9,16
    travel agents vs. operators,
        40-41,51
Formal interpersonal
        communication, defined, 58
Francken, D., 208

Frequent-stayer programs, 5
Frequent travellers. *See* Repeat
        visitors
Friedman, H., 200
Friedman, L., 200
Friends. *See* Families
Funding. *See also* Costs
    in hiring celebrity spokesperson,
        200
    of state advertising campaigns,
        101

Gaebler, T., 221
Gartner, W., 201,205
Geller, A. Neal, 232
Gender
    in focus groups, 130
    response to environmental
        messages and, 156-160
    sources of information, 179,181
Georgia state slogan, 96,105
Getaway trips, information needs
        study, 136-143, 137t,138t,
        140t,*141*,142t
Ghosahl, Sumatra, 245
Gilbert, D., 122-123,129,198
Gilson, C., 172
Gitelson, R., 127,128,207
Gitelson, R.J., 6,59,173
Globalization of tourism industry
    collaborative alliances, 220,221
    competitive advantage in,
        237-238
    CRS (computerized reservation
        systems) networks, 242
    network development, 243-245
    of tourism demands, 234
Goodall, B., 192-193,196
Government agencies
    constraints to collaboration, 219
    entrepreneurial approach, 221
    network development, 244
    partnerships with private sector
        and other agencies,
        220t,221-222,224

Grassroots tourism development, 103
Gray, B., 220,224
Greco, A.J., 172
Greco, G., 208
Greenleaf, E.A., 135
Group composition. *See* Travel
    groups
Group depth interviews. *See* Focus
    groups
Group travel. *See* Tours
Growth pole model of networks, 239
Guidebooks, 46-47
Gunn, Clare A., 23,196,219,233,243,
    244
Gyte, D.M., 6

Hampe, Gary D., 99
Hawes, Douglass K., 99
Haywood, K.M., 13
Heskett, James L., 240
Hickman, Craig R., 239
Hilton International, 221,237,242
Hirschman, E.C., 135,145
Hitchins, Fred, 234
Hodgson, P., 115,116
Hoffman Research Co., 122
Hogan, Paul, 200
Holbrook, M.B., 135,145
Hopper, Max D., 241,243
Hotel representatives, 231
Hotels
    distribution channels, 235
    frequent-stayer programs, 5
    product, 244
Hotel value system, 232
Houghton, P., 122-123,129,198
Hunt, J., 205,206

Illinois state slogan, 97,108
Image formation. *See* Destination
    image
Impersonal communications
    British travelers, 63-64,64t,67-72
    defined, 58

Income
    of British travelers, 66
    source of information and,
        177,179,181,184,187
    travel propensity and, 87
    trip expenditure and, 83,84
Indiana information needs study,
    136-143
Indirect distribution channels, 231
Induced image formation,
    196,205-207
Industry-university partnerships,
    220,221
Informal communication
    British travelers, 63-64,64t,72-73
    characteristics, 7
    defined, 58
    management control of, 15
    in marketing of services, 40
    repeat travelers' use of, 4,11-13,
        16-17
    in tour purchasing decisions,
        48,49,52
Information acquisition
    factors encouraging, 172
    importance in tourism, 172-173
    need arousal and attention to
        stimuli in, 134
Informational brochures, 112
Information needs
    functional vs. nonfunctional, 136
    future research, 144-145
    in information acquisition,
        133-136
    marketing implications, 143-144
    study of, 136-143, 137t,138t,
        140t,*141,*142t
Information search. *See* Information
    acquisition
Information sources, 135
    for automobile travellers in Texas,
        127
    for British travelers, 61-62,64t,72-74
    demographic characteristics and,
        173-174

in destination choice, 128
in external searches, 172
in information acquisiton, 172
relative importance and visitor
    characteristics
    demographic variables,
        179-187,180t-181t,184t,
        185t
    media, 185-187
    motivation, 186t,187
    repeat visitors, 185
    study and methods, 175-179
    word-of-mouth and
        experience, 179,182t,183t,
        183-184
    social-psychological factors and,
        174-175
    tour operators vs. travel agents,
        39-41,46-47,49
    travel expenditures and, 85t,85-86
Information technology, 229-230
    in competitiveness, 236-238
    in network development, 245
    in tourism demand, 234
Informative promotion, 6
    for repeat visitors, 9
Infrastructure, 233-234
Interaction. *See* Personnel-visitor
    contact
Internal communications
    characteristics, 7
    management control of, 14
    repeat travelers and, 4,9-11
        strategic use of, 16
Internal stimuli, 192
Interpersonal communications
    British travelers, 63-64,64t,72-73
    defined, 58

Jamaica, 202
Johnstown, Pennsylvania, 202

Kagan, David S., 93

Kamins, M., 200
Kanuk, L.L., 72
Kassaye, W. Wossen, 33
Kaven, William K., 231,232,
    235-236,240
Kendall, K.W., 234
Kent, W., 202
Kentucky state slogan, 97,108
Key corporations, 239
Khan, S., 206
Kinnear, T., 115, 116
Korea, 203
Kotler, P., 191

Lake Superior Circle Tour, 102
Lambooy, J.G., 239
Length of trip for British travelers,
    70
Leven, Michael A., 231,235
Lime, D.W., 174,219,224
Local tourists
    attitude toward the environment,
        149
    brochure design for, 121-122
    in focus groups, 130
    source of information and,
        178-180,184,187
Lukeman, G., 200
Lundberg, C.C., 14,15
Lure brochures, 112
    brochure design research on, 114
    effectiveness, 129
    in motivating travel, 124-125
    use of, 122

McArdle, Jill, 240
McAvoy, L.H., 219,224
McCann, J.E., 223,224
McCarrol, Thomas, 241
McDonough, M.H., 59,72
McGuffie, James, 230
Magazines
    British travelers' use of, 64-65
    in destination image formation, 198

importance as source of
information, 182,183
media selection practices study,
24-31
Maine state slogan, 96-97
Males
in focus groups, 130
response to environmental
messages, 156-160
sources of information, 179,181
Management
choice of inputs and channels, 232
control of marketing
communications, 13-17,14t
media selection practices, 21-34.
See also Media selection
practices
in network development, 244-245
sharing of knowledge, 238
Mandese, J., 198
MANOVA technique, 178
Maps in brochures, 123
Marion, L.J., 148
Marital status
of British travelers, 66
response to environmental
messages, 156-160
Marketers. *See* Destination
marketers; Management
Marketing communications. *See also*
Brochures; Media
categories, 58
channels as basis for market
segmentation, 57-74,59-74
channel and information
sources, 63-64,64t
destinations, 65, 67t
interpersonal vs. impersonal
channels, 72
media habits, 64-65
promotion and, 73-74
sociodemographics, 65,66t
study method, 60-63
travel characteristics,
67-71,69t-70t,71t

channels of distribution and,
39-41,46-47,47t,51-52,232-
235
defined, 7
in destination image formation,
197-199,205-207
link between industry and target
market, 57-58
media selection practices, 21-34
data and method, 24-26
differentiation by firms, 22-23
effectiveness, 33
market structure analysis of,
23-24,32-33
media mix decisions,
28-31,29t,30t,32
media use decisions,
26-28,27t,31-32
repeat travelers and, 7-17
formal external, 9
internal, on-site interaction,
9-11
management control,
13-15,14t
strategies, 15-17
word-of-mouth messages,
11-13
response to, 198-199
strategies based on tourist
information needs, 143-144
unique selling proposition (USP)
advertising
components, 92-94
in state slogans, 94-105,*95*
Market penetration
of destination image formation
agents, 201,210
in USP advertising, 92
Market segmentation, 23
brochure design, 127
communication channel as basis
for, 57-74,59-60
channel and source of
information, 63-64,64t
destinations, 65,67t

interpersonal vs. impersonal, 72
  media habits, 64-65
  promotion and, 73-74
  sociodemographic variables,
    65,66t
  study methods, 60-63
  travel characteristics, 67-71,
    69t-70t,71t
  communication needs as basis for,
    40
  for local attractions, 78
  search behavior, 175
  variables, 59
Market structure analysis of media
    selection practices, 23-24,
    32-33
Marriott, 237, 242
"M.A.S.H.," 203
Mass communications. *See also*
    Media
  British travelers, 63-64,64t,67-72
  defined, 58
Mazanec, J., 192
Media
  British travelers' use of, 64-65
  in destination image formation,
    197-199,200-203
  importance as source of
    information, 174,177,182t,
    183t,184-187
  influence on tour purchasing,
    46-47,47t,49t
Media habits
  of British travelers, 64-65,72
  promotion strategies and, 58-60
Media selection practices, 21-34
  data and method, 24-25
  differentiation by firms, 22-23
  effectiveness, 33
  for environmental
    communications, 165-166
  market structure analysis, 23-24,
    32-33
  media mix decisions, 28-31,29t,
    30t, 32

media use decisions, 26-28,27t,
    31-32
Men
  in focus groups, 130
  response to environmental
    messages, 156-160
  sources of information, 179,181
Mexico, 206
Midwest trips, information needs
    study, 136-143, 137t,138t,
    140t,*141,*142t
Milepost (magazine), 24-32
Millar, Victor E., 242
Milo, K., 202
Minnesota, 224
Montana tourism bureau, 102
Morgan, D., 115,116
Moriarty, Sandra E., 93
Motives for travel
  brochures in, 123-127,125t,126t,
    128-129
  information searching and,
    174-175
  source of information and,
    178,183,184,186-187
Motives in activity choice, 192
Moutinho, L., 172, 174, 175
Multi-national tourism companies,
    220, 221
  competitiveness, 237
  value system, 232
Murphy, P.E., 224

National Tour Association, 42
Need arousal, 191-192
Negative word-of-mouth messages,
    reasons for, 12
Network concept, 238-245
  characteristics, 238-239
  current developments, 242
  developing, 242-245
  information technology in, 241-242
  reasons for, 240-241
  types of, 239
New customers

external communications to,
13-14
perception of service quality, 10
promotional approaches, 15
service quality expectations of,
14-15
vs. repeat visitors, 5-6
Newell, S., 204
New Environmental Paradigm
(NEP), 152
New Horizons Conference, 221
New Jersey state slogan, 100
Newman, J.W., 173
Newspapers
British travelers' use of,
64-65,73-74
in destination image formation,
198,200-203
importance to visitors as
information source,
177,182-187
media selection practices study,
24-31
trip expenditures and, 85
New York state slogan, 96
Noe, F.P., 152,153
Nolan, S., 208
North Carolina Zoological Park
(NCZP), 176-188

Occupation
of British travelers, 66
response to environmental
messages and, 156-160
Ohio state slogan, 97
Okoroafo, S., 206
Oliva, T.A., 135
Olympic Games in Calgary, 202-203
On-site interaction. *See* Internal
communications
Operational decisions, 22
Organic image formation agents,
204-205,210
Organic images, 196

Organizational variables and media
selection practices,
23,26-31
Organization set theory, 223
Osborne, D., 221
Outdoor advertising
importance to visitors as
information source,
177,182t,183t,184-187
media selection practices study,
24-31
Overt Induced I image formation
agents, 197-199,210
Overt Induced II image formation
agents, 199,210

Pacific Travel News, 203
Packages and British travelers,
63-64,64t,67-71
Pamphlets. *See* Brochures
Parasuraman, A., 25,26,33
Parsons, Talcot, 33
Past experience. *See* Experience
Peers, 174,208
Penetration
destination image formation
agents, 201
in USP advertising, 201
Pennsylvania
regions in tourism literature, 100
state slogan, 97,107,108
People's Republic of China, 201,203
Persian Gulf War, 222
Personnel-visitor contact
critical nature of, 9-10
employee feedback and
initiatives, 16
management control of, 14-15
service quality, 11
word-of-mouth messages in, 13
Persuasive promotion, 6,9
Phelps, A., 6,196
Phillips, S., 148
Planning time for trip. *See* Decision
time for trip

Pleasure-seeking in information
    search, 135
Popular culture in destination image
    formation, 203
Porter, Michael E., 232,235,236,242
Previous experience. *See* Experience
Primary images, 196
Product
    characteristics, 233
    misconceptions, 244
Promotion. *See* Marketing
    communications
Promotional brochures, 112
    brochure design research on,
        114-115
    in motivating travel, 124-127
Propensity to travel
    and brochure use, 86-89,87t,88t
    and motivation, 175
    in targeting market, 78
Propositional advertising, 92-93
    in state slogans, 94-98,*95*
Psychological factors and source of
    information, 174-175
Public agencies. *See* Government
    agencies
Pull in USP advertising, 92

Quality of product, 10-11,206

Radio ads
    in destination image formation,
        197-198
    importance to visitors as information
        source, 177,182-187
    media selection practices study,
        24-31
    trip expenditures and, 85-86
Raitz, K., 172,174
Recognizable spokesperson in
    destination image
    formation, 199-200
Reeves, Rosser, 92

Referrals. *See* Word-of-mouth
    messages
Regional tourism bureaus, 102-103
Reid, R., 113
Relatives. *See* Families
Reliability in service quality, 10
Reminding in promotion, 6
    for repeat visitors, 9
Repeat visitors, 3-17
    brochure use of, 86-89,87t,88t
    importance of, 3-7
    information searching of, 174
    marketing communications and,
        7-13,*8*
        formal external, 9
        internal, on-site interaction,
            9-11
        management control,
            13-15,14t
        word-of-mouth messages,
            11-13
    source of information and,
        178-183,185
    strategies for building, 15-17
    targeting for local attractions, 78
Reputation of travel service,
        consumer decisions based
        on, 44,48-49
Residence
    response to environmental
        messages and, 149,160-164
    source of information and,
        178-180,184,187
Resort patrons, 208
Responsiveness in service quality, 10
RFM criteria (Recency/Frequency/
        Monetary value) in tracking
        repeat visitors, 15
Rhode Island state slogan, 97-98,109
Rietbergen, Ton van, 238
Rio Grande Valley, 6
Risk in consumer decisions,
        40,50-51,58
Ritchie, B., 202
Ritchie, J.R.B., 10

Rivoli, Pietra, 245
Robertson, T.S., 174
Roehl, W., 201
Ronkainen, Ilkka A., 245
Runyon, K.E., 174
Rural residents, attitude toward the
    environment, 149

SABRE, 237,241
Salient beliefs, 204
Satisfied customer in advertising,
    200
Schatz, C., 219,224
Schiffman, L.G., 72
Schreyer, R., 174
Schuett, M., 112
Schuett, Michael A., 172
Schul, P., 72
Schweiger, G., 192
Scotland. *See* United Kingdom
Scott, W., 193
Scottish Tourist Board, 122
Secondary images, 196
Service quality, measures of, 10
Service quality control, 11
Servqual approach to service quality,
    10-11
Shen, J., 201
Silva, Michael, 239
Slogans. *See* State slogans
Small businesses
    advertising, 33
    induced image formation, 208
    network development, 244
Smith, B., 202,221
Snepenger, D., 174
Snow, B., 152,153
Snow, R.E., 150
Social network, 239
Social-psychological factors, source
    of information and, 174-175
Sociodemographics
    attitude toward the environment
        and, 149

    of British travelers, 65,66t,72
    induced image formation
        effectiveness, 208
    promotion strategies and, 58-60
    response to environmental
        messages, 156-160,165-166
    source of information and,
        173-174,177-187
Solicited Organic image formation
    agents, 204,210
Sources of information. *See*
    Information sources
South Carolina state slogan, 97,100
South Dakota state slogan, 98,107
Spain, repeat visitors, 6
Spanish, M., 115,116
Spokesperson in destination image
    formation, 199-200
State slogans, 91-104,206-207
    dealing with geographical
        heterogeneity, 99-102
    dealing with political
        heterogeneity, 102-103
    problems in, 91-92
    public knowledge survey,
        105-109,*106*,107t,108t
    recommendations for, 103-104
    unique selling proposition (USP)
        advertising in, 92-99,*95*
State tourism bureaus
    cross-border alliances, 102-103
    literature, 100
    regional vs. centralized, funding
        of, 101-102
Stewart, D.W., 174
Strategic decisions, characteristics,
    22
Strategic Planning Institute at
    Cambridge, 12
Stutman, R., 204
Sykes, G., 150
Symbols in communications
    messages, 149-150,165-166

Tangibles in service quality, 10
Targeting
  brochures, 77-89
    effectiveness, 77-78
    market segmentation in, 127
    pre-testing in, 120
    site specific or general
      purpose, 80t,80-81
    study methods, 79
    travel expenditures and
      brochure use,
      81-86,82t,83t-84t
    travel expenditures and
      information source, 85t
    travel propensity and brochure
      use, 86-89,87t,88t
  environmental communications,
    165-166
  induced image formation,
    207-208
  repeat visitors, 5-6
Task specific factors and media
    selection practices,
    23,26-28,29-31
Taylor, David T., 99
Taylor, J., 115, 116
Technology. *See* Information
    technology
Television
  in destination image formation,
    197
  importance to visitors as
    information source, 177,
    182-187
  media selection practices study,
    24-31
Texas
  information sources for travellers,
    127
  repeat visitors, 6
Thurstone, L., 202
Tiananmen Square, 201,203
Time constraints, marketing
    implications of, 81
Tour brokers, hotel rooms, 235

Tourism channel system, 38. *See also*
    Direct sales
  network concept, 238-245
    current developments, 242
    developing, 242-245
    information technology in,
      241-242
    reasons for, 240-241
    types, 239
  shifting demand and, 232-235
  turbulent environment and
    competitive advantage,
    235-238
  value chain and, 230-232
Tourism industry. *See also*
    Management
  collaboration vs. competition, 225
  collaborative alliances, 217-225
    antecedents to, 220t,220-222
    constraints to, 218-220,219t
    theory of, 222-224
  demand in, 232-235
  direct vs. indirect distribution,
    230-232
  network concept, 238-245
  pay for representation system,
    219-220
  technology in, 229-230
  turbulent environment and
    competitive advantage,
    235-238
Tourism product
  characteristics, 233
  misconceptions, 244
Tourism supplier services and repeat
    travelers, 3-17. *See also*
    Travel agents
  importance of, 3-7
  management control, 13-15,14t
  marketing communications,
    7-13,8
  strategies for building base of,
    15-17
Tour operators in destination image
    formation, 199

Tours, distribution channel study,
37-54
consumer attitudes toward
channels, 38-39
demographics of, 52-53
domestic vs. foreign travelers,
41,47-52,48t,49t,50t
marketing communications,
39-41,51-52
methods, 41-44,45t
respondent characteristics, 43t
tour operators vs. travel agents,
44-48,46t
Tour wholesalers and British
travelers, 73
Transnational model, 245
Travel agents, 37-54,174. *See also*
Tourism supplier services
and repeat travelers
British travelers, 63-64,64t,72,73
in brochure effectiveness, 129,
198
as distribution channel, 231
hotel rooms, 235
information technology, 234
tour purchasing attributes
consumers' age and, 52-53
consumers' attitudes toward,
38-39
domestic vs. foreign travelers,
41,47-51
purchase decision parameters,
44-47,46t
study methods, 41-44,45t
tourism communications,
39-41,51-52
use of computer reservation
systems (CRS), 237
Travel characteristics
of British travelers, 67-71,69t-70t,
71t
promotion strategies and, 58-60
Travel distance and source of
information, 178, 181
Travel expenditures

brochure use and,
81-86,82t,83t-84t,89
information sources and,
85t,85-86
Travel groups
British travelers, 69,70
response to environmental
messages and, 160-164
source of information and, 180,182
trip expenditure and, 83
use of Biscayne Bay National
Park, 155
Travel guides in media selection
practices study, 24-31
Travel motivation
brochures in, 128-129
factors in, 128-129
Travel patterns of brochure
requesters, 86,88t,89
Travel philosophy of British
travelers, 68,71,71t
Travel propensity
brochure use and, 86-89,87t,88t
motivation and, 175
in targeting market, 78
Travel writers, 200-201
Trip length for British travelers, 70
Trip planning, brochures in, 123
Trist, E.L., 222
Turbulent environment of tourism
industry, 222,235

Um, S., 121,128
Unique Selling Propositions (USP),
91-103
components, 92-94
in state slogans
dealing with geographical
heterogeneity, 99-102
dealing with political
heterogeneity, 102-103
evaluation, 94-99,95
United Kingdom
communication channel
segmentation, 60-74

channel and source of
     information, 63-64,64t
destinations, 65,67t
interpersonal vs. impersonal
     channels, 72
media habits, 64-65
promotion and, 73-74
sociodemographic variables,
     65,66t
study method, 60-63
travel characteristics,
     67-71,69t-70t,71t
use of focus groups in, 116
United States
     perceptions of, 207
     use of focus groups in, 116
United States Forest Service, 224
University-industry partnerships,
     220,221
Unsolicited Organic image formation
     agents, 203-204,210
Urbanization, attitude toward the
     environment and, 149
U.S. Travel Service, 202, 207
USP. *See* Unique Selling
     Propositions
Utah, 205
     intergovernmental collaborations,
     222
Utell, 231
Uzzell, D., 206

Vaccaro, Joseph P., 33
Value chain, 236
     information technology in,
     241-242
     tourism channel system and,
     231-232
Value system, 232
Van Liere, K., 149,152
Van Raaij, W., 208
Verbal messages. *See* Word-of-mouth
     messages
Victoria, Canada, 224
Virginia state slogan, 97

Visual information needs, 135-144
Vogt, C.A., 59

Wahlers, R., 198
Wales. *See* United Kingdom
Weekend getaway trips, information
     needs study, 136-143,137t,
     138t,140t,*141,*142t
Wholesalers
     and British travelers, 73
     as distribution channel, 231
     hotel rooms, 235
Wicks, B., 112
Wicks, Bruce E., 172
Williams, D.W., 174
Wisconsin, 206
     state slogan, 96-97
Women
     in focus groups, 130
     response to environmental
          messages, 156-160
     sources of information, 179,181
Woodside, A.G., 189
Word-of-mouth messages, 58
     British travelers and, 63-64,64t,73
     characteristics, 7
     in destination image formation,
          204
     importance as source of
          information, 179,182-183
     management control of, 15
     repeat travelers and, 4,13,16-17
World Tourism Organization (WTO),
     221

Yale, D., 113
Yoder, S., 202

Zagreb, 193,196
Zeithaml, Valarie A., 25,26,33

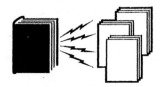

Haworth
DOCUMENT DELIVERY
SERVICE
and Local Photocopying Royalty Payment Form

This new service provides (a) a single-article order form for any article from a Haworth journal and (b) a convenient royalty payment form for local photocopying (not applicable to photocopies intended for resale).

- *Time Saving:* No running around from library to library to find a specific article.
- *Cost Effective:* All costs are kept down to a minimum.
- *Fast Delivery:* Choose from several options, including same-day FAX.
- *No Copyright Hassles:* You will be supplied by the original publisher.
- *Easy Payment:* Choose from several easy payment methods.

Open Accounts Welcome for . . .
- Library Interlibrary Loan Departments
- Library Network/Consortia Wishing to Provide Single-Article Services
- Indexing/Abstracting Services with Single Article Provision Services
- Document Provision Brokers and Freelance Information Service Providers

MAIL or *FAX* THIS ENTIRE ORDER FORM TO:

Attn: **Marianne Arnold**
Haworth Document Delivery Service
The Haworth Press, Inc.
10 Alice Street
Binghamton, NY 13904-1580

or FAX: (607) 722-1424
or CALL: 1-800-3-HAWORTH
(1-800-342-9678; 9am-5pm EST)

PLEASE SEND ME PHOTOCOPIES OF THE FOLLOWING SINGLE ARTICLES:
1) Journal Title: _____
     Vol/Issue/Year: _____ Starting & Ending Pages: _____
Article Title: _____

2) Journal Title: _____
     Vol/Issue/Year: _____ Starting & Ending Pages: _____
Article Title: _____

3) Journal Title: _____
     Vol/Issue/Year: _____ Starting & Ending Pages: _____
Article Title: _____

4) Journal Title: _____
     Vol/Issue/Year: _____ Starting & Ending Pages: _____
Article Title: _____

(See other side for Costs and Payment Information)

COSTS: Please figure your cost to order quality copies of an article.

1. Set-up charge per article: $8.00

                    ($8.00 × number of separate articles) _____

2. Photocopying charge for each article:

                    1-10 pages: $1.00 _____

                    11-19 pages: $3.00 _____

                    20-29 pages: $5.00 _____

                    30+ pages: $2.00/10 pages _____

3. Flexicover (optional): $2.00/article _____

4. Postage & Handling: US: $1.00 for the first article/

                    $.50 each additional article _____

                Federal Express: $25.00 _____

                Outside US: $2.00 for first article/

                    $.50 each additional article _____

5. Same-day FAX service: $.35 per page _____

6. Local Photocopying Royalty Payment: should you wish to copy the article yourself. Not intended for photocopies made for resale. $1.50 per article per copy (i.e. 10 articles x $1.50 each = $15.00) _____

                              GRAND TOTAL: _____

METHOD OF PAYMENT: (please check one)

❑ Check enclosed   ❑ Please ship and bill. PO # _____

                (sorry we can ship and bill to bookstores only! All others must pre-pay)

❑ Charge to my credit card: ❑ Visa;   ❑ MasterCard; ❑ American Express;

Account Number:_____ Expiration date:_____

Signature: **X**_____ Name: _____

Institution: _____ Address: _____

City: _____ State:_____ Zip:_____

Phone Number: _____ FAX Number: _____

MAIL or *FAX* THIS ENTIRE ORDER FORM TO:

Attn: **Marianne Arnold**
Haworth Document Delivery Service
The Haworth Press, Inc.
10 Alice Street
Binghamton, NY 13904-1580

or FAX: (607) 722-1424
or CALL: 1-800-3-HAWORTH
(1-800-342-9678; 9am-5pm EST)